Armed For
Personal
Defense

Jerry Ahern

Published by

Gun Digest® Books, an imprint of F+W Media, Inc.
Krause Publications • 700 East State Street • Iola, WI 54990-0001
715-445-2214 • 888-457-2873
www.krausebooks.com

To order books or other products call toll-free 1-800-258-0929
or visit us online at www.krausebooks.com, www.gundigeststore.com
or www.Shop.Collect.com

Library of Congress Control Number: 2010925141

ISBN-13: 978-1-4402-1408-0
ISBN-10: 1-4402-1408-5

Cover Design by Tom Nelsen
Designed by Paul Birling
Edited by Dan Shideler
Photos by Sharon Ahern unless otherwise noted

Printed in United States of America

Dedication

This book is dedicated to all the good, honest, decent people who carry concealed weapons to protect themselves, their loved ones and other innocents from predators who would prey on the weak and defenseless. The right to be armed is not granted by any government or any person. It is a natural right to be cherished and never surrendered.

Acknowledgments

Of course, there would never be an Ahern book of any sort without the most wonderful girl in the world helping to make it happen. Sharon's the best. I'd also like to thank the manufacturers and others in the industry who assisted by loaning product samples and providing some additional photographs. Thanks as well to Bradley Fielding for assisting us with this project. A special thanks to our son-in-law, Danny Akers, who tirelessly aided us in the completion of this work. Thanks to the always great looking Tracy for being extremely patient with our photographic demands.

Contents

Armed For Personal Defense

Introduction

For many of us, being armed in preparation for the possibility of defending oneself, the family, or an innocent stranger, has always been a part of being a free human being. In the world of today – as this is written it is the waning years of the first decade of the 21st century – the need to be armed at all times when it is possible is greater than ever before.

One of our dearest and oldest friends, an intelligent and gentle soul, as fine a fellow as one could hope to meet, in the aftermath of the September 11, 2001 attacks, made the decision to stop carrying the pocket knife he had carried all his life. He reasoned that the knife might inadvertently set off a magnetometer and draw security personnel away from a real threat. He's a brave and good man, one of the best. Most persons reading this book, however, likely thought just the opposite following that deadly series of events. Of course, no one wants to divert security personnel from a bad guy who is up to no good. Similarly, though, most readers here would be less concerned with that unlikely event and more worried about responding to an attack.

After the attack on America by radical Islamic fundamentalist killers, most of us have – and, I think, rightly so – perceived the need to arm up rather than down, to be better equipped on a daily basis than before that awful morning. Assuming that it is legal for you to do so, man or woman, it is silly to venture forth these days without at least one handgun, one reliable knife and a reliable cellular telephone. For the handgun, there should be readily available reloads. The knife should be sharp and your cellular phone's battery well-charged.

If one is properly armed and properly schooled in the use of arms, one has the ability to dispense death. It is incumbent upon the rational person to accept this awesome responsibility with the gravest seriousness. Those who view this power otherwise are sociopaths or sadists, like the murderous savages responsible for September 11, 2001. We all cheer when, in the movies, the good guy or guys (or girls) arrive in the nick of time and prevent gruesome slaughter through the skillful use of weapons against persons who see no intrinsic value in human life. Sadly, we may need to go to the movies to see the good guys win, but we can just check out the day's news to be informed of the latest atrocities committed by the bad guys.

In modern society, many people fear weapons and view those who use weapons as suspect, and they blame the weapons themselves when evil persons use them in evil ways. In America, alone among the major industrialized nations, men and women of all races, ethnic backgrounds and religious creeds still have the freedom to be armed – as this is written. In the last few months of 2008, with the serious likelihood of firearms-unfriendly politicians taking over Washington, sales of ammunition and arms soared, this trend continuing and intensifying in 2009 in light of the reality of election results. In the aftermath of the November 2008 election, firearms and particularly ammunition were found in short supply, when found at all. Oddly, some might think, the most difficult to find cartridge became .380 ACP, a cartridge associated with firearms kept for concealed carry or home/business defense. The majority of the fifty states allow concealed carry. Individuals are armed, as they should be.

To be armed for one's own protection and the safeguarding of others, however, one must carry's one's weapons concealed in one manner or another. Indeed, intrinsic to the issuance of concealed carry permits in most or all jurisdictions is that weapons must be kept concealed and never brandished unless they must be brought into play. Sloppy concealed carry leads to difficulties for the man or woman carrying the concealed weapon or weapons and consternation and possible panic for the habitually weaponless.

For most or all persons reading this book, it is incomprehensible that any rational person would intentionally render himself or herself defenseless. Beyond that, though, many of these same "irrational" people wish to see everyone weaponless, as if this is some great good. In order to derail such persons – and, out of common courtesy to these persons – concealed weapons must be concealed.

How to carry concealed weapons is one thing, but detecting that others are armed is a skill from which even the most weapons-abhorrent person can benefit. Because of the unabated risk of terrorist attack, the potential for distraught individuals to flip out and opt for suicide by cop, and myriad other situations in which the thoroughly evil or the thoroughly crazy crave the commission of murder, every teacher, every high school or college student, every shopper who frequents a mall, every person who uses any sort of public transportation, needs to learn as much as possible about spotting concealed weapons.

Read this book and learn.

Stock Photo

WEAPONS SELECTION

Chapter One

For many persons, the only gun worth carrying is a full-size 1911 and they wouldn't go out into the world without one. Others swear by North American Arms mini-revolvers as all the protection they need when going about their daily errands.

In years gone by, the snubby .38 revolver was the most common concealed carry weapon for those who were professionally armed. Before the advent of firearms of convenient size and reliability, daggers were hidden in one's clothes. Walther PP series pistols in .22 LR and Beretta 70S pistols in the same caliber were, at one time, the weapons carried under the outer garments of Israeli executive protection agents and undercover aircraft security. Whether from Beretta or Browning or Raven Arms, .25 automatics used to be and likely still are among the most commonly carried personal defense or backup handguns.

There is nothing wrong with any of these choices – even daggers. Depending on circumstances, however, some of these choices may be more "right" than others. The important thing is to be armed, when and where legally possible. The requirements imposed by the need to conceal a weapon rather than wear it openly are considerable. If it were legal to do so, rather than dropping a small caliber pistol in your pocket when you ran out to the store late at night or took the dog for a walk, many of us would just as soon buckle on a full-size handgun or snatch up a lightweight, high capacity carbine and sling it on in a patrolling carry. Most areas, however, frown on openly displaying weapons on one's person. Obviously, an assault rifle – even the civilian legal, semi-auto kind – is a better defensive choice than any handgun. Yet rifles get set down and are not always on one's person. A handgun can always be worn, when legal to do so.

Because of the fact that in order to legally carry we must almost always carry concealed, as far as projectile weapons are concerned, handguns are usually it, save for the occasionally encountered "witness protection" shotgun or little submachineguns like the mini-Uzi. Handguns, of course, vary widely in size and in caliber – not to mention effectiveness. Historically, much effort within the arms making community has concentrated on getting the greatest caliber into the smallest and (often) lightest package. This movement really gathered steam in modern times during the 1970s with the original Detonics .45s. The Seattle-made Detonics CombatMaster was a production gun, albeit a pistol that involved a great deal of handwork to build. Up until that time, taking full-size semi-automatic battle pistols – usually 1911s, sometimes Hi-Powers – and chopping them down to convenient carry size was a custom gunsmithing operation exclusively. At the time of the inception of the Detonics, the little-seen Thomas DA pistol came and went and the hand-cycled Phil Lichtman-designed Semmerling came on the scene in limited numbers. The Detonics has seen several revivals and, as this is written, is coming out of southern Illinois. The Semmerling is still available in extremely limited quantity – handmade – from American Derringer. A cut down version of the Browning Hi-Power, from FN, was offered some years ago, appearing to be not too dissimilar in size to the small Glocks. I've never seen one "in person," as it were.

This Smith & Wesson .38 Double Action, in .38 S&W caliber, is a late Fourth Model, produced prior to 1909. All the parts work, there's plenty of rifling in the bore and .38 S&W cartridges are still available.

During World War II, a limited number of Walther P-38s were produced for the Nazi Gestapo with barrels cut to about two and one-half inches, rather than the usual uncut length of five inches. Some P.08 Lugers were given this snubbing treatment as well. Of course, on this side of the Atlantic, before and after World War II, there were S&W and Colt .38 Special revolvers with shortened barrels.

After the war, more .38 Special snubs were created by Smith & Wesson with the introduction of their Chiefs Special J-Frame (then-new small frame, slightly larger than the I-Frame) Model 36 in 1950. An entire line of variations with round and square butts, two-inch and three-inch barrels, enclosed, shielded or exposed hammers, and even some with adjustable sights emerged. After legendary modern gunfighter Bill Jordan's successful campaign to get S&W to make a K-Frame (medium frame) revolver in .357 Magnum, his brainchild Model 19 four-inch was soon thereafter offered by Smith & Wesson as the round butt Model 19 with 2-1/2-inch barrel in .357 Magnum. It proved quite popular and the stainless 66 2-1/2-inch which followed it became one of the most sought-after sixguns in the S&W line.

But the 19th century had raised a bumper crop of concealable handguns, whether one considers the early S&W rimfires, the Remington derringers, the occasional examples of Single Action Army revolvers with no barrel at all and the more common Sheriff's models, or the ubiquitous small caliber handguns from Hopkins & Allen and others which were made to be carried in the side pocket of a jacket or inside a woman's purse.

Toward the close of the 19th Century, the Borchardt of the early 1890s and the more successful (and still formidable) C-96 Mauser Broomhandle semi-automatics were to help usher in an entirely new era in handguns. As automatics came into their own after the turn of the century, the pioneering medium-frame .32s and .380s from Colt and FN, both based on Browning designs, were revolutionary. It would be more than three-quarters of a century before that entire size range in those calibers of 7.65mm Browning (aka .32 ACP) and 9mm Kurz (aka .380 ACP) came into question. 1985 started the miniaturization craze in earnest when Larry Seecamp stopped making his .25 and started making the LWS .32 – but the guns were exactly the same size.

This was a pistol the size of an average .25 ACP ("ACP" stands for "Automatic Colt Pistol"), almost identical in size to the Colt-marked Spanish produced semi-automatics in .25, so much so that many holsters for one will fit the other. The Baby Browning .25 was smaller, and some other .25s were larger. What mattered was that, instead of a pistol of this size being restricted to one variation or another of the slow moving 50-grain .25 ACP cartridge, larger bullets moving more rapidly could be fired from the same package.

According to Marshall and Sanow's ground-breaking ballistics analyses, the 71-grain .32 ACP solid has a 50% one-shot stop rating, while the 60-grain .32 Silvertip hollow point has a 63% rating.

> ### *"Downsizer" pistols, offered in .45 ACP and other calibers, require heroic recoil management skills due to the combination of major caliber, minor size and negligible weight.*

This performance from a gun the size of a .25 was radical. That "gee-whiz!" quality is somewhat diminished in recent times by other guns following in the Seecamp .32 ACP's footsteps and Seecamp himself producing a .380 ACP version of exactly the same size and identical (6+1) capacity ("6+1" means six rounds in the magazine and one in the chamber for a total capacity of seven shots). More small .380s followed from North American Arms, Kel-Tec and Ruger. The diminutive Rohrbaugh 9mm Parabellum (literally, in Latin, "for war") is in a more performance-intensive – not to mention recoil-intensive – caliber still, for what is essentially .25 automatic size. The "Downsizer" pistols, single shots smaller than a pack of unfiltered cigarettes, were offered in .45 ACP and other calibers requiring heroic recoil management skills because of the combining of major caliber and minor size and negligible weight.

The medium frame automatics, in their customary calibers of .32 and .380, would be largely obsolete as this is written, except for the fact that they are so likeable. Sitting on my desk as I write this is a Century International Arms imported Walther PP police turn-in pistol in .32 ACP. It even sports Crimson Trace LaserGrips (technically made for the PPK/S, but the grip frame is identical) and it's loaded with .32 Silvertip hollowpoints. I have another handgun in a more substantial caliber on the desk as well. But, these medium frames have a certain je ne sais qua that cannot be denied and will likely enable them to retain reasonable popularity for long years to come.

What has brought about this sunset syndrome for the true medium frame is two-fold. The .32s and .380s of current design are the same size as the .25s (and .22 Shorts) of decades earlier. The .32s are extremely pleasant to shoot and the Seecamp and North American Guardian in .380 – the only two .380s of this size with which I have personal experience – are also perfectly pleasant to shoot. That being the case, why have a much larger .32 or .380 when their entire purpose is close concealment (effective close concealment is, essentially, undetectability without physical search or electronic assistance)?

The other mitigating factor here is that arms manufacturers have discovered ways – radical design engineering and better metallurgy chief among them – to chamber medium-frame-sized handguns in .45 ACP, .40 S&W, .357 SIG, and 9mm Parabellum (9x19). The frames are usually slightly wider, but length overall is, essentially, the same as the .32s and .380s designed in the early and middle 20th century. Most of these handguns are pleasant enough to shoot, and certainly so in the self defense context and for defense-related practice. They may weigh a bit more, but not much more. Models such as those from Glock (the Glock 26 9mm and Glock 27 .40 S&W, for example) also offer increased cartridge capacity over the standard six- or seven- or eight-round magazine capacity of the .32s and .380s. A SIG P-225 single column 9mm with eight-round magazine is only three-quarters of an inch longer in the butt than a Walther PP single column .32 ACP with eight-round magazine. The SIG P-225 is only one-eighth-inch longer at the muzzle. The Walther PP .32 in question is essentially identical in overall length and height to the Detonics CombatMaster .45. The Detonics has a six-round magazine, so the Walther is two rounds up on it. The Walther throws a 60-grain Winchester Silvertip, in this particular case. The CombatMaster, as I load it, is stoked with 230-grain

The Fourth Model Smith & Wesson .38 Double Action is a break top five shooter that, despite its age, could well serve in a pinch as a reliable concealed carry personal defense weapon. The cartridge is weak by today's standards, but .38 S&W has been used as a military cartridge and getting shot with one wouldn't be exactly healthy.

Hydra-Shok hollow points; one of the bullets from this cartridge is 3.833 times the weight of the little .32's bullet.

Both the SIG 225 and Detonics CombatMaster are heavier than the Walther and the Walther is heavier than the Seecamp. The Seecamp .32 weighs fourteen ounces fully loaded, with 6+1 capacity. With the same Silvertip ammo, only 8+1, the Walther PP weighs 26 ounces (including Crimson Trace LaserGrips). Length for the Walther is about 6-5/8 inches; the Seecamp only 4-1/2 inches. Height of the Walther, sans magazine, is 4.25 inches, while the Seecamp is right on 3 inches.

The logical conclusion one draws from these comparative measurements is inescapable. If diminutive size is all that matters, take the Seecamp or similar pistol in .32 or .380. If size is important, but caliber effectiveness is of similar or greater concern, take one of the larger caliber guns in size approximating what used to be known as a "medium-frame automatic." Stick with the original medium frames – generally quite accurate and reliable, albeit not the ultimate caliber in the size package – if you just like them. There's nothing wrong with that and that is why my Walther PP .32 is sitting loaded on my desk and not heavily greased and socked away in the back of a safe or stashed in a safety deposit box at the local bank. I like it and it shoots great.

Whether the gun is ultra small or just kind of small or medium sized or sort of on the large side, no weapon in and of itself is proof against being spotted as armed. As the old expression goes, "it's all in knowing how!"

Revolvers vs. Semi-autos

Because of the renaissance in semi-automatic pistol design which took place in the closing decades of the 20th century, choices in handguns are richer than ever before.

The two major categories of handguns are, of course, semi-automatics and revolvers. Revolvers bear some considerable mention. .45 ACP fans not withstanding, the .357 Magnum cartridge fired out of a four-inch barrel or longer is still the most reliable manstopper available out of a conventional handgun. The reason the .357 SIG was designed was to match this round's performance, but from an automatic rather than a revolver. It's no coincidence that the .357 SIG is offered in 125-grain JHP form, because 125-grain JHP in .357 Magnum is generally considered the knockdown champ from a revolver.

The operative concept when one considers .357 Magnum, however, should be barrel length. I am one of the world's most ardent fans of the J-frame Smith & Wesson revolver, most especially the Model 640, steel-framed and stainless, enclosed hammer, round butt and chambered in .38 Special – not in .357

Magnum. Why would I want a super lightweight Scandium or Titanium gun in a reasonably heavily recoiling cartridge? Why would I want a muzzle flash looking more like a flame from a torch? Why would I wish to inflict such pain on myself that I would eschew practice and, should the weapon be needed, be unskilled in its use? I mentioned barrel length as the operative concept. Out of a nominal two-inch barrel, the typical .357 Magnum round has little if any terminal effectiveness over .38 Special because there is no time/barrel length for that velocity to develop anywhere near the way it would if fired from a longer barrel. The old Model 19 and Model 66 2-1/2-inch revolvers were easier to handle because of size, but their ballistic performance wasn't much better. You need a four-inch barrel or longer for .357 Magnum to be worth the effort.

Smith & Wesson still offers two J-frame .38 Specials in its Classic line, as this is written, and there are good quality J-frame .38s to be found on the used gun market. Charter Arms and Taurus also offer snubby .38s; there are old Colt revolvers to be had, as well as overseas makes.

> *Because semi-automatics do not have a cylinder and have generally flatter grip profiles, larger semi-automatics are easier to hide on the body than similarly sized revolvers.*

Although the snubby .38 hasn't really been substantively improved since 1950 – except for the introduction of stainless steel – these handguns are still quite viable and, although in the initial surge of interest in high capacity semi-automatic pistols some thought the revolver for defensive purposes had gone the way of the passenger pigeon, revolvers are still a force in the market place. A good snubby .38 Special revolver is something I have always considered an "essential" weapon for every arms battery.

Choices are vastly wider in semi-automatic pistols for concealed carry. Because semi-automatics do not have a cylinder – which makes a natural bulge – and have generally flatter grip profiles, larger semi-automatics are easier to hide on the body than similarly sized revolvers.

As concerns construction, large frame semi-automatics in full-size and compact form are classifiable in several different ways. Large frame autos can be true full-sized pistols, such as the .45 ACP Colt or Kimber or Springfield or Taurus or Smith & Wesson or Detonics 1911-style pistols with five-inch barrels. They can be "Commander" length pistols, wherein the barrel has been reduced to 4-1/4 inches, but the grip frame remains the same length. They can be the size of the Kimber SIS Pro, with full length grip and 4-inch barrel. They can be the size of the rather rare Detonics "StreetMaster," with full-length 5-inch barrel and a height of only 4 inches from the top of the slide to the base of the grip frame.

In certain other contexts, that length matters less than height might be heatedly argued. Those concerns aside, when it comes to carrying concealed weapons, that statement couldn't be more true that length matters less than height. That StreetMaster is an excellent example when compared to the Commander-sized guns. Reducing a .45 automatic's length by three-quarters of an inch achieves absolutely nothing when it comes to concealment. There is a weight reduction – minimal – and, certainly, this individual or that may find the slightly shorter length hangs better in his or her hand. All that is fine, but leaving that slightly shortened pistol with a full-length grip makes it no easier to conceal. Reducing grip frame length and, correspondingly, the overall height, does make a difference. The grip is what will be far more likely to profile or bulge under a covering garment than any normal barrel or barrel/slide length. Therefore, a gun with a 5-inch barrel length and a 4-inch height will generally conceal better than a gun with a 5-inch barrel length and a 5-inch height, as found in the typical Government Model 1911. This is most noticeable with the various types of belt carry and vertical shoulder holster carry, least noticeable with diagonal shoulder holster carry (one of the few carries where length can make more difference than height).

Semi-autos can also be categorized as "single column" or "double column" magazine pistols, these latter sometimes referred to as "High Cap" or "wide body" magazines. Often, the term High Cap may be reserved for wide body magazines with their original capacity. During the period of the Clinton magazine capacity limits, the 12-round magazines found in a SIG 229, for example, were mandated to be replaced in guns sold after a certain date with politically correct 10-round magazines. As this is written, that foolishness is gone from the scene; hopefully, it will remain so.

Under some circumstances, pistols with single column magazines (with lower capacity) will conceal better than those with double column magazines (whether the politically correct variants or the originals). Think flatness and height/grip length and you'll understand one of the most elemental aspects of concealed carry.

Semi-autos are also classifiable as "single action," "double action," or "other." By "single action," we actually mean that two actions are required to fire a cartridge already loaded in the chamber (or the cylinder of a revolver): cocking the hammer and pressing the trigger. A "double action" requires only one action to discharge a round, namely making a long double action pull, which cocks the hammer and releases the hammer. Traditional double action semi-automatics and revolvers can be fired as double actions or can be manually cocked, like a single action, so only a shorter, lighter squeeze of the trigger is necessary to fire a shot. There are certain revolvers and a large number of semi-automatics which are DAO, meaning "double action only." New York City Police revolvers, in days gone by, were rendered DAO, in order to prevent possible unintentional discharge when a weapon was cocked or when a hammer was lowered. In DAO trim, the hammer could neither be cocked nor de-cocked, except by double actioning the trigger. The popular S&W Model 640 "Centennial" variants have a totally enclosed hammer which cannot be cocked manually.

Single action revolvers have been passed by for defensive purposes, used these days only in the game fields for handgun hunting and in sports such as Cowboy Action Shooting. The notable exceptions are North American Arms mini-revolvers. These super-tiny revolvers couldn't incorporate a double action mechanism because there wouldn't be enough room. Watch-like in their precision, the most practical of these are the smallest .22 Long Rifle (1-1/8-inch barrel) and the .22 Magnum models with similar or longer barrels. The NAA "Pug" .22 Magnum is one of the firm's newest models. The bull-barreled Pug has useable sights and the gun can be had with Tritium night sights as well. With a slightly larger grip, but not so large as to hinder concealability, the Pug is an outstanding choice, if .22 Magnum will be adequate for your needs.

Although the full-size cowboy-style single action revolvers are almost never carried for defense, these days, make no mistake. A skilled person with a Colt or Colt-like Single Action Army would make a formidable adversary. The really

The Little Ace .22 Short single shot, made around the middle of the 20th Century, may well be the smallest handgun in a conventional caliber. Made from brass, steel and wood, if one were used defensively it would have to be a contact distance against a very soft target.

good single action shooters can operate these guns with a cyclic rate better than many machine guns and can reload a chamber at a time as they go when firing more slowly. I own a 7-½-inch-barrel Cimarron Arms stainless Model P in .45 Colt; it is a serious revolver. Remember that the Colt Single Action Army came on the scene in 1873, which means it debuted only 38 years before that other most famous .45, the 1911.

Although you'll likely not find too many people carrying single action revolvers larger than a mini-revolver for defense, there's no shortage of persons armed with single action semi-automatics. Only the first shot requires that the hammer be cocked in advance. Subsequent hammer cocking is taken care of "automatically" as the slide moves rearward. If not the majority, then certainly the vocal minority of persons carrying single action automatics don't cock the hammer before firing a shot. They cock the hammer and leave it cocked, maybe all day long, maybe for days or longer at a time. After cocking the hammer, they raise the thumb safety present on these types of pistols and carry the weapon cocked and locked. Preparatory to actually firing, the thumb safety is lowered, and then the trigger pressed.

Carrying cocked and locked is popularly known as "Condition One." "Condition Two" is carrying the hammer down over a live round. "Condition Three" is hammer down over an empty chamber. Almost without exception, no single action semi-automatic should ever be carried with the hammer on the safety intercept notch, what's known as "half-cock." That safety intercept or half-cock notch is usually considered not strong enough to withstand a stout blow to the hammer.

"Other" Handguns

The "other" category of handguns is comprised of striker fired weapons, which would be best typified by the ubiquitous Glock "Safe Action" pistols. The striker – like a firing pin, but not requiring any hammer action – is cocked or partially cocked and pressing the trigger either releases the already cocked striker or finishes the cocking action and then releases the striker. This latter situation, overly simplified, is at the heart of the Glock firing mechanism.

A final classification of handguns used in defense and, thus, carried concealed is one of the oldest specifically designed for use as a concealed weapon: the derringer. The classic derringers of the 19th century were those of the Remington Arms Company in .41 rimfire, the famous "Remington double derringer." They were extremely concealable, dangerous to carry and fired a round that was dubious at best. They were very popular nevertheless. Many modern derringers, loosely patterned after the original Remington over/under derringers, are somewhat larger than the originals, yet are quite concealable,

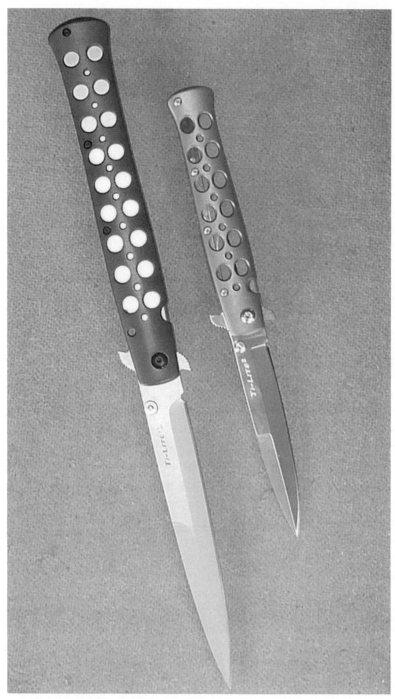

Two versions of the Ti-Lite from Cold Steel, Titanium handled knives designed to look like "switchblades" from the 1950s teen exploitation films.

likely feature manual safeties and, even in the smaller calibers, are much more effective than the .41 rimfire.

As an aside, how many readers would volunteer to be shot with a .22 Short, a .25 ACP, a .32 ACP or the historic .41 rimfire? I doubt there will be much of a show of hands. Even the most disrespected defensive cartridges can kill you. The virtue of the bigger cartridges lies not in whether they will or will not kill an attacker, but rather in putting an attacker down and thus ending the fight. If the bad guy dies, he dies. Unless we are self-styled vigilantes or congenital sociopaths, we're not out to kill people in a defensive context; all we wish to do is end the fight without ourselves or an innocent getting killed, maimed or hurt. Those .41 rimfire rounds, if they penetrated the clothing of one's assailant, would have carried grease, dirt, powder residue, bits of fabric and enough bacteria to kill an elephant into the shootee's body. Given 19th century medical techniques and the lack of antibiotics, blood poisoning might very well put one's assailant into the grave – but quite possibly not before said assailant pulled his gun, shot you dead, got the local sawbones to remove the bullet you'd put in him, had a few drinks, maybe rode off to the next town and got into another gunfight or two before the fever became so bad he couldn't stand up.

Rifles & Shotguns

Concealed weapons needn't always be handguns, of course. As mentioned earlier, the smaller submachineguns by Uzi and others are to be considered. They can be carried in special shoulder holsters or slung, to be hidden under winter outerwear or raincoats, etc., even, with varying degrees of concealability, under a loosely fitting sportcoat or bomber jacket or M-51 Field Jacket.

When we were in the holster business, we made a shoulder rig for short barreled shotguns. It worked rather well with an eighteen-inch-barreled pistolgrip Remington 870 pump. Custom holstermaker Sam Andrews makes a rig which carries a semi-automatic pistol along with spare magazine on one side and accommodates a short barreled shotgun on the other side, with loops for spare shotgun shells, of course.

The ideal shotgun for such an assignment, also mentioned earlier, is what is generally categorized as a "witness protection shotgun." These are weapons which require special Federal licensing to possess – not too difficult to obtain, if you have a clean background and don't live in a weapons-unfriendly state or police jurisdiction. The barrels are quite a bit shorter and the shotguns are pistol gripped. The shorter barrels make these arms much more easily concealed. If you watched Miami Vice on television, the "Ricardo Tubbs" character carried a witness protection shotgun quite often.

Folding stock Mini-14s and AK-47s, when fitted with shorter magazines, can be worn under longer length outerwear. Full length magazines for an AK, for example, would be essentially impossible to hide when in the weapon. Such rifles offer increased range over a handgun or shotgun and, if a large capacity magazine were carried in an offside pouch, then slammed into the weapon, considerable firepower. Take a semi-automatic AK-47, for example. With a sixteen and one-quarter-inch barrel and folding stock, it is thoroughly legal in most areas. An executive protection specialist (bodyguard), or someone who needed such considerable response capability to an attack, could swing the weapon forward out of its holster or on its sling while the offhand drew a 30-round magazine from beneath the other side of the covering garment. Getting an AK magazine inserted quickly takes some practice, of course, but our subject would certainly perform such practice. Getting an AK magazine un-stuck after improper insertion can be extremely difficult.

A folding stock Ruger Mini-14 – magazine insertion is quite similar to the AK-47 – is an even better proposition for this sort of carry, since Ruger offers five-round magazines which seat flush in the rifle. One could get the first five rounds going while snatching a larger capacity magazine from the offside. AK magazines are available in reduced capacity versions and warrant serious consideration. Mine came from Maine Military Supply. The advantage to any rifle velocity round at close range, of course, is penetration. Terrorists, for example, of the non-suicidal variety, might well be expected to wear soft body armor. A standard hardball .223 round will easily punch through quarter-inch steel plate. A good friend of mine once put a hole in a reactive pistol target of mine with the exact same round. SIG-Sauer offers a pistol version of the AR-15 known as the P556 and Century International Arms offers a pistol version of the AK.

Knives

But, there are other excellent weapons to be carried in conjunction with firearms or, in some situations, perhaps, on their own. I've heard the Japanese Katana (Samurai sword) described as the most deadly close range weapon ever devised. Be that as it may, unless we're in the movies or on television and happen to be immortal (unless another immortal lops off our head, of course), we can't regularly conceal an edged weapon with a blade 27 inches or longer. However, we can conceal quite a wide variety of fixed blade and folding knives.

Included among fixed blade knives for concealment are various types, generally classifiable as push knives, neck knives, sleeve knives, belt knives, boot knives and specialty clandestine knives.

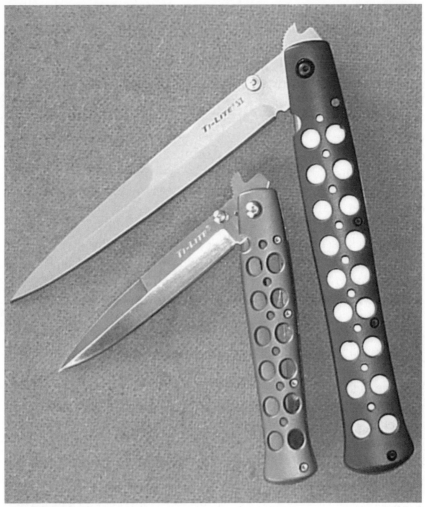

The Cold Steel Ti-Lites open.

Push knives – called "push daggers" by some – are extremely concealable when properly designed because the surface to be grasped by the hand is at right angles to the blade, forming a "T" shape. The blade needn't be long, either, in order to be effective. Traditionally, one holds the push knife (or two of them, one in each hand) in the clenched fist, then punches the blade into one's adversary. If the blade is well-constructed, it will re-emerge to be stabbed with again, should that prove necessary. Most are double edged, making push daggers illegal to carry in a great many areas. Those few that are single edged, however, make not only superb clandestine defensive tools, but can also serve as handy knives for more mundane chores. We are fortunate to possess two since-discontinued early Cold Steel push knives with single edge blades. These are considerably more legal in more areas and are ideal, for example, for a woman to carry in a purse or on body. Everybody can ball up a fist and punch, however frail one might be in comparison to an attacker. The slightest contact and one's adversary is cut. In a close encounter of the horrifically unromantic kind, such a knife could be a woman's ideal close range defensive weapon. They're great for men, too, of course. If assaulted by a physically superior person or by multiple assailants, even one push knife could make a definite difference; one in each hand could do even better. There are many sources for push knives, but two I would recommend are Blackhawk Products and Wild Boar Blades. Wild Boar offers push knives in double-edged and single-edged configurations.

A.G. Russell is a household name in knives and his various versions of the Sting are considered to be among the finest boot knives ever designed. From left, the original Sting, the Sting I, both of these with Micarta handle slabs, the most famous of the knives, the Sting IA Black Chrome (modern versions of this classic are being made again), the most recent, a folding Sting and the non-metallic CIA Letter Opener. Taking one of these "letter openers" into an airport is a federal crime.

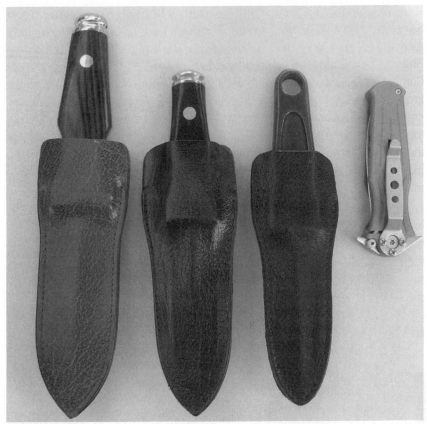

The Sting, the Sting I, the Sting IA, each with sheath. The folding Sting is closed.

Neck knives are designed to be worn on a chain around one's neck. Consequently, they are usually small, thin and light. They can also be quite effective. These days, the scabbards for neck knives will be tightly fitted synthetics and may also include some sort of locking device. The scabbard is important, because the knife is most often worn upside-down. One reaches through or under one's shirt, grasps the haft of the knife and jerks it clear of the scabbard and into action. The idea with neck knives and some of the push knives is to avoid detection in a light frisk. That's possible, of course, but not to be counted on in these days of electronics. Some of the current push knives are all synthetic and would, theoretically, not trigger electronic countermeasures. Carrying a synthetic knife, like A.G. Russell's classic CIA Letter Opener, for example, can make good sense, but only where legal. Walking into an airport with such a knife is a violation of Federal law and not worth the potential trouble.

Sleeve knives can be extremely practical. My favorite is the (discontinued)

H.G. Long produced replica of their original sleeve knife, made for the British S.O.E. (Special Operations Executive) and American O.S.S. (Office of Strategic Services) during World War II. These perfect replicas were imported from England in stainless steel years ago by the original (Illinois) Blackjack Knife Company and feature a meticulously crafted sheath and belt. The belt wraps around the inner forearm and the sheath can be worn with the haft of the knife pointed toward the wrist or the blade pointed toward the wrist. I prefer the former arrangement. Reach up your sleeve with the offhand and you have the knife. In the instance of the H.G. Long sleeve knife, it is a triangular, spikelike blade, ideal for stabbing. Atlanta Cutlery offers a similar knife, but you may want to get a longer strap for securing the sheath to your arm.

The discussion of the sleeve knife seems the perfect point at which we should briefly digress. When discussing serious concealed weapons, it should be remembered that, in a civilian context, they will most often be used when circumstances are horribly dire and inaction will result in death or worse. That is when such weapons must and will be employed. So, there should be no politically correct worries about the idea of stabbing someone with a triple edged spike. The eye, the ear, the throat, the area around the neck's carotid artery, and the femoral artery on the inside of the right thigh – these are the targets. It should not be

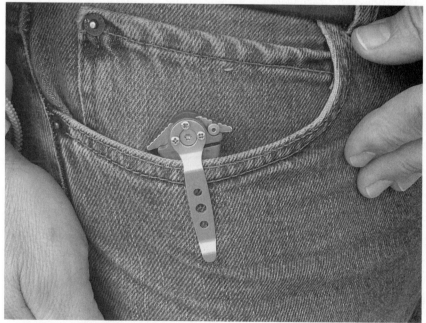

The folding Sting works well in a jeans pocket. Unlike the fixed blade knives, the folder is single edged.

taken lightly, this power of life and death over an attacker. But, the exercise of this power should not be avoided. To do so is suicide.

Chemical Sprays and Stun Guns

As a way around making life and death decisions – a tactical alternative, if you will – many persons will choose to carry some sort of chemical spray or stun gun. Carrying such a product in addition to a firearm is the best way to capitalize on the concept. Noted writer and trainer Massad Ayoob advocates escalation of force, as needed, and this makes great sense. Being able to demonstrate to a court that you chose non-lethal alternatives before resorting to a firearm could make a real difference in how your actions are perceived. And, really effective alternatives may very well obviate the need for using a firearm.

Chemical sprays have come a very long way since the days of tear gas units about the size of a small flashlight. State-of-the-art today in non-lethal weaponry is the Kimber JPX-Jet Protector. Kimber is, of course, noted for its fine firearms, both handguns and long guns. The JPX is built in the shape of a handgun and operates similarly to a handgun. This facilitates both accuracy and training. When the JPX is fired, what Kimber describes as "…a pyrotechnic drive launches near pharmaceutical grade OC solution at 270 miles per hour." This unit really has everything. It fires two bursts and is effective out to twenty-one feet. The magazines are replaceable, so large numbers of persons can be zapped with the JPX, if need be. An oleoresin capsicum (hot pepper) solution is the top choice, as powerful as can be had in this type of device. The unit is available in black or orange and, although I like black, I'd probably opt for orange, so it wouldn't be mistaken for an actual firearm. And, much like a firearm, this unit is available with a laser that will allow enhanced accuracy. Additionally, a blue dye practice magazine is offered, so one can get the feel for accurate use of this non-lethal defender in a safe, yet realistic, manner.

Tactical Illumination: Flashlights & Lasers

The other non-lethal alternative involves a surge of electricity that will stun the person. The problem with this choice is that it is possible, however unlikely, to kill the person such a device is used against. Some types of heavy outerwear may well obviate such a product's effectiveness. In short, if you elect to use electricity as a weapon, learn all that you possibly can about the product and its advantages and potential limitations, before taking such a device into the field.

Two other non-lethal alternatives, but ones which must be used in conjunction with a firearm, are the laser and tactical illumination (high tech, high intensity flashlights).

There are many excellent laser products on the market, and I have been using lasers since the mid-1970s. In those days, a state-of-the-art laser sighting system was the size of an automobile muffler and could cost more than the gun to which it was mounted. As price and size reduced, more and more lasers were coming into use in tactical applications. I always liked the idea of a laser sight, but never actually got into wanting a laser on a gun full time until the advent of Crimson Trace LaserGrips. Although Crimson Trace Laser-Grips really don't alter gun shape, holsters which cover the upper edge of the right grip panel may or may not fit properly. Not to worry, makers ranging from Galco to Ken Null offer most or all of their holsters tweaked so that they will accommodate guns with or without Crimson Trace LaserGrips.

> *Drop a red dot on someone's chest and, unless that someone lives in a vacuum, he'll realize that where the red dot is a bullet will soon follow.*

The tactical advantages of any laser sight are considerable. Drop a red dot on someone's chest and, unless that someone lives in a vacuum, he'll realize that where the red dot is a bullet will soon follow, if he persists in his anti-social behavior. A laser can be a terrific fight-stopper. And, a laser allows the user to practice shooting from hip level without using the sights. Of course, as any competent trainer will point out, you should not count on a laser to replace your sights and you must train in sighted fire as you would if lasers didn't exist. That's all true. However, knowing how to accurately shoot from the hip, let's say, is much more easily learned with a laser. Why would one wish to learn to shoot from the hip? Contrary to some tactical dogma, there are times when there will not be sufficient time or distance involved to bring your pistol up into a Weaver or isosceles stance and use your sights. A laser can enhance your development of this skill to the point where, should your laser fail because the battery has run out, etc., you won't need it for close range point shooting. It will have become instinctive. The virtues of hip shooting, by the way, were not initially revealed to me by an instructor, but rather by a man who used handguns in an anti-personnel context, in live or die situations. I don't question the validity of that kind of experience. Remember, he's the one who lived!

With the continuing engineering efforts at Crimson Trace, it is possible, as this is written, to have a laser on a truly small pocket pistol. My North American Arms Guardian .380 is so equipped. Lasers of various makes and descriptions are available for a surprisingly large variety of handguns that one might well carry concealed. They are the wave of the future, certainly, and extremely practical additions to your concealed carry firearms. Crimson Trace has a special design for the Ruger .380. This is not a LaserGrip, but a LaserGuard. The laser is mounted under the frame, forward of the trigger guard, the mount mating to the outer side of the trigger guard and ending at the grip front strap where the activation button is positioned. Very slick indeed.

Tactical lighting covers an even broader spectrum of use. With a tactical light, you can do anything from something as mundane as shedding light on your front door so you can find the keyhole to temporarily trashing an opponent's night vision in a potential gunfight to punching someone. We're not talking about police flashlights, of course. Actual police flashlights – like

SureFire Tactical Lights are among the best of the breed. From left, the L4 Digital Lumamax, the AZ2 Combat Light and the Backup. Each light has its own special features and these are three out of a wide range of SureFire Lights. The little Backup is extremely convenient to tuck into one of the pockets of a pair of Woolrich Elite Series Tactical Lightweight Operator Pants.

Note brilliance of the Surefire X-300 WeaponLight, even in full daylight.

the MagLites from Mag Instrument – are something everyone should have. At our house, we couldn't get along without them. That said, a full-size three D-cell flashlight is a little large to carry concealed.

The most well-known name in high-tech concealable tactical lighting is SureFire. I've been carrying SureFire lights for years and they just keep getting better and better. A tactical light can be as small as the hand held L4, which runs about 5 inches in length and operates on two SureFire Lithium batteries or the even smaller 4-inch long E1B Backup, an LED tactical light that allows you to switch between faint and brilliant illumination, thus giving phenomenal service with a single battery. High Beam is eighty lumens and will last for a little over an hour with a light that will "...overwhelm night-adapted vision." This E1B Backup is one of my favorites. Low Beam is only five lumens, giving you as much as 37 hours use on a single battery for normal stuff.

These days, tactical lights are often mounted beneath the weapon, on a Picatinny rail. Without arguing the various merits of mounting a light thusly, it is possible to get concealed carry holsters that really work and allow one to hide a pistol with the light mounted below the frame. I use a SureFire X300 with my Crimson Trace LaserGripped Glock 22. A full size gun, the Glock on its own will demand careful attention to detail for effective concealed carry. Add the SureFire X300 tactical illumination device and concealment holster choice becomes seriously limited. One of the best available is the Halo Belt Holster from Galco. Putting the name "Galco" in the same sentence with the

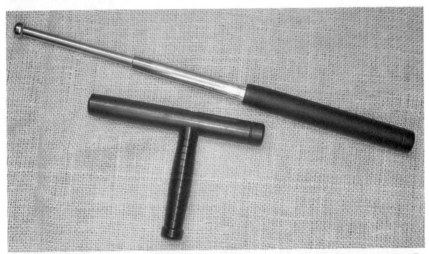

An ASP collapsible baton, extends quite easily and with a distinctive sound as well. Collapsible batons are useful for police officers, not only as a weapon, but as a tool for breaking glass, etc. Below the ASP is a Tonfa-shaped collapsible baton. These and other impact weapons may be illegal for carry where you live; such impact weapons frequently are.

phrase "...one of the best available..." is a pretty routine thing for anyone writing about concealed carry holsters.

Tactical light developments are going almost exclusively toward LEDs, pressure switches on the tail cap and rugged construction from anodized aircraft grade aluminum. Tactical lights are not inexpensive, but they are a necessity as part of your concealed carry battery.

But just as we must broaden our horizons concerning technical innovation, we must also remember that there are other kinds of defensive tools besides firearms and edged weapons. One of the great things about full-sized aircraft aluminum flashlights was/is their ability to be used as an impact device when needed. I smashed a window with one, once – intentionally. The high-tech tactical illumination units don't demand any sort of delicate treatment, of course, but they often aren't well-suited to use as a weapon, either, because of their small size. At least, not in the conventional sense, that is. Using your tactical flashlight with the brightest illumination possible will disrupt your opponent's night vision, giving you a momentary edge, a tactical advantage. One tactical light, from the handgun company Detonics, features a 20 Hz strobe function which is designed to temporarily disrupt the transmission of visual data to the brain. It's essentially over in – forgive the pun – the blink of an eye, but the resultant disorientation can provide tactical advantage.

Although the police flashlights did double duty as a light and an impact weapon, because most tactical illumination utilizes tail cap button-type switches, you may prefer to use the business end of the light, if the tactical light is to be used for an impromptu yarawa stick. However, impact weapons come in various styles and sizes, to meet most tactical needs. The archetypical impact weapon is the police night stick, which has been replaced most notably by batons like the Monadnock Rigid PR24, which is designed to be used as a control device more than a club. But, collapsible batons – from Monadnock, ASP and others – can be carried concealed and work quite well in close range defense. Make no mistake. An impact from such a device can do serious damage; so, just because your defensive weapon doesn't launch a projectile or have an edge, don't think it's any safer to use. It's not.

The classic concealed carry impact weapon, of course, is the blackjack, otherwise known as a flat sap. The spring sap, otherwise known as a cosh, is another personal size impact weapon. Sharon's dad used to keep a spring sap near his front door in the event of an intruder. One of my oldest friends, a former Chicago cop, used a blackjack to save his life, once, and learned how to use it not only for impact, but to cut, as well.

The important thing to remember is that a concealed carry permit will usually not include concealed carry of a blackjack. Let's see! I can carry a gun without worrying about breaking the law or I can carry a blackjack and do something illegal. Hmm? In short, things like blackjacks, nightsticks and brass knuckle "paperweights" are nice to have and fun to collect, but don't carry them as concealed weapons. Leave them home – with the inert practice grenades.

Using Common Items as Weapons

There are certain pens on the market, from SureFire (no, theirs doesn't light up), Benchmade (it doesn't turn into a knife) and others. These pens are made for writing – and do so elegantly and excellently – but are also made for impact applications. One from SureFire features a glass shattering device on the butt. A second from SureFire doesn't incorporate this device. The one I use from Benchmade doesn't have a glass shattering application, either. All three are easily grasped and held firmly. All three are made from anodized aerospace grade aluminum and all three could be used in close range combat against soft targets, etc. Not inexpensive, they are first quality writing instruments which can do double duty in a pinch. In the case of the original Sure-Fire model with the glass breaker, make that triple duty.

As my son pointed out to me and to his oldest son when I showed them one of these, an ordinary pen can be used as a weapon. This is true. However, these non-ordinary pens are designed with the sort of unparalleled toughness one doesn't find in the typical ball point.

If you are entering a weapons-free environment, that does not mean you have to be unarmed. It only means you cannot have actual weapons. A metal ball point pen of any type can be used against eyes, the windpipe, etc. Men's belts are more sturdily made than those made for women, and a man's belt can be turned into an excellent flail. Time permitting, remove the belt and wind the belt through the buckle several times, making a mace of sorts at the end. You can swing the belt – your improvised mace and flail – for use as an impact weapon or to deflect or parry a knife, box cutter or the like. When used as an impact weapon, go for the face, the eyes, and the throat. Leave enough tail on the belt that you'll have a good grip and good reach and, if you get into a grappling situation, hopefully you'll be able to grasp both ends and use the belt to throttle your attacker. If time does not permit – usually the case, of course – just whip the belt off, get a good twist of the belt's tail around your fist and use the buckle end against your attacker's eyes and face. Keep in mind that on an aircraft, for example, cabin headroom will limit the space in which you can wield the belt.

We all remember the shoe bomber whose murderous intent made it necessary for us to step out of our shoes before boarding an aircraft. I have a pair of slip ons that that I keep for aircraft use, otherwise wearing shoes that lace and tie. Those shoes you're wearing can make an excellent weapon. One of my relatives taught his son how to reach back and pull off a shoe in a hurry and use it against an opponent's head or face. Women have used high-heeled shoes as impromptu weapons for years. Thrusting one's hand into one's shoe armors the hand to a degree and increases the felt impact against an attacker. With your hand inside the shoes, palm open and down, slap the shoe against an opponent's face, your hand and the shoe around it functioning much the same as a large, flat sap (blackjack).

Most of us will have a cellular telephone, a calculator, a pocket-full of change, etc., on or near our person at all times. Time permitting again, take off a sock and put that phone or calculator inside the sock, then use the sock like a mace and flail. If you have a pocket-full of change, that's great. If you are aboard a conveyance that is under attack, you can always take up a collection!

Another variation, if you wear over-the-calf socks, is to remove the sock, put the shoe inside the sock and use this as a mace and flail.

The key to all of this is to think creatively. Remember that your brain, combined with your free will, is the ultimate weapon.

When I write here about attacking an opponent's eyes or throat, some may think this is sounding more than a bit bloodthirsty. Not so. Let's take a terrorist who attempts to seize an aircraft. This person, through this act, has stepped out of the human community. He'll kill you, your great aunt who can't get out of a wheelchair, your grandchild who's still an infant, anyone at all because he hates with a vengeance. Hatred is counterproductive, a waste of energy. Using whatever means possible to foil such a thing's vile intent is a positive, life-affirming act.

ANYTHING CAN BE A WEAPON

Chapter Two

The human mind is the greatest weapon known, because from it arises all innovation and invention. If this ultimate weapon is properly maintained – kept sharp, as it were – then it will enable you to see the potential for use as a weapon of a surprisingly wide array of everyday objects. Traditional weapons generally, whether designed as such or improvised, can be divided into certain basic categories, among which are edged weapons, impact weapons and projectile weapons. A projectile weapon can be as simple as a rock one picks up and throws at an adversary, or launches from a sling, *a la* David versus Goliath in the Bible. A projectile weapon can also be a shoulder fired missile, or a blowgun or a crossbow. It all depends on perspective and what is available to counter a perceived threat.

The typical home is a veritable arsenal of improvised weapons. Certainly, actual weapons – like firearms – are more well-suited to defensive applications; but, absent guns and knives and swords and clubs, when at home one is still well-armed. Attacked in the basement or the garage or the storage shed? Chain saws often times take a few tries to start up and this can waste precious seconds. But, an ordinary saw of any type – a carpenter's saw is better than a coping saw and a hacksaw is another ideal size – can be a serious weapon when used as a cutting implement, rather more like a saber than a thrusting weapon. As with a sword, only the most foolish attacker will grab for a saw wielded against him, because of the very real risk of sustaining deep cuts and possible loss of a finger or fingers.

Edged Weapons

An axe is a terrific weapon, so long as it is wielded aggressively and correctly. It is more easily grasped by an assailant because the cutting surface is much reduced over the edge surface of a saw; and, this being the case, a long handled axe can become the focus of a grappling match between the attacker and the attacked. If taking up an axe for defense, the shorter length camp axe style is to be preferred over the longer handled types. When our daughter began driving, she was, of course, too young to legally carry a handgun in her car. We wanted her armed, however, for self-defense. We struck on an axe, even going so far as to take it to a local jeweler and have her name engraved on the head. And, we taught her how to use it, striking in an upswing, edge up, the action rather like the movements associated with a "granny shot" in basketball. If the attacker tries blocking the up-swinging axe head, his hands will be injured. If he doesn't block, the axe may strike in his genitalia. Even missing the attacker's genitalia, as the swing continues upward, it will definitely encounter flesh, possibly the underside of the jaw. A down swing leaves the defender's torso far too open and vulnerable and is more easily sidestepped by the attacker. An axe is a great weapon, because, when it is brandished, the attacker will likely consider the possibility of losing some pieces of his body.

Years ago, I encountered a marvelous truism: Few of us have been shot, but every one of us has been cut at one time or another; edged weapons are universally feared. That makes great sense. And, your home is a fine source for edged weapons. Say someone breaks into your home and you have the good fortune to be in the kitchen. The higher end modern chef's knife is essentially identical to the fighting knives used in the early days of American frontier expansion, only better made. The ones my wife uses have a blade a little over eight inches in length, two inches at maximum width and are an eighth-inch thick, this with a full-length, full-width, full thickness tang. No guard, that's true, but the early knives used on the frontier had no guard, either. Jim Bowie's

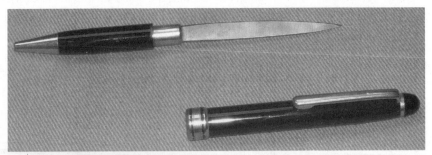

This is a functioning ball point pen which houses a spike blade. It's an example of the sort of weapon one conceals in plain sight.

original knife may not even have had one. When such a knife is used in a defensive context, don't try stabbing with it. Instead, use that long, sharp edge for what it was intended, to cut.

If you still favor the idea of impact along with cutting, a full-size Chinese cleaver, found in many kitchens, ours included, is deadly. These days, Chinese criminal societies are most frequently referred to as "Triads." In years gone by, however, they were often called "Tongs." The Chinese Cleaver, wielded in hand-to-hand combat or thrown by an assailant, was a favored weapon of the Tongs.

Impact Weapons

If impact weapons are more your style, as is the case for many women, the old practice of hitting someone with a frying pan, although it often elicits a laugh in the movies, is not a laughing matter. By far, the best choice in impact weapon cookware is cast iron. Cast iron cookware wears like, like – well, like iron! As such, it's a lifetime investment. And, for the purposes of this chapter, it cannot be surpassed as a close range impact weapon. Certain specimens of the cast iron cookware Sharon uses weigh 6 pounds (a 10-inch skillet) and 7 pounds (an 8-inch stovetop Dutch oven).

Although it was a weapon made out of a wooden boat oar, the legendary samurai and author of *The Book of Five Rings,* Miyamoto Musashi, used such a "bokken" in a duel to the death with Sasaki Kojiro. Sasaki Kojiro was renowned as a superior practitioner in the use of the "nodachi," a two-handed sword. Musashi drew his blunt wooden weapon as his opponent was about to strike, crashing it down over the swordsman's head and taking the fellow's life. Remind yourself of that incident if a frying pan or a wooden rolling pin (not the plastic kind that is filled with water) or a large can of baked beans is all you have to hand (I prefer Bush's original recipe over other variations).

From the Kitchen ...

Let's not forget another category of weapons which will be found in the kitchen, namely chemicals. Spraying an attacker in the eyes with an aerosol cooking spray, window cleaner, bug spray, furniture polish, household deodorant and the like will, at the least, buy you some time.

> *Spraying an attacker in the eyes with oven cleaner will likely buy you some time.*

Not a chemical but always around the kitchen, salt and especially pepper can be hurled into the eyes of an attacker. Sugar and flour and corn starch and anything else like that will, at the very least, disorient an attacker. They are, after all, abrasives.

Hot items on the stove – especially liquids – can be used in self defense. A hot steam iron can do serious harm to an attacker, but even a cold one can be used as a bludgeon against the face and head.

Various other common household items make wonderful weapons as well. Power strips for the computer can be used as a bludgeon and the cord can be employed to choke an opponent. Scissors and letter openers are other home office-related items which can do good service. As already mentioned, a pencil or a pen can be used to thrust into sensitive soft tissue areas of an attacker's body, such as the throat, face, etc. Win a bowling trophy? If it's a good quality trophy, it'll make a fine impact weapon. Older telephones were wonderful weapons, even well-designed to stay in the hand. Modern telephones are best used to "smack someone upside the head," as the saying goes. Chairs of any kind can be flung or used as impact weapons, metal chairs against the head or neck of an attacker or any sensitive, nerve intensive area, especially effective.

In the Bedroom

Once one departs the kitchen or home office and goes to the bedroom, weapons options will be somewhat different. The bedroom should be as fortified as possible against attack, since such incidents often take place during the hours when many of us are abed. If someone is silly enough to invade my home, the person (that term used quite loosely) will be greeted by a variety of projectile weapons, edged weapons and impact weapons. Aside from more than one handgun, I sleep with a Katana and Wakazashi beside the bed. And, of course, my cellular phone.

You should always have a large, powerful, police-style flashlight beside your bed in the event of a power failure. It can also serve, of course, as an impact weapon. If you end up grappling with an attacker – something to be avoided when at all possible – try strangling with an electrical cord or the sash-like belt from a bathrobe. You can always smother an attacker with a pillow. The important consideration is to disable the bad guy, not set out to kill him. If you interfere with your attacker's airways, for example, you must make certain that the attacker is really subdued and not just faking in order to get you to stop your defensive action. Once you do suspend your defense, if you haven't done so already, call the 911 operator, ask for law enforcement and for medical assistance to hopefully revive the attacker. Take whatever precautions you can as you wait for help.

A belt with a heavy brass buckle can easily be used as a flail. This was a street gang weapon in gentler times than these, but is a weapon anyone can have on his person with impunity, because it is just an ordinary belt. Work the flail in a circular motion to hold off an attacker or strike.

Making the belt flail is easy, if you have the right buckle. The kind that is ideal is a rectangular Garrison Buckle, the type used in work/gun belt styles commonly referred to as Garrison Straps, what used to be the Chicago Police Department gunbelt. Start the belt winding through both sides of the rectangle, as if you were making a slightly irregular ball. For an adult male, you'll have filled the gap on both sides of the buckle tongue by the time you have about eighteen inches or so of belt remaining, especially if you have a lined/double thickness belt. Don't worry about the tongue (the little thing that is at the center of the buckle and penetrates the holes when the belt is worn normally). This will be pointing toward the business end of the flail and merely support the belt. If used properly, this is a serious self-defense weapon against a physically superior assailant or multiple assailants.

The belt is used as a flail, spun and swung, to keep an attacker back or to counter-attack. The heavy brass buckle makes this have the heft necessary for the task.

Your Vehicle

If you are in your car, you are in control of a serious weapon, indeed. A Chevrolet Impala, for example, has a curb weight of 3,550 pounds. Curb weight is usually calculated fully topped off with fuel and fluids and absent passengers. If you are surrounded by attackers trying to haul you out of the car with the apparent intent of killing you, stomp the gas pedal. Some years ago, during a violent and protracted civil dislocation (a riot) in a major Midwestern city, an innocent woman stupidly stopped for a traffic light, the street and sidewalks crowded with angry people she'd never met. They surrounded her car, hauled her out from behind the wheel and beat her to death.

The Great Outdoors

Otherwise, local laws permitting, make certain to have an accessible firearm available. If there is no firearm and you are outside the vehicle, get to the jack handle from the trunk (assuming no other impact or edged weapons are secreted there). Rather than trying to use the jack handle as a club, utilize it as a thrusting weapon, employing it against soft tissue areas and the eyes of your attacker. If you carry tools, screwdrivers don't need to be sharpened in order to be used quite effectively as a thrusting/stabbing weapon. Claw hammers are great, too.

Push the alarm button on your "key" and start your horn going to draw attention to what is happening.

Just for safety and convenience in everyday driving, an automobile should always be equipped with an entrenching tool and an axe at the very least. Trench shovels can be used very effectively as a weapon and were, as I understand it, employed as such against human wave attacks during the Korean War.

And, let's not forget chemical weapons here, either. Various lubricants and other aerosol products are often found in automobile trunks. There should always be a fire extinguisher in every car. Get the metal ones and these will serve as an impact weapon, of course, but the contents can be sprayed into an attacker's face. Fire extinguishers should be found in various locations throughout the home, as well.

If weaponless in the usual sense and surprised in the out of doors, whether in the woods or on the street, again, try to be versatile! Fallen tree limbs make poor weapons, often because they are likely partially or almost totally rotten and will crumble when striking an adversary. Smaller sticks – say eighteen inches long or so – can be used as thrusting weapons against eyes and soft tissue. Rocks can be good, larger ones to be held in the hand and used like telephones, "smacked" against the malefactor's head. Smaller rocks may well have jagged edges, but don't count on finding one of these in the crush of the moment. Throwing dirt or leaf material or other detritus into an opponent's eyes can buy precious seconds.

In the urban environment, metal trash can lids can be employed as impact weapons or as shields against an opponent's knife, etc. Picking up a loose brick or a piece of paving could be useful, but shouldn't be counted on. Similarly, that trash can lid is more likely to be rubberized plastic these days, instead of metal.

If you are totally without any sort of conventional weapon and no improvised weapons possibilities present themselves, for a man, at least, there is a frequently available item which can be a terrific counter against an opponent's fists, edged or impact weapon. That's a trouser belt, as earlier elaborated upon. Women's belts tend to be lighter weight and more flimsy. A good man's belt, of the kind one might wear if supporting the weight of a gun is a concern, is an outstanding accessory. And, don't forget the shoes. Sharon used to work with a girl whose father had her carry a brick in the bottom of her purse. In the event of an attack, she was to smack the attacker with her purse, run, then dump the brick.

This scratched up Mag-Lite three D-Cell police-style flashlight is of a type that can be used as an impact weapon, yet it's an innocuous light. The body is of aircraft aluminum. You hit with the butt end, preferably. It must be remembered that impact to the head or the abdomen can precipitate a wide range of somatic complications, some of which can lead to death. Taking a blow to the head – or administering one – is nothing like it is in the movies.

The modern era doesn't lend itself as well to improvised weapons on the street. These days, you can't even count on finding an automobile antenna to break off and use as a whip!

On the other hand, modern times can have advantages. With your cellular phone, you can dial 911 and hope for the best. With modern cars incorporating electronic locking capabilities, you can push the alarm button on your "key" and start your horn going to draw attention to what is happening.

If almost anything can be a weapon in the hands of a creatively thinking "warrior," this prepared individual should evaluate options and practice. There is no reason, for example, that anyone's automobile trunk should be devoid of at least something as useful as a long screwdriver.

Even in the most weapons paranoid cities in the USA, a good, solid, aircraft aluminum three D-cell police-style flashlight can be carried with impunity in any vehicle. These flashlights were made to be rugged and make a fine impact weapon. Flashlights, which are often smaller, but made for superior brightness, can temporarily blind and/or disorient an attacker and buy a second or two of reaction time for you, time in which to flee or to acquire an improvised weapon.

Swordsmith Angus Trim makes some special shorter length blades which are frequently carried by drivers in areas where having a firearm in the vehicle is illegal. Swords, like an axe, will scare away many attackers because the long blade of even a shorter sword is intimidating.

Blackjacks, spring saps, brass knuckles and the like require getting up close to one's attacker and are often categorized as offensive rather than defensive weapons by law enforcement. Such weapons, as mentioned earlier, are best left to those who are experienced in their use. Getting so close to an attacker is dangerous in the extreme.

Where legal to do so, it is only good sense to be armed at all times. If I am dressed, I'm armed. Unless I'm in an area or a facility in which being armed is legally prohibited, there is always one weapon (or weapons) on-body or within reach. This is as natural to Sharon and me as breathing – and it's a very good way to continue breathing!

The title of this chapter aptly states what should be a mantra for the prepared individual, that, indeed, anything can be a weapon. A rolled up newspaper or, better still, a magazine, can be utilized as a thrusting weapon against soft targets on an opponent's body. A number of years ago, an old friend actually used this technique to evade his enemies and fight his way out of a transportation center. Had he failed, he would likely have died in an unpleasant manner.

Ordinary objects – ranging from obvious choices like a full-size umbrella or a cane to a woman's cologne atomizer – have tremendous potential when your life is in the balance. A gun is best, obviously, but when no gun is at hand, one doesn't throw up one's hands in surrender and hope for mercy from an attacker.

Think! Then, do!

Library of Congress Photo

SNUB–NOSED REVOLVERS

Chapter Three

Whether a cop was a "detective" or a "chief," he could be "special" with the classic short-barreled .38 Special revolver, used by everyone from real-life Untouchable Elliot Ness (as mentioned in Chapter Five) to movie and TV private eyes. The origin of the snub-nosed .38 Special revolver, perhaps the most recognizable good-guy gun in the world after the Single Action Army, is closely linked to the legendary Colt cowboy guns. In the percussion era, of course, there were "pocket" models of various revolvers, the Pocket Navy being one of these; but such guns were not really snubbies. Indeed, the first seriously radical barrel shortening of an otherwise full-size revolver was the total barrel removal on a small number of Colt revolvers, to include percussion models as well as the Single Action Army. Persons who needed maximum close-up handgun firepower, yet worried not at all concerning accuracy beyond point blank range, would employ these guns when it was kill or be killed, often across or under a card table.

The application of such a modification was seriously limited, however. Since there was no barrel at all, beyond very close range, the bullet might go almost anywhere. A better solution was needed and the Sheriff's and Storekeeper's Models of the Single Action Army were the answer. These guns could be had with a factory barrel length as short as 2-1/2 inches. There was a cosmetic issue to these guns, in that the short barrels necessitated more cautious application of factory roll markings. That same short barrel length also precluded any sort of ejector rod. I've seen holsters made to accommodate Sheriff's Models which incorporated a tubular sheath holding a knockout rod for punching the empties. Such "snubby" Colt six-shooters (although knowledgeable pistoleros almost invariably loaded only five rounds) would have

ARMED FOR PERSONAL DEFENSE

been at least marginally more concealable than the commonly encountered barrel lengths of four and three-quarter, five and one-half and seven and one-half inches; remember too, the traditional 19th century Colt "plowhandle" grip is smallish by comparison to many other revolver grips.

In 1927, the first truly modern snub-nosed revolver debuted. It was the 2-inch barreled version of the swing-out cylinder Police Positive Special, called the Colt Detective Special. Over 400,000 of these guns were produced in various incarnations, most in .38 Special. The guns were dropped from the line in the 1970s, brought back, continued until the 1990s and, at last, left the scene as part of Colt's discontinuation of most civilian-oriented arms production. Although Robert Stack's turn on Elliot Ness had the famous Treasury Agent in weekly gunfights using a four-inch .38 Special, and Kevin Costner's Ness, who carried a Government Model .45, got into gun battles as well, the real Elliot Ness never had occasion to fire his "Dick Special" in anger during those romanticized Chicago gang-busting days.

> *The Colt versus Smith & Wesson controversy is analogous to the debate over the merits of Fords versus Chevrolets.*

The "Dick Special" – a nickname derived, of course, from the hoodlum slang term for "detective" – was a robust handgun. As many a veteran cop would recount, the Colts had a reputation for being the sort of guns one could drop on the pavement without incurring damage. Colt's principal rival was thought to be a little more accurate and a little more delicate, although there is little if any truth to the delicacy part. As to the other, any quality handgun will almost invariably be capable of greater accuracy than a human being can muster. Colts held six rounds, while the little Smith & Wesson revolvers held only five. Of course, the narrower five-round cylinder was a little easier to conceal. The Colt versus Smith & Wesson controversy is analogous to the debate over the merits of Fords versus Chevrolets – both will do what they are intended to do and failure in the field is almost always traceable to human error, neglect or fuel issues. One common complaint about .38s in general, and more a concern with snubbies, was directly traceable to the 158-grain round nose lead .38 Special ammunition which was almost universally used in these guns up until the ammo renaissance led by Lee Jurras and his Super-Vel Cartridge Company in the 1970s.

The old 158-grain round nose lead .38 Special load just couldn't be relied upon to reliably knock down the bad guys.

Up until 1950, Smith & Wesson snubbies couldn't even handle this mild, basic .38 Special load. The I-Frame Smith & Wesson Hand Ejector, from which the Smith & Wesson Terrier sprang, was great for .32s and the .38 Smith & Wesson cartridge. The .32 Smith & Wesson was an oft-encountered cartridge well into the last half of the 20th century, frequently issued to police women because of its milder recoil back in the days when police women didn't perform regular patrol duty, but rather served as Youth Officers, etc.

When American gun makers resumed normal handgun production at the close of World War II, Smith & Wesson leadership wisely determined that a new frame size was needed, a frame which would allow use of the more powerful .38 Special cartridge in a small, concealable package. Introduced at the International Association of Chiefs of Police (IACP) convention in the fall of 1950, a vote was held to come up with the name and "Chiefs Special" won. And, a true winner it was. The original gun, the Model 36, was available blued or nickel plated. Almost immediately, S&W began producing the gun in three-inch barrel configuration because of demand. The Airweight Model 37 was the Model 36 with aluminum frame. Aluminum cylinders were incorporated, but the use of other than standard velocity ammunition resulted in several problems and Smith & Wesson wisely gave up on aluminum cylinders in favor of steel.

Smith & Wesson was quickly getting the edge on Colt when it came to snubby .38s, Colt having only three basic models: Detective Special, Cobra and Agent. The Agent had a differently configured grip frame, the Cobra a lightweight frame. Soon, S&W had not only its basic snubbies, but the Centennial Model with completely enclosed hammer and a grip safety, the hump-backed Bodyguard with the modified frame which formed a shield on either side of the hammer spur, even guns with adjustable sights. Both the Centennial and the Bodyguard, also available in Airweight versions, were designed for rapid deployment from a pocket or even firing from within the pocket. Colt offered a screwed on shield which could be affixed to their guns, thus achieving the same hammer shrouding effect as the S&W Bodyguard. Colt would, eventually, redesign the grip shape of the Dick Special to provide a more substantial handhold and more modern looking appearance.

The one-upsmanship contest continued.

Smith & Wesson held the trump card and used it: the Model 60, in all stainless steel. The Model 60 was the Model 36 two-inch .38 Special, but with the metal parts made of stainless steel, the first time such a handgun had ever been manufactured. S&W not only launched a product, the company started a revolution which spread throughout the company's revolver line and, eventually, into semi-automatics and became an inexorable tide which swept the handgun industry.

Colt and Smith & Wesson were always the classic rivals, of course; but throughout their history, there was competition from other sources, sometimes domestic, sometimes foreign. The modern era was no exception. Three names emerged in the snub-nosed .38 lists: Taurus, Charter Arms and Rossi.

Anyone who follows the firearms business knows that Smith & Wesson has several times changed ownership. For a time, Smith & Wesson was owned by a firm called Bangor Punta, the name derived from the geographic diversity of the company's holdings. Forjas Taurus entered gunmaking in 1941. In 1970, Bangor Punta acquired majority ownership interest in Taurus. For the next six years, a considerable amount of information sharing went on between Taurus and Smith & Wesson, and not all one way. Although Taurus is known in the USA as a gun company, Taurus is actually quite diverse, renowned in a wide range of manufacturing venues, motorcycle helmets (not sold in the USA) being one noteworthy example. In 1980, Taurus acquired the Beretta plant in Brazil, including all manufacturing equipment, drawings and personnel, then in 1982 forming Taurus in Miami as a separate entity with ultra-modern manufacturing capabilities.

> ## Quality of Taurus handguns in the modern era is second to none.

Taurus is a serious international firm and the principal competition to Smith & Wesson in the snubby revolver market, as well as a force to be reckoned with concerning handguns generally. Quality of Taurus handguns in the modern era is second to none.

Charter Arms came on the scene in 1964; its first gun, as a matter of fact, was a snubby .38. Called the "Undercover," it was an all-steel design weighing a quarter-pound less than the all-steel Smith & Wesson. Like the weight, prices also were lower. Charter expanded and became best known for a later entry, the .44 Special Bulldog. Whether .44 or .38 or the "Undercoverette" in .32, all the guns shared the same grip frame, but not necessarily the same grip plate size. The original Charter Arms entity experienced difficulties and suspended operation.

As this is written, the popular Charter Arms handguns are back, offered also in stainless steel. And, Charter makes a snubby .38, the Southpaw, that's unlike any from any other source ever. It is a perfect mirror image of the standard right hander's gun, the cylinder release catch on the right side of the frame, the cylinder opening to the right, rather than the left.

Third among prominent competitors in the .38 Special snubby market is Amadeo Rossi. Braztech International is the importer and Taurus actually manufactures the handguns on the Rossi equipment at a special facility in Brazil. Amadeo Rossi, the man, founded the company which bears his name in 1889 and his descendants still run the firm. Rossi snubby revolvers are less expensive than most of the competition; but, considering their history and who currently manufactures the guns, there's no reason to think a Rossi wouldn't be a good bet.

Firing a .357 Magnum out of a 2-inch barrel gives precious little additional performance value over firing a well-designed .38 Special round.

With Colt – at least as this is written – no longer producing any revolvers except Custom Shop Single Action Army models, the snub-nosed revolver market has only five significant players, namely Smith & Wesson, Taurus, Charter Arms, Ruger and Rossi, these ranked generally in this order for both pricing and share of the snubby .38 market.

Of course, these days, caliber choices go well beyond mere .38 Special in these guns. The little ".38s" can be had in .17, .22 Magnum and .357 Magnum. Stainless steel is still sought after, but lighter weight guns in Titanium and Scandium are readily available.

Here are some facts which should be hard to ignore, but apparently can be ignored quite handily. The .357 Magnum round achieves its significant oomph when fired from 6-inch, even 4-inch barrels. As barrel length diminishes, so does performance, but not noise and muzzle flash, as well as perceived recoil. What this means is that firing a .357 Magnum out of a 2-inch barrel gives precious little additional performance value over firing a well-designed .38 special round, either +P or +P+. If you fire .38 Specials through your .357 Magnum, which is perfectly fine to do, with the passage of time, you will risk leading the forcing cone (that portion of the barrel on the inside of the frame which receives the bullet as it is fired). The reason for this is that .38 Special rounds are one eighth-inch shorter than .357 Magnum rounds, so the bullet fired out of the .38 Special length cartridge has an extra eighth-inch or so more to jump than a .357 would.

Right profile of a Crimson Trace Laser-Gripped old style Smith & Wesson Model 640 .38 Special.

As muzzle flash increases, since a deadly encounter is at least as likely if not more likely to occur under diminished light conditions, the shooter firing a .357 Magnum out of a J-frame-sized gun has a heightened chance of losing night vision, being temporarily blinded for critical seconds.

Excessive noise is always disorienting.

Recoil is still another concern. One could be the manliest guy on the planet and there would still be a level of perceived handgun recoil which could be described as unpleasant. Let's be honest and say, "painful." Even the toughest or stupidest person will get tired of this sort of repetitive pain. Therefore, one either gets rid of the gun, stops practicing with the gun or swaps down to a lower energy round. So, why a .357 Magnum small frame snubby in the first place? Beats me.

If you want a short barreled .357 Magnum, why not move up to the Smith & Wesson 686 2-1/2-inch, for example? This is built on the larger of Smith & Wesson's two medium frames, the L-frame. L-frame revolvers are terrific guns. You'll still have the noise and muzzle flash, but you'll be able to fire .357 Magnum ammo without crippling your hand. And the gun will hold up longer.

The lighter the weight of the gun, by the way, the greater the perceived recoil when it is fired. My wife had an "Uncle," a fine family friend who was a policeman. He once showed me his perfect looking J-Frame S&W snub-nosed .38 Special. I remarked about how pristine it looked. He told me that it should, because he had never fired it. Don't worry; "Uncle" survived to retirement and lived to a healthy old age. He had no excuse for not firing his weapon, the revolver an all-steel Model 36, the ammo in it certainly the mild old 158-grain RNL load. Move into lighter gun, heavier caliber and those diminishing returns really start to add up. You may fire your super lightweight small frame revolver a little bit; you won't fire it enough. You will, like as not, find every excuse that you can so you don't have to fire it.

My wife and I own and frequently carry snubby .38 Special revolvers. Our daughter has one, too. All of them are stainless steel, not some lightweight metal. The guns are chambered for .38 Special, not .357 Magnum. Sharon's and Samantha's are fitted with Crimson Trace LaserGrips. As much as I like

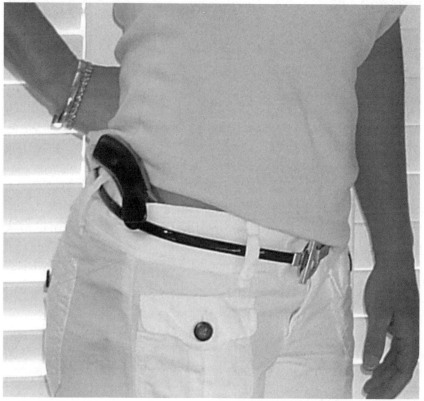

An old style Smith & Wesson Model 60 .38 Special with a Barami Hip Grip.

Loading the old style Smith & Wesson Model 640 .38 Special, sans speedloader or Bianchi Speedstrip.

and use Crimson Trace products, I also utilize a Barami Hip-Grip with a snub-by Smith & Wesson. So, I switch from one to the other.

Humanity was born to complain, it seems, and the grips that used to come on snub-nosed revolvers were a constant source of consternation to many people, namely lamenting that the grips weren't large enough. Aftermarket grips were designed which greatly increased the gripping surface of the revolver. In some cases, this was just great; but, if you increase the size of the grips too much, the gun loses some of its concealability. I had a pair of Smith & Wesson J-frame target stocks that I tried on my original old J-frame Smith & Wesson. The replacement grips didn't stay on the gun for more than a few hours; yet I will always remember how they looked, reminding me, as they did, of putting combat boots on a ballerina.

These days, most snubby revolvers come from the factory with black neoprene (or some other type of synthetic) grips, all of these increasing the front to rear surface, most not increasing the length. My Model 640 came with smooth walnut skinny grips. It's also marked as suitable for +P+. One is not likely to find something like that at the local gunshop.

The Hip-Grip essentially duplicates the skinny old J-Frame S&W factory grip shape. I'm quite used to that shape. When shooting a snubby revolver fitted with the older, skinny grips, I have absolutely no difficulty. I wrap my fist around the grip, holding it as tightly as possible, rather like holding a piece of rod or a roll of quarters in the fist before firing off a punch. When possible, I settle the revolver – which is held in a death grip inside my right fist – into my left hand for a proper two-hand hold. Accurately firing double action – what one should do with a snubby – is easily accomplished.

My first J-frame, which was my first handgun, was a snubby .38, specifically a Smith & Wesson Model 36 Chiefs Special, blued. I bought that gun in 1967. These days, when I carry a snub-nosed .38 Special, it's the aforementioned Model 640, the stainless steel .38 Special re-introduced Centennial Model. Although my revolver is rated for +P+ ammunition, I only use +Ps, specifically the 158-grain lead semi-wadcutter hollowpoint, which used to be called the FBI load. And, yes, I know this was the load carried by the Agents who were involved in the disastrous Miami shootout against a bad guy armed with an assault rifle. Remember, also, though, that it was this round that ended the conflict when a wounded and quite courageous FBI Agent shot the perp in the head. This is the same round that my wife and my daughter have in their J-frame snubbies. I no longer find this round listed from Federal, but Remington offers it as the R38S12. There are also other sources.

The old Smith & Wesson ammunition company offered a 125-grain Nyclad hollow point that was loaded for maximum efficiency from a two-inch barrel, while keeping recoil extremely manageable and cutting down on lead emissions. This round was made by Federal but isn't currently cataloged, as far as I can tell.

Because of the proliferation of .357 Magnum snubbies, perhaps, the available .38 Special loads have dwindled. Yet, there is still sufficient variety to answer one's needs.

With one of the 158-grain lead semi-wadcutter hollowpoint loads, firing my Smith & Wesson Model 640 double action, of course, I can consistently hit what I'm aiming at. Most of my practice with .38 Special snubbies has always been at practical ranges for these guns, between 21 and 30 feet. In really skilled hands, the typical good quality snubby can be relied upon out to 25 yards and beyond; but that is not what these guns are designed for. Although I've shot all of the major brands of snub-nosed .38 Special, the preponderance of my experience

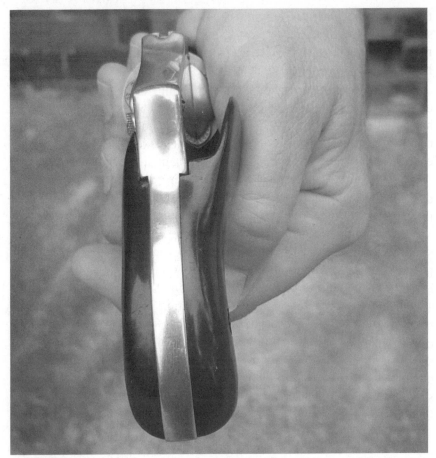

Hip-Grips feature a hook or shelf on the right grip plate, used to suspend the gun over the waistband.

is with Smith & Wessons. Typically, these guns are inherently accurate right out of the box. Unlike the larger Smith & Wesson revolvers, J-frames do not usually lend themselves as well to action jobs. Most of the time, however, trigger pull is quite satisfactory, both as concerns smoothness and weight. Lock-up – easily checked – has always been very good, in my experience.

There are a few things I've learned in four decades of using these little guns. When you are utilizing particularly dirty ammunition for range practice, revolvers generally can pick up so much lead and powder fouling that the cylinder doesn't spin as freely as it should. I discovered this the hard way when the cylinder of that first .38 snubby I owned would no longer turn by hand. That was when I learned how to properly clean a revolver. You should remove the crane screw (the crane on which the cylinder is positioned to rotate is secured with a single screw), slide the crane off the frame, replace the screw, then slip the cylinder free of the crane. Clean this whole area. When the revolver is reassembled, the swung-out cylinder should spin as freely as an honest roulette wheel.

As one becomes experienced with good-quality double action revolvers, one learns how to control the hammer fall by taking the trigger only so far back, hesitating and tripping the action in the next split second, after accomplishing that last check on sight alignment. With DA only guns, like the enclosed hammer snubbies, this is an extremely useful skill.

To further enhance accuracy potential, unless one is addicted to Hip-Grips or dislikes lasers, I recommend the Crimson Trace LaserGrips. They are offered for the J-frames from Smith & Wesson and the similarly-sized Taurus revolvers.

By now, some readers may be wondering why I have barely mentioned Sturm-Ruger. One of the most successful and well-respected firearms manufacturers in the world, the firm did not offer a true small frame revolver, the closest thing to a snub-nosed .38 Special-sized revolver being their SP-101. The SP-101 is a medium frame revolver with shorter barrel and shorter grip offered in .357 Magnum. If, indeed, a slightly larger revolver which will more comfortably handle .357 Magnum is what you need, then these fine guns should be given full consideration along with the slightly larger guns from other manufacturers. With the introduction of Ruger's unique LCR .38 Special snubby, Ruger can be added to the list that already includes S&W, Taurus, Charter Arms and Rossi.

Service revolvers are no longer seen in most parts of the country. Indeed, revolvers were always more popular in the USA than overseas in the post-World War II era. Revolvers hold sway for handgun hunting and, of course, are enormously popular for cowboy action shooting and similar sports. The only non-sporting area in which the revolver still maintains a strong position is with the smaller, personal defense hideout/backup guns, predominantly in .357 Magnum and .38 Special.

And, this last bastion of the fighting revolver shows no sign of crumbling away.

REVOLVER AND AUTOLOADER DIFFERENCES

Chapter Four

The issue of firepower – how many projectiles of what size can be delivered on target in how much time – has spurred arms development from long before the era of firearms ever began. The recurve bow, fast to operate, provided more penetrative power than a standard bow. The hand-cranked crossbow could launch a bolt with more oomph than the arrow from any normal bow, but even the most experienced operator could not match the speed with which conventional arrows could be fired. Firearms, of course, were initially cumbersome, inaccurate and unreliable. Once the size, accuracy and reliability issues started getting under control, the pursuit of increased firepower could begin again.

Actually, accuracy was of little concern outside of hunting or dueling, because long arm battlefield accuracy was not an issue. Smoothbore muskets were fired in volley at targets which stood their ground in good European military fashion. It was considered bad form to take cover. American Colonial riflemen were able to pick off enemy personnel at considerable distances because their hunting guns had rifled bores. When it came to handguns, these, too, were single shots. Attempts were made – in retrospect, some of them

The 1 5/8-inch barrel North American Arms .22 Magnum Mini-Revolver is an ideal extreme close range backup.

silly – to have more than one round available without reloading, but nothing quite solved the problem until Sam Colt's invention of the revolver. Although probably apocryphal, we all know the story of how, as a young fellow, Colt supposedly watched the paddle wheel of a steamboat turning around a central axis and was struck with the inspiration for his revolutionary handgun design. Firing multiple rounds before reloading one's handgun became an almost instantaneous hit.

For another half century, a handgun with a revolving cylinder was the ultimate in handheld firepower. If you wanted more than five or six rounds, you had to get a lever action rifle. In Europe, however, names like Borchardt, Luger and Mauser were becoming synonymous with a new type of handgun, one which fired multiple shots without reloading, had no cylinder at all and, when reloading was needed, could be reloaded more quickly (if the operator had the proper equipment). Add to that the fact that such handguns were capable of holding more than the customary five or six shots. The 1896 Mauser "Broomhandle"—which usually carried ten rounds – and the Luger were soon followed by the designs of John M. Browning. The age of the semi-automatic pistol was upon us.

Semi-automatic pistols began to encroach upon the supremacy of the military revolver, so much so that in World War I, the United States used revolvers only as substitute for the standard Colt Automatic of 1911. By World War II, even though the USA employed some revolvers left over from World

Two ultimate cop guns, one European, one American. The Walther PP .32 saw considerable law enforcement use in Europe, while American plainclothes officers often carried an old style Smith & Wesson J-Frame .38 Special. This is a Model 640, modernized with the addition of Crimson Trace LaserGrips.

War I and some other revolvers as special purpose weapons, the .45 automatic was the handgun of the American G.I. Our great allies, the British, clung to the revolver until the last, even Russia adopting a semi-automatic after the War. Eventually, the British adopted the Browning High Power, although, during World War II, after Belgium was overrun by the Nazis, P-35 Hi-Powers were produced for Third Reich consumption. The pistol was used by both sides, however, High Powers having been manufactured in Canada by the John Inglis Company.

Clearly, the selection of semi-automatics over revolvers for military issue was multi-faceted. The late marksman and firearms pundit Colonel Charles Askins made a point in an article which appeared in *Guns* magazine in the mid-1970s that cannot be ignored. He was always into revolvers for social

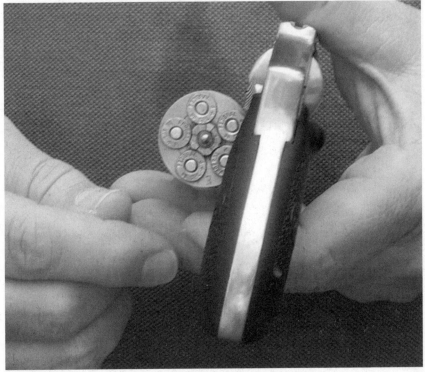

The cylinder of a revolver is the ammunition delivery system.

shooting situations, and took one with him into combat in World War II. The dirt and debris of the field did its work and did the gun in. He switched over to an automatic. Speed of reloading, less complicated mechanism, etc., aside, the automatic is more rugged. More ammunition sensitive, true, but the gun will hold up longer and better under adverse field conditions.

This military popularity eventually had a trickle-down effect within the general population of American shooters. Europeans, when they could have firearms at all, had been into semi-automatics for quite some time. America was wheelgun country. But, in the USA, too, the virtues of the autoloader became more and more obvious.

Civilian concealed weapons carriers were using semi-autos quite a bit. Cops were using semi-autos for backup guns some of the time, occasionally for their off duty weapons. These latter ran the full gamut of what was available, from a good-hearted Chicago Gang Intelligence cop I knew who carried a Walther PPK in .32 ACP to another officer – a really small guy – who carried a chrome plated 1911. One cop I knew switched back and forth between a Smith & Wesson revolver and a Colt World War I commemorative 1911.

A partial reload of a revolver can be accomplished by working the ejector rod only part way, so spent cases can be plucked out and replaced by hand or from a Bianchi Speedstrip. The revolver is a Smith & Wesson Model 681, no longer produced.

In 1967, the Illinois State Police became the first major American law enforcement agency to adopt a semi-automatic pistol, the Model 39. The theory at the time was that the gun could be carried on duty and off duty and that this would be a real asset. The Model 39 had its problems, eventually worked out in successive generations, and gave rise to the large capacity Model 59, the first "wondernine," as such guns came to be called. The world changed – at least so far as American law enforcement uniform sidearms was concerned. Between then and now, 9mms and .40s and some other calibers in larger capacity semi-automatics have become the standard for duty use across America.

The matter of concealed weapons carriage was a lot less forthrightly resolved in the issue of revolvers versus automatics, a greater grey area to be examined and understood.

Examination of the basic differences between the two types does not fully

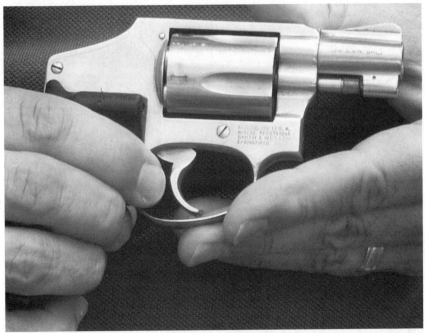

With a double action revolver, the trigger is in a forward position between activations, the trigger drawing back when an exposed hammer weapon is cocked.

The barrel of a revolver is almost always fully exposed. Some revolver styles – some Dan Wesson revolvers – shrouded the actual barrel.

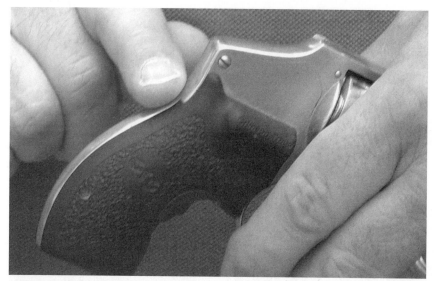

This particular style of revolver has a hammer that is fully enclosed within the frame, making the weapon double action only.

explore the questions involved. The semi-automatic has the following features going for it as a concealed weapon: flatness, greater number of rounds between reloadings, faster reloading (when spare loaded magazines are available to hand), the potential for better accuracy in average hands (although that point is more or less moot at average man on man confrontation distances) and enhanced reliability when neglected or subjected to dirt.

The revolver has the following features going for it as a concealed weapon: less ammunition sensitivity, simplicity of operation and less physical strength required from the operator.

Looking first at the revolver, although double action revolvers are more complicated, watch-like mechanisms in their operation, nothing else is usually required – assuming the gun is loaded, which is simpler than loading an automatic – than to point the weapon and pull the trigger. Certainly, most double action revolvers can be manually cocked and, if not fired, the hammer must be lowered. But, if the operator is taught to use the weapon properly in the defensive context, most of the time the weapon will – hopefully – never be manually cocked unless at the target range. So, to make the gun go bang, the cylinder is swung out, cartridges are loaded into the cylinder (they can only be loaded bullet end first) and it's usually pretty obvious if a cartridge is too big, small, long or short for the cylinder's charging holes.

The cylinder is closed (even flicking the cylinder closed, a potentially damaging practice in which some movie private eyes of old were wont to indulge,

Note the very basic, yet effective, sights on the revolver.

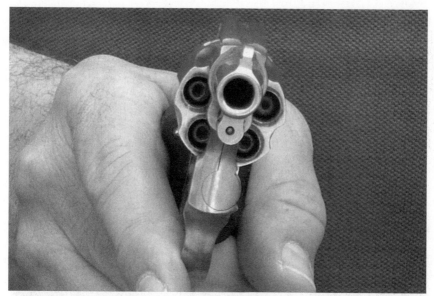

An opponent can look at a revolver and get a good idea of its loaded condition when the weapon is pointed at him. Note also that this J-Frame revolver has Crimson Trace LaserGrips.

would have to be done a lot in order to render the revolver inoperable) and the gun is pointed and the double action trigger is pulled. If the operator changes his or her mind while squeezing (more like pulling) the trigger, easing trigger pressure will let the hammer down with insufficient force to ignite the primer; and, anyway, hopefully the revolver was originally pointed at something or someone that needed to be shot. When the gun has been fired five or six (or more, these days) times, it will click, just like in the movies, but no bullets will come out and there will be no noise other than the click. Our inexperienced operator realizes that the weapon is empty and elects to reload or leave the gun empty.

The double action revolver is simple.

No great level of physical strength is required – especially hand strength. If the operator has trouble with recoil from something as mild as a standard velocity .38 Special or a .32 S&W Long, .22 Magnum revolvers exist. Even a .22 Long Rifle double action revolver can serve, when needed. So perceived recoil becomes a non-issue, one way or the other. As long as the operator can lift the double action revolver into a firing position, even an extremely weak person who could not successfully complete a double action pull can, out of necessity, cock the hammer of the typical double action revolver and exert the miniscule amount of finger pressure required to pull the single action trigger and fire a defensive shot.

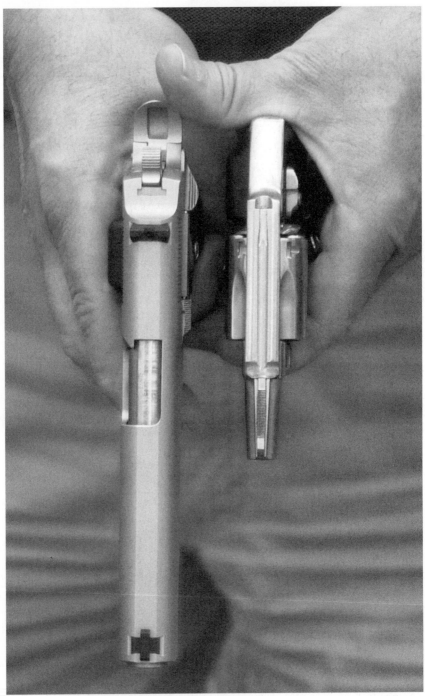

The revolver is always a little wider at least than an automatic, the automatic generally easier to conceal because of its flatness.

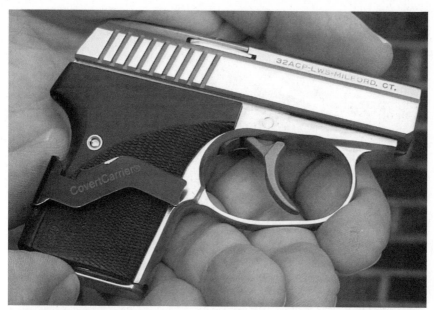

The Covert Carrier replacement grip makes this Seecamp something easily tuckable inside the waistband, especially with a dark belt. The unit is made as replacement grip panels or as attachable clips and really works.

In short, double action revolvers are a no-brainer to operate and can be successfully manipulated by almost anyone, regardless of sex, age or physical health. And, under normal circumstances, they are ridiculously dependable, despite their greater degree of mechanical complexity. Whenever I am asked, for example, what sort of weapon I would recommend for a woman (not someone sufficiently experienced or knowledgeable to select her own firearm), I always suggest a S&W two-inch J-frame .38 Special (not .357 Magnum) with a steel frame. The 640 in .38 Special (which means finding one on the used gun market) is, unequivocally, the very best choice of all. After that, any good S&W or Taurus would be an excellent choice.

Although I carry semi-autos almost exclusively, I keep a .38 Special Model 640 with Crimson Trace LaserGrips handy at all times when I am at home (and I work from home). I acquired one of these for our daughter as her 21st birthday present and got one for Sharon, as well. Both of their revolvers have Crimson Trace LaserGrips, as an aftermarket accesssory. One of the most well-known semi-automatic pistol designers in the United States keeps a Crimson Trace LaserGripped two-inch J-frame .38 as his bedside handgun.

First among the semi-automatic's attributes is flatness. Even my pet Model 640 S&W is five-rounds chubby at the midsection – its cylinder. With five rounds, it is almost identical in thickness – side to side width – to a .45 auto-

A removable magazine, erroneously called a "clip" by some, even some who know better, is the ammunition delivery system for a semi-automatic pistol. They are called "automatics" because they "automatically" load the next round into the chamber in the barrel until the supply in the magazine is exhausted.

matic. A gun like a Walther PP series auto is thinner still. Not only thinness, but size overall is a consideration when discussing the relative virtues of revolvers versus automatics.

Everyone who follows my writings, whether magazine articles or Sharon's and my novels, knows I'm a fan of the Detonics CombatMaster. The basic S&W two-inch J-frame, regardless of model, is about the same length and thickness as the CombatMaster, which is a .45 capable of six rounds in the magazine and one round in the chamber (I only carry 5+1, stripping the top round from the magazine into the chamber), as compared to five rounds in the cylinder. Those rounds – in my CombatMaster – are 230-grain Federal Hydra-Shoks, as opposed to five 158-grain lead semi-wadcutter .38 Special +Ps. I would not volunteer to be shot with either, and the .45s will not realize their full potential out of a three and one-half-inch barrel. Suffice it to say, you can pack more into a semi-automatic, when it comes to size, than you can in a revolver.

There is a greater number of rounds between reloadings, even despite the flatness issue. Most knowledgeable handgunners would concede that, although somewhat an apples-to-oranges comparison, a .380 ACP is a close equivalent to the better standard velocity .38 Special rounds. Let's take two of my favorite handguns, my S&W Model 640 .38 Special and my Walther PP .32 ACP. But let's say the Walther is a .380, instead. In that chambering, the PP (or PPK/S) holds seven .380s in the magazine and one in the chamber. The S&W still only holds five. Well, say I get into it hot and heavy with an arch-enemy or

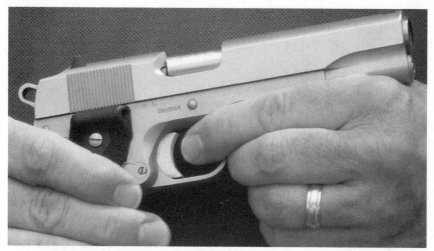

A single action semi-automatic's trigger will frequently look like this when the hammer is at rest or cocked preparatory to firing.

two and I burn through the five rounds in my 640. I have to open the cylinder, hit the ejector rod (with the revolver oriented properly for the empty cases to fall out), use a speedloader or manually load one or two charging holes at a time, close that cylinder and resume firing as needed. In an alternate universe, I blow my eight rounds of .380 from the Walther PP. In the properly functioning pistol and magazine combination, the slide remains open after the last shot has been fired and the last piece of empty brass is ejected. If I have a typical PP-series weapon, it has a push button magazine release (rather than heel-of-the-butt as some comparative few runs of the Walthers had). I hit that button with my thumb and the empty magazine falls clear (if it were a Glock, the magazine might have to be withdrawn after partially ejecting, but I'd have lots more rounds). Assuming that I have a spare magazine previously loaded, I ram that new magazine up the butt of the weapon, draw the slide back just a tad and let it go. The slide strips the first round from the magazine and I'm ready to continue shooting for another seven rounds, with a nice, smooth, single action pull for the first and subsequent shots, I might add. If I don't have a spare, previously loaded magazine, reloading is much slower than with a revolver.

When we turn to a more modern weapon than a Walther PP series pistol, we can have far greater firepower between reloadings. The Glock 26, for example, a 9mm Parabellum caliber pistol somewhat fatter than the Walther, but more or less the same size otherwise, holds ten rounds in its magazine, exactly twice the capacity of the J-Frame S&W, eleven rounds when carried with one round in the chamber and a full magazine. For a greater number of

With most but not all semi-autos, the barrel is concealed within the pistol's slide.

rounds between reloadings and faster reloadings, the semi-automatic is the obvious winner.

What about accuracy? Many people will say that, because of the grip shape of the typical semi-automatic, and in some cases the grip angle (the Luger, the Glock, etc.), semi-autos are more natural feeling in the hand and, because of this, point more naturally at the intended target than do revolvers. More to the point, though, is the fact that pinpoint accuracy – the sort of thing high-end target semi-auto pistols can produce with low-recoil-impulse target ammunition – is not important in the context of concealed carry. Certainly, it's always good to strive for accuracy, but any quality handgun in proper working order, whether revolver or semi-automatic, is capable of better accuracy than the typical human being can achieve with it.

Defensive shooting from concealment can take place at contact distance and, despite those who claim one must always – ALWAYS – look across the sights when shooting, in self-defense scenarios there just sometimes isn't the time or the distance. The wise concealed weapons carrier will learn the skills needed for hip level point shooting at seriously close range.

I am no terrific marksman and have never claimed otherwise. That said, what has always seemed practical to me has been this: Be prepared to shoot from the instant the weapon has cleared the holster and all the while you are raising the gun to eye level and firmly seating it with the support hand.

The typical semi-auto is more of an enclosed system than the revolver. Because of that, it is more forgiving of the dirt and debris associated with everyday use. But, again, we're not debating the merits of revolvers versus semi-autos under prolonged battle conditions in a harsh climate. If we were, there would be no contest; the revolver would lose because it has more moving parts

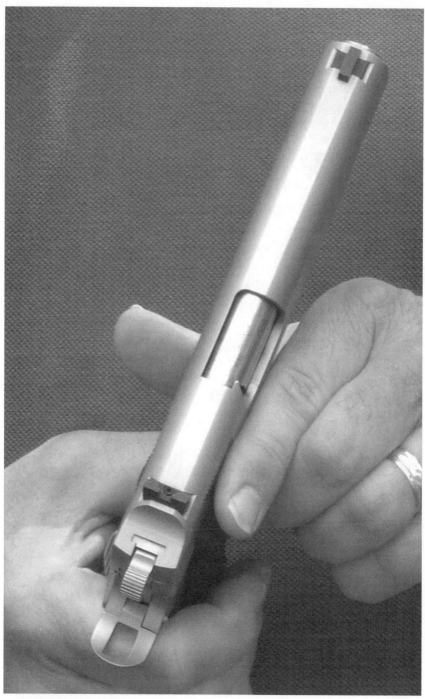

These are not target sights at all, but typically – although not always – fixed (non-adjustable) sights on a semi-automatic will be a little larger than those on hideout revolvers.

and is, typically, less robust. We are, instead, considering what to carry under our clothes for use in an emergency.

The real concern with a semi-automatic is reliability. In years gone by, there was great worry over magazine spring failure. Then, as now, if the spring is properly heat treated, the magazine could well be loaded for years without the spring taking a set (i.e., failing to spring back) and no longer functioning. This assumes, however, quality magazines. If you fit your weapon with

The Kimber SIS was designed for LAPD's Special Investigative Service, but generated controversy because of the special markings on the slide. It has been discontinued. The Kimber SIS is shown here with a DeSantis shoulder rig, a Benchmade Presidio Axis auto, a Covert Carrier equipped Seecamp .32 and cartridges.

cheap magazines of questionable construction, you should not be surprised when the magazine fails. Some of the things that can happen, besides the spring taking a set, include the follower getting jammed on a rough spot in the body or on the follower itself, the magazine becoming compressed on the sides and jamming the follower, the follower nose diving because the magazine spring has the wrong tension, etc. With original equipment magazines or aftermarket magazines from purveyors of high quality components, encountering such difficulties should be rare, indeed. When you first get a magazine, take a dowel rod or unsharpened pencil and depress the follower fully, letting it rise, then repeating the procedure several times. If the follower doesn't stick, you're probably okay. But, of course, the ultimate test is to shoot your weapon and observe how the magazine performs. If all goes smoothly and you take decent care of your magazines, even cleaning them periodically, you shouldn't experience any difficulties.

Indeed, the ultimate reliability issue with a semi-automatic pistol concerns ammunition. Revolvers will generally function with any ammunition of the appropriate caliber. It is difficult to make them jam. Assuming no harsh field conditions, either an extremely heavy amount of powder residue is needed on the cylinder base pin – heavier than I've ever seen – or the primers were not seated deeply enough and they block cylinder rotation. This I have seen, but with hand loaded ammunition.

Semi-automatics, on the other hand, can be very sensitive when it comes to ammunition. A different bullet shape may alter feeding characteristics or a different powder charge may slow down or speed up the slide, thus producing anything from a "stovepipe" on the way out to a feeding jam on the way in. It is important that the ammunition which will be in the weapon when it is carried is the ammunition with which you do at least some of your practice. If, let's say, you can get some really inexpensive ammo and you want to burn it up for practice, fine. Just make certain that you have run enough ammo through your semi-auto of the type that will be carried on the street. The popular wisdom – and I wouldn't dispute it – is that a minimum of two hundred failure-free rounds should be put through the weapon before carrying the weapon for defense.

In brief, if you are a gun knowledgeable person of satisfactory adult strength, either a revolver or a semi-auto will get you through.

The final question is, however, which type is more easily concealed? Because the semi-auto is flatter and the grip doesn't flare outward, the semi-auto wins over all revolvers except the five-shot snubby .38. Full size revolvers are rarely concealed at waist level, these days; if carried concealed at all, they are more likely going to be worn in a diagonal shoulder holster. Full-size

The Kimber SIS is one of the best looking .45 automatics on the planet and proof that looks don't have to be only skin deep. The pistol is also a great shooter.

semi-autos, on the other hand, are worn concealed at waist level by droves of concealed weapons carriers.

Earlier in this chapter, we compared the two-inch J-frame with five shots to the Detonics CombatMaster with six or seven rounds. Comparing my old six-shooter version of the Smith & Wesson Model 686 .357 Magnum to a full-size 1911 with seven round magazine plus one in the chamber, we see that both handguns are a nominal 8.75 inches long, the 686 revolver 5 inches in height while the 1911 runs about 5.25 inches. The 686, measured at the cylinder (the widest part of the revolver), goes 1.5 inches. The 1911, measured at the ejection port, is under 7/8 of an inch wide. The 686's barrel is only 4 inches long and the 1911's barrel is 5 inches in length.

I like a good revolver as much as the next guy – and maybe more. But in a package not much over half as wide as a revolver, I can have two more rounds, reload lots faster and still have an extra inch of barrel for enhanced cartridge performance and accuracy, all while being able to hide the gun on body more easily and more comfortably. If I shift to the slightly fatter large capacity semi-auto, regardless of manufacturer, I can have twice as many rounds as even the more modern seven-shooter revolvers. If I were to compare capacities between a six-shot revolver loaded with light .357s or moderate .38 Specials and an ordinary Glock 17 9mm with the best possible ammo choice, the Glock would have three times the capacity and, depending on loads chosen, not identical but comparable useful oomph on the target. The facts speak for themselves.

OTHER THAN A HANDGUN

Chapter Five

Weapons other than a handgun can be viewed in the context of concealed carry in two radically different ways. The first of these two categories is use as backup or auxiliary concealed weapons to augment the effectiveness and/or versatility of the handgun or handguns. The second category is the use of non-handgun weapons in lieu of a handgun or handguns because firearms are not available or, for some reason, cannot be employed.

Let us identify and examine the types of non-handgun concealed weapons, to include noteworthy examples of same; and let us subsequently examine how these weapons can be employed successfully, either in concert with, or in the absence of, a handgun or handguns.

The basic types include such weapons as are designed for cutting/piercing, impact, airway constriction, or stunning (in this latter classification, both chemical dissemination and electrical current devices). I will avoid electrical current weapons for two reasons, both of which are, admittedly, quite subjective. I consider such weapons at once terribly iffy in terms of halting the attack of a physically strong, hyper-violent adversary; alternatively, such weapons have been known to cause heart failure, thus precipitating or contributing to a death with a supposedly non-lethal weapon.

One of man's oldest tools is the knife. Indeed, not just fixed blade knives, but folding knives, as well, go far back in history. When the Knife Maker's Guild Museum was located in Chattanooga, Tennessee years back, one of the more fascinating items on display was a folding blade knife actually dating from ancient Rome.

The fixed blade knife has its origins in animal horns and claws, sharp and sharpened stone implements, flint-knapped blades and, eventually, in manufactured and/or wrought metals, such as bronze, iron and finally steels of various formulae, some good, some not so good. Fixed blade knives were and are used by themselves or along with larger and longer blades such as swords. But the personal knife or dagger could always be on the person when a sword or more primitive firearm could not and served mundane purposes ranging from cutting and/or eating one's food to staking one's cards to the table in a poker game with untrustworthy companions.

Used with a rapier, the dagger was not a backup to the sword. Used in blade to blade combat on the battlefield, the dagger or knife might be used for any number of tasks, ranging from emergency self-defense to the coup de grace for a valiant enemy.

Motion pictures from the latter decades of the 20th century aside – the *Rambo* films, *Commando*, etc. – the era of the really large or long bladed knife being used as a self defense weapon, most notable among these in the USA being the Bowie Knife and the Arkansas Toothpick, all but vanished when reliable, multi-shot handguns, such as Colt's 1851 Navy, came into wide circulation. What replaced such knives as popular man to man weapons were folding knives, push daggers, straight razors and similar edged weapons, which lent themselves to concealment under conventional urban attire.

Automatic Knives

A subset of folding knives, long considered to be of inferior quality, poor reliability and symbolic of bad character or criminal intent, was the automatic knife, most commonly known as a "switchblade" or "push-button."

Some knives that were not strictly automatic in nature, yet opened in an unconventional manner, were known as a "gravity." A gravity knife uses a blade set into a track. Depress a lever and the blade of the fully inverted knife should slide out by means of gravity alone, possibly aided by a flick of the wrist. My only experience with a gravity knife is from my youth. To get the blade out of the haft or handle, one had to depress the release, then snap the knife in such a fashion that the blade would continue outward and downward, once handle movement ceased (Although such knives can indeed be reliable, the one with which I experimented was not). Once the blade is clear, the activation mechanism can be released and the blade locked in place. To close such a knife, one must activate the mechanism once again and push the point of the blade against a hard object, thus starting it inward.

Until fairly recently, the reputation for dubious automatic knife quality persisted. In recent times, however, the automatic knife from an unimpeachable source – such as Benchmade Knives – has become the gold standard in tactical/defensive/utility folding knives.

Automatic knives can be broken down into categories in several ways, but one very important classification involves how the blade emerges from between the handle scales. Does the blade rotate out the side, or is the knife an "out-the-front?"

Automatic knives that are "out-the-front" style may or may not require some sort of lockout device for heightened safety when carried. Out-the-front knives are like gravity knives, but use a spring loaded mechanism to propel the blade. With many out-the-front styles, closing is accomplished as with the gravity – the point of the blade must be pushed against a hard object when the activation mechanism is worked, starting the blade to retract.

True switchblades – where there's actually a switch that must be flipped for the knife to open – are, generally, going to be fine without an added safety lockout. Push button automatic knives, to be truly safe when carried in a pocket rather than in a belt pouch or some other piece of equipment, do require a lockout. Benchmade automatic knives of the push button variety – of which I am a great fan – have incorporated such a lockout feature for quite some time. Years ago, I used an original Benchmade AFO – Armed Forces Only – push button automatic for a wide range of mundane tasks, including cutting leather and working with construction materials on my front porch.

Benchmade offers a fine selection of folding knives and is one of the leaders in the field. This automatic opening Presidio with its Axis lock a perfect example of rugged dependability and ease of operation.

The knife never failed me, held an edge terribly well, touched up easily and is still not only 100% reliable, but as tight and strong as if factory new. However, since it wasn't in a pouch much of the time, we made a little leather strap which snapped together and secured around the closed knife. This kept the blade from flipping open if the button were inadvertently actuated. The reason for this device was that once I accidentally worked the button on that knife while it was in my pocket. As I started to reach into the pocket, I found that I had a partially open knife with which to contend and I almost gave myself a potentially serious cut.

Double-edged knives are illegal for civilians to carry in most jurisdictions.

An example of an out-the-front knife is the Benchmade Infidel. The original version of this knife takes unique advantage of the out-the-front opening method by incorporating a double edged blade, although a subsequent version became available with a single edged blade. The Infidel, quite popular with American troops, features a switch-like device, this not flipped, but slid, instead. Slide the switch forward and the blade snaps from the front of the knife. Sliding the switch rearward retracts it without the need to "start" the blade by pushing the tip against a hard object. The arrangement found in the Infidel is quite sturdy and the blade shows no tendency to pop open, unless one activates the switch. Remember that double edged knives are generally lumped together with daggers and dirks, hence illegal for civilians to carry in most jurisdictions within the United States and, in some parts of the USA where draconian weapons laws are passed at legislative whim, illegal even to possess. Unless you are military and may need the knife for sentry removal or similar tasks, the single edged version of Benchmade's out-the-front is the better choice.

Indeed, when it comes to legality, automatic opening knives are illegal to carry in many parts of the country and of dubious legality in some others. It is wise to make oneself well-informed concerning such potential restrictions.

Assisted-Opening Knives

Bridging the gap between automatic and manually opening folding knives are the "assisted opening" knives. These can either be viewed as a semi-automatic knife or a semi-conventional folder. Assisted opening knives are not, according to popular wisdom, considered automatics, this because the blade must be started opening manually. Once the blade is through, let's say, ten percent of its opening arc, the spring mechanism is actuated and the blade

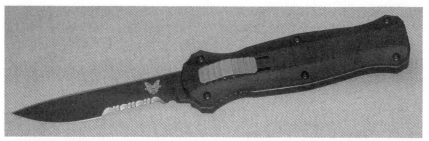

The Benchmade Infidel Out-The-Front comes in two basic styles, this version with a single edge blade. Benchmade OTFs have a unique activator. Slide it forward and the blade pops out; slide it rearward and the blade retracts. Benchmade's unique opening/locking system truly works.

flicks out the rest of the way. This gets around anti-automatic knife laws quite handily. Such knives are available from a wide range of makers, many of these some of the better overseas producers.

My own personal choices in a lockblade folder are quite basic. If an automatic knife cannot be used, I prefer the original Benchmade McHenry & Williams Axis folder. I've worn this knife concealed in swimming trunks in the ocean surf and at the swimming pool. It had neither been spotted nor failed to open when required nor suffered any serious damage from exposure to salt water – all it needed was a little cleaning up after repeated immersions in salt water over a period of several days.

Next on the list of favorite lockblade folders is the Benchmade Benchmite, a super small knife with a unique locking system which must be actuated in order to open the knife or close it. This is so small that it looks perfectly innocuous and is. Yet, because of its construction and locking system, it could serve well in a pinch. And, pinch is exactly what one does in order to work the Benchmite's lock. Also a McHenry & Williams design, the Benchmite is unlocked to open or close merely by depressing a lever in the left handle scale, thus allowing the blade to be manually opened with the aid of the cut-through thumbnail slot or folded closed by pressing on the blade spine as one would close any other knife.

I also have some old favorites. One of these is the original Buck 110, which I like because it is so similar to my original old favorite, a Puma Plainsman. Both of these very similar knives feature standard lock backs, Bowie pattern blades and brass bolsters. Neither employs a thumb stud, but both have been retrofitted with One Armed Bandit thumb studs. These attach to the blade spine wherever it suits you, get turned in with an Allen wrench and are crafted from steel softer than the Rockwell for a typical high quality folding knife blade; they cannot scratch your blade. They work great.

I carried the Puma for years without the One Armed Bandit stud, adding that only a dozen or so years ago. I bought the knife over forty years ago for $18. Used a lot, it's in beautiful shape still.

Butterfly Knives

An entirely different class of folding knife is composed of those knives wherein the blade does not fold out, but the handles fold open, instead. This class of folder would be best exemplified by the Butterfly style knives, known as Bali-Songs. I'm not trying to sound like a commercial for Benchmade, but theirs are the original high-end American Butterfly knives. The Bali-Song originated in the Philippine Islands, albeit the design may have been brought to the Philippines by an American seaman. The well-known stunt co-ordinator, second unit director and Hollywood stunt man Jeff Imada has written the

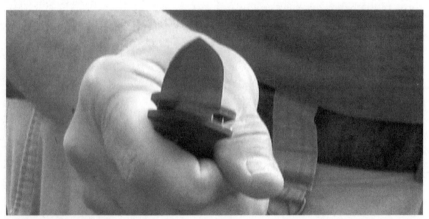

The blade is presented with blade flats horizontal, edge inward.

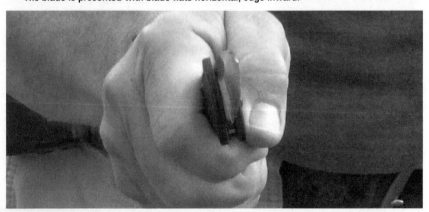

Presenting the blade in a rapier hold, edge downward. Holding the knife edge upward is another option.

Using a dagger hold, the blade can be held close against the forearm and swiveled outward against an attacker. A skilled knife person may be able to keep the presence of a blade hidden, revealing it only to counter a bare hand or impact weapon strike.

definitive book on the handling of these knives, which can, in itself, be quite spectacular to behold. Basic operation for reliable one-handed opening and closing is simple enough to master, and is certainly an attention getter if you must open it for some sort of social encounter. Be advised, perhaps because these knives are spectacular looking in action and exotic looking even when not in use, there are cheapies on the market that one should avoid. Similarly, a Butterfly knife from an otherwise respected source should serve you well. Remember, however, that these knives are prohibited in some areas, most likely because they are reliable and can be useful in self-defense. One of mine, an original Pacific Cutlery/ pre-Benchmade model, features a handmade Wee-Hawk blade by the late Jody Sampson, the designer and fabricator of the original "Conan" Atlantean swords.

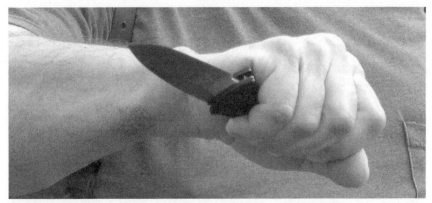

The knife is pivoted outward, edge toward the opponent. A stout lockblade folder – this one is from Benchmade – is an essential element of concealed weapons carry.

The advantage a stout folding knife has is that it can be used as a tool just as easily as and far more often than it is used as a weapon. Without even opening the knife, it can be used to hammer an object – or an attacker. With a combo edge, its cutting versatility is considerably enhanced, although its tactical utility may be slightly compromised – saw teeth can get caught on an adversary's web gear on the way in or the way out. And, such stout, dependable knives are often worn in plain sight, either by means of a pocket clip or a belt pouch. Frequently, the pocket clips can be switched around to accommodate different blade orientation preferences or handedness. Pouches can be worn for a straight upward withdrawal, positioned for a downward draw or, in some cases, worn horizontally for added concealability. A really small folder, like the little Benchmite, can be dropped in the pocket along with one's keys, etc.

Boot Knives

Most boot knives are double edged,
making them illegal to carry.

Once one gets past these knives, one enters the realm of clandestine carry. The most commonly encountered clandestine knife carry besides a folder hidden in a pocket is the boot knife. In eras gone by, many a frontiersman might carry a knife in his boot top. Although this might be a hidden knife, often the boot top was simply a convenient place to carry a hunting knife, the haft fully exposed to anyone who wished to notice it. The modern boot knife is intended to be hidden, either within a boot, the top of which is covered by a garment, or inside the waistband, rather like an inside waistband holster. When worn

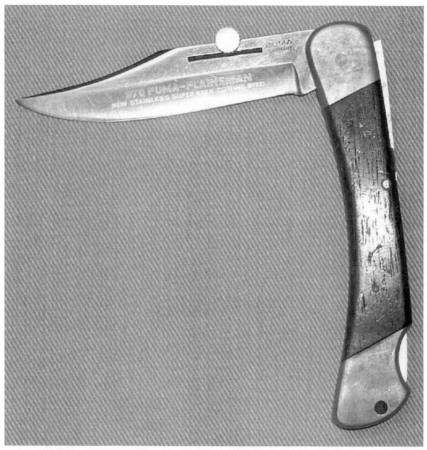

The handle scales of this Puma are Jacaranda wood, the bolster solid brass and the blade stainless "Super Keen Cutting Steel."

in either way, a clip – like those often found with inside holsters for firearms – secures the sheath. For true boot carry, the prepared man or woman will have a leather craftsman position a sheath within the boot top, which will keep the pommel area of the knife – the butt, if you will – just below the top of the boot, thus allowing quick access and total concealment.

Most boot knives are double edged, making them illegal to carry in many jurisdictions. One solution was recounted many years ago in an A.G. Russell catalog, referencing what may well be the world's classic boot knife, the original A.G. Russell Sting IA. A resourceful customer, who loved the knife, couldn't legally carry it because it was double edged. He had one of the edges rounded off so that the knife was a single edge and was, thusly, able to carry the knife legally – he used it on his boat, if I recall.

A lockblade folding knife – manual, assisted or automatic – can often work well in a boot top by means of the pocket clip. For most purposes, I would find this more practical than a fixed blade knife in this application.

When I was a kid, I would sometimes carry a very small fixed blade knife with the help of an ordinary key chain passed through the top of the sheath's belt slots, then passed through the top of a trouser belt loop over my hip. The knife was completely hidden within my pants, but could be fished up when

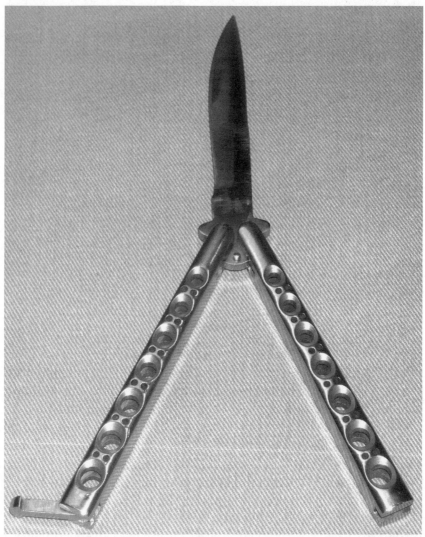

An original Bali-Song knife, the Weehawk blade handmade by the late Jody Samson, the knifemaker who crafted the sword Arnold Schwarzenegger used as "Conan." Bali-Songs, or "butterfly knives," are fast into action in the right hands and spectacular to watch in motion.

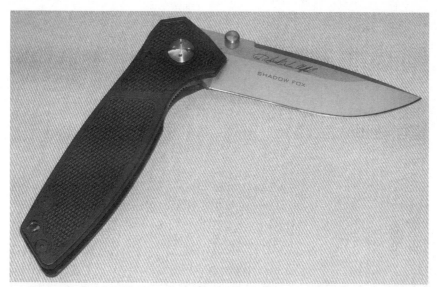

This Shadow Fox folder is a comparatively large knife, roughly twice the size of a conventional lockblade folder.

needed. Innovation in carry technique can be the true key to effective conceal-ment – as long as it works reliably.

Another way in which to carry a fixed blade knife concealed is on the fore-arm. During World War II, some British Special Operations Executive (SOE) and, quite possibly, some Office of Strategic Services (OSS) personnel had ac-cess to a marvelous little spike blade sleeve knife. It was worn in a thin leather sheath, the sheath fitted with two sets of belt slots. A narrow belt accompanied the knife and sheath, the belt wound through the four slots, forming an "X" on the outside of the forearm, then buckled closed. The knife sheath held the knife, inverted, butt toward the wrist, on the inside of the forearm. When one reads in the late Ian Fleming's earliest James Bond novels that Bond carried a knife on his forearm, it was this sort of arrangement of which Fleming was likely thinking.

The sheaths for small fixed blade knives were sewn behind lapels or any other likely spot in one's clothing. These "lapel daggers" and "thumb dag-gers" were duplicated in sharpened plastic during the First Gulf War to help our personnel who might have been captured have a weapon which would not be found out by metals detectors. Non-metallic can still be had. A.G. Russell's justifiably famous CIA Letter Opener is a non-metallic version of the Sting IA Boot Knife. It is remarkably strong and effective as a weapon. It is also a felony to bring one into an airport, let alone past security. Cold Steel has also offered Tanto-shaped and spike-shaped non-metallic knives.

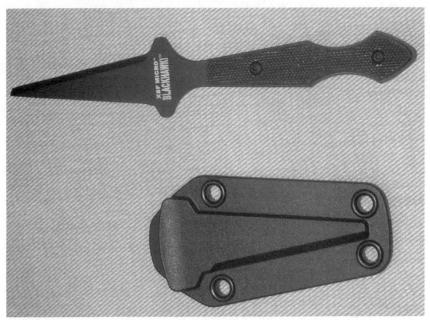

The Blackhawk! XSF Micro dagger has a short blade, but plenty of haft or handle, comparatively.

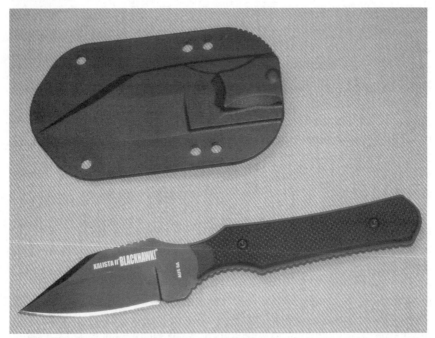

The Blackhawk! Kalista II at first glance might look not at all special. When one considers the grip possible with this handle and realizes how little edge is really needed in most defensive contexts, the Kalista II's potential becomes clear.

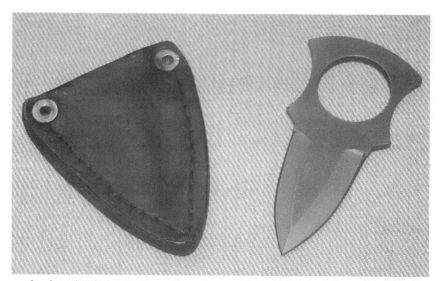

A unique thumb dagger that would be slipped over a finger like a ring. Like as not, this design would dictate using the weapon with it positioned on the underside of the hand, cuts delivered with a slapping motion.

Push Daggers

The push knife, often called a push dagger, is a fine close quarters defensive weapon, enabling a physically smaller or weaker person to make a good account of himself/herself against a stronger and bigger opponent. These knives enjoyed great popularity during the 19th century. Modern versions, using neoprene handle materials and stainless steel blades, are otherwise little different from their more antique counterparts. One fists the knife so that the blade emerges between the second and third finger. Such knives are sometimes used in pairs, one in each hand. The classic way to use a push knife is to punch with it, just as if one were punching bare-handed. Most such knives are double edged.

Cold Steel offered a fine version with a single edge that was versatile enough to be used as a regular knife, as well as a defensive tool. Sharon carried one of these single edged Cold Steel knives in her purse for years. They are an ideal close quarters weapon for a woman in the event she is attacked. Wild Boar Blades offers a single edged push knife, stag gripped. The sometimes larger, double edged push daggers are great backup weapons in the tactical context and all these unique knives can be worn in a variety of ways. Blackhawk Products offers a push knife that is small, light, easily concealed and extremely effective. I have a pair of them, and that's the best way to use push knives. They can even be worn on a chain suspended from the neck.

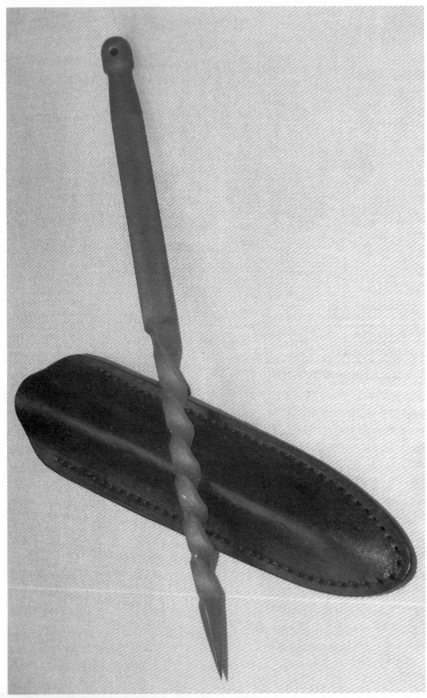

A spike with a twist – literally and figuratively – from Pat and Wes Crawford, this is called the Dragon Tooth and would be easily hidden.

Neck Knives

The Crawfords and many other makers offer various types of knives which can be brought together under the title of "neck knives." The term "neck knife" is pretty self-explanatory, really. The knife sheath is designed to handle a neck chain attaching to its tip. The sheath – typically fabricated so that it will hold the knife securely with a friction fit – is worn inverted under one's clothing. Someone may notice the neck chain, but that chain could serve a variety of purposes, from the wearing of a religious symbol to an article of jewelry to a small handgun (NAA once offered a neck chain option for certain mini-revolvers). I knew a juvenile offender from the long ago time before widespread use of metals detectors. He'd been caught by the police after repeatedly burglarizing an electronics store during a snow storm; the cops tracked him to his stash. He did time in a major metropolitan juvenile detention center. I learned, well after he was released, that he had worn a .25 automatic on a chain around his neck the entire time of his incarceration. Gives you a comforting feeling, doesn't it?

Most non-automatic, non-butterfly knives, open rather conventionally. Another classification of knife opening mechanism, unique to Benchmade, is the sliding lock system pioneered in the Benchmade McHenry & Williams Axis folder. Ambidextrous, the sliding lock can be accessed with equal ease, regardless of handedness. Fold out the blade as one normally would by levering the thumb against the thumb stud. The Axis lock slides to release the blade and lock it open. To close the knife, draw the Axis lock rearward, until the blade

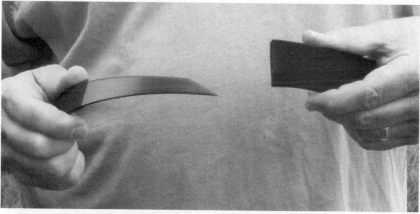

The Razor Dagger from Razor at Beltswords.com was designed at the request of a federal agency as a frisk-proof backup weapon for "undercovers," a dagger that could be carried hidden under one's regular belt, then drawn with lightning speed and used for stabbing and slashing – read as, staying alive. There's also a sword that can be had, but the Razor Dagger, curved to fit the body, is trouble enough for a bad guy.

releases from the locked open position. This system is fast, sure and elegant. The Presidio automatics from Benchmade use this same locking mechanism, making them perfectly ambidextrous.

Many accomplished knife people can pinch a folding knife blade partially open and reliably snap it open the rest of the way with a flick of the wrist. I can't! Some will invert the knife, pinching the blade and flicking the handle away from the blade, then roll the knife into a saber hold. A lockblade folder of decent size, whether an automatic or a conventional knife, need not be opened to be effective in the anti-personnel context. The butt of the knife – useful for hammering in the field at times – can be useful for hammering in a fight, too.

Impact Weapons

Impact weapons can be anything that will inflict pain and/or injury. The classic, of course, is the ever-popular blackjack, otherwise known as a flat sap. Such a device is sometimes referred to as a "kosh." A skilled man with a flat

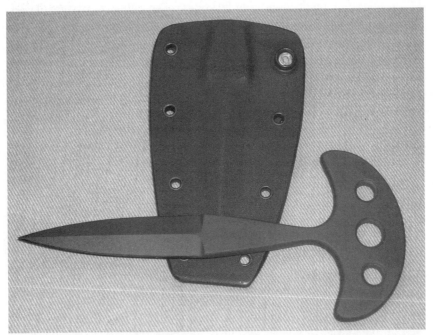

The Crawford All Steel Push Dagger shown with its sheath. Pat and Wes Crawford make some of the most uniquely designed close range defensive implements to be had.

The Crawford All Steel Push Dagger is double edged, as are most push daggers. When clenched in a balled fist, a push dagger makes a formidable weapon. Push daggers – ornate ones, often – were popular weapons in the nineteenth century, easily hidden and effective.

Pat and Wes are known for equal parts of imagination and superb craftsmanship.

sap can use it for everything from inflicting impact blows to cuts, but impact is its principal purpose. In days gone by, no self-respecting uniformed Chicago cop would be caught dead without his blackjack sticking out of his hip pocket. Filled with powdered lead and constructed of heavy leather, blackjacks come in various sizes, the compact ones most often seen and the most practical. Before continuing, it is well to remember that some impact weapons – blackjacks among them – can get you into more legal trouble than a handgun, assuming you have a concealed carry permit.

Again, the movie image of the impact weapon is deceiving. In films or television, the bad guy sneaks up behind the good guy and smacks him across

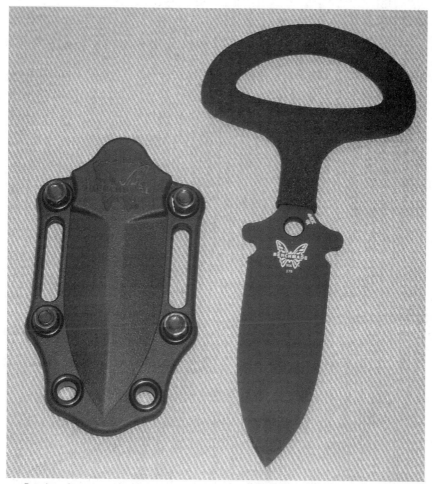

Benchmade makes this push dagger as a hideout weapon, the sort of thing a police officer might carry in case he/she is disarmed. This little push dagger would be easily missed in a hasty body search.

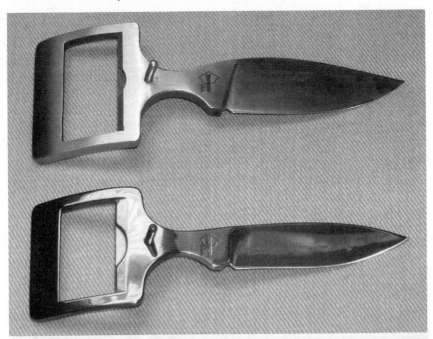

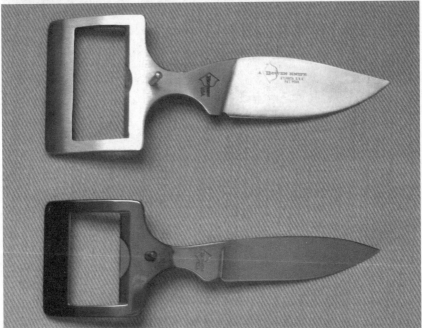

An assortment of blade shapes in Bowen Belt Buckle Knives, the belt buckle becoming the knife handle, the belt the sheath itself. Finely made from stainless steel, they are elegant looking, available either single or double edged. The single edged versions make good work knives in a pinch.

the back of the head. We're not talking about cold-cocking a shamus in the context of this book, nor are we talking about someone getting his jollies by inflicting pain on somebody. Indeed, perhaps the best example is that of an old friend of mine who was, at the time, a policeman. He became embroiled in a fight with a man who was vastly larger and quite powerfully built. My friend's firearm had fallen to the floor when the attack began. As this physically overpowering man was choking the life out of my friend, my friend's only weapon was his blackjack, with which he not only subdued the attacker but saved his own life. He has that blackjack to this very day. I might have been tempted to have it bronzed.

To use a blackjack or any impact weapon in the defensive context, you must attack. You have to get close enough to your assailant to rain blows on his head, face or neck. If you have a rigid impact weapon, you can also use it to thrust

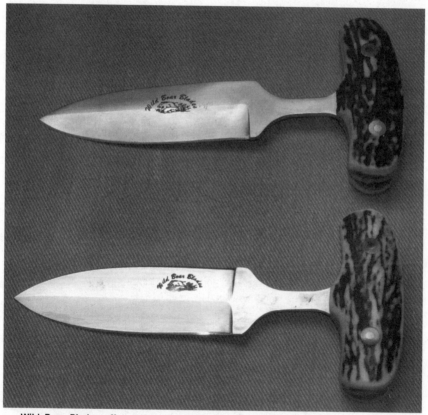

Wild Boar Blades offers a very practical push dagger that is single edged, hence not automatically classifiable as a dagger from a legal standpoint. This matched pair allows taking full advantage of push dagger technique, one balled in each fist. Think of this technique as boxing with an "edge."

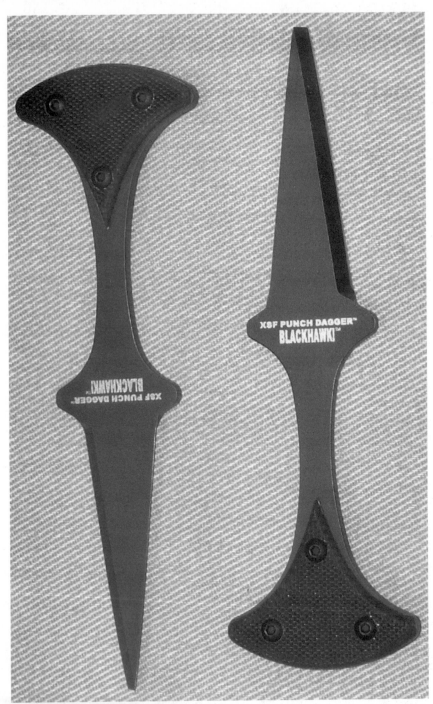

These Blackhawk! XSF Punch Daggers can be used with one in each fist. Skeletonized, they weigh next to nothing and can be secretly worn on body in a variety of ways.

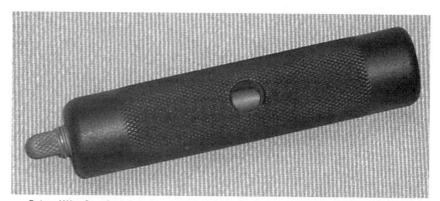

Pat and Wes Crawford, father and son knifemakers, create some marvelously original knives and edged weapons. The Push Pick conceals a spike in the handle. One can use the handle as shown as an impact weapon.

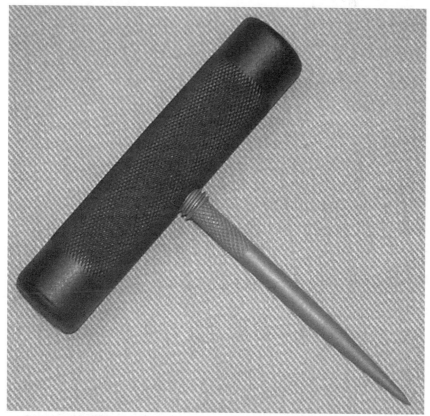

Or, one can position the spike at the center of the handle, wrap the fist around the handle and use the Push Pick like a push dagger. Not shown, one can unscrew the Push Pick's spike from the center position and screw it into the end from which it was initially unscrewed and drawn only with the spike pointing outward. This way, it's held like a conventional knife, for stabbing and thrusting.

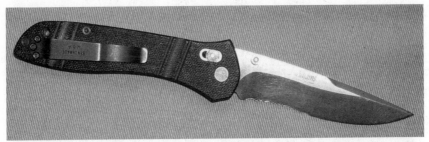

This McHenry & Williams Axis folder opens rapidly, can even be flicked open with a gentle nudge, and is rugged in the extreme. It holds an edge, and the serrations on the combo edge really cut remarkably well and can be touched up just like the primary edge. The Axis lock is found in conventional, automatic and assisted opening models.

against the softer parts of the body – the throat, the abdomen, the groin, for example. Rigid impact weapons can be used, of course, to deal head blows, as well. Again, movie imagery must be considered. Whether the impact weapon is a cast iron skillet or a blackjack or a piece of pipe or a gun butt (and, semi-automatic pistol magazines can be damaged when striking something as hard as a human head), blunt trauma doesn't work like it does in fiction. After being rendered unconscious, the good guy usually gets up a little slowly, rubs his head or neck, shakes his head to clear it and is, otherwise, unscathed. Not in reality. My wife and I were privileged some years ago to hear a fascinating lecture by a writer who was also a board certified physician, well versed in head injuries. She confirmed much of what we already knew. A knockout blow to the head may well cause anything from a skull fracture to a subdural hematoma. If you're a private detective who gets hit on the head so severely that you are knocked unconscious, assuming that you do wake up, seek medical attention immediately – the babe and the bottle of scotch can wait.

There are other handy impact weapons to carry concealed besides the blackjack or flat sap. There is a spring sap. The spring sap is designed to inflict a glancing blow, "springing" toward the target, then snapping back. There are a number of variations on the sap or kosh, some even disguised as key rings. One of the more interesting and versatile variations is the sap glove. Sap gloves typically have powdered lead shot in the knuckles, extending along the four fingers as they comprise the flat of the fist. One can use these like a flat sap and slap with them – I've seen saps described as "slappers" – or one can backhand an assailant or just wear the gloves while delivering punches. These gloves are, of course, winter weather wear; in warmer seasons, they would attract too much attention. As an aside, sap gloves are not terribly warm. So, if you do wear sap gloves in the wintry months, you might be well advised to get woolen G.I. glove liners to wear with them.

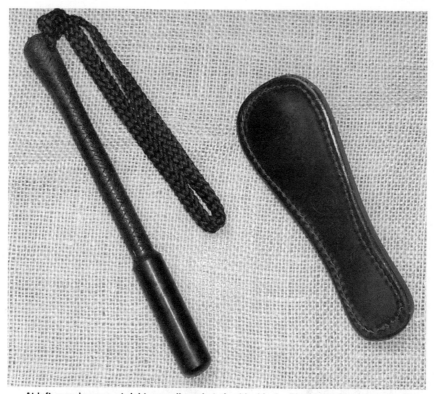

At left, a spring sap, at right a small, pocket size blackjack. Blackjacks like this were seen in almost every uniformed officer's hip pocket years ago. It is probably illegal for you to carry one of these.

The classic gentleman's impact weapon, of course, is the cane. Although not concealable, it is an ordinary object and, if one affects a limp, a cane will go largely unnoticed. If someone complains, just grouse about your rights being violated under The Americans with Disabilities Act and the complaints will likely stop. Although sword canes are readily available, an ordinary cane – not a weapon at all – can do yeoman service as a defensive tool. Don't swing with it unless the opportunity presenting itself is a sure thing. If you can swing it, someone else can catch it. Instead, use your cane as if it were a rapier, the tip of the cane – even if it has a rubber cap – employed against hard or soft body targets, just as one would employ the sharp point of a rapier.

Not only can a cane be used to counter-attack an assailant, it can also be used to deflect or parry attacks your assailant might make with an edged weapon or a blunt instrument. In close quarters grappling, of course, a cane can be utilized to crush a windpipe. The problem there is that, in doing so, regardless of the fact that this is self-defense, such an act might also be considered deliberate homicide, going beyond the boundaries of mere defense. Be careful not to allow victimhood to be construed as aggression.

The noted firearms writer and teacher Massad Ayoob has often made the point in print that, in order to keep the law on one's side when responding against an attack, one should be able to show a continuum of force. That goes like this: Sure, you have a handgun, but you also have a pepper or mace spray and use this to ward off the attack, only moving up the force continuum when and if necessary. Hopefully, I'm getting Massad's idea across properly. And, it is sound reasoning in the extreme. One never wants to be viewed by the legal establishment as a wannabe vigilante avenger.

Someone accosts you on the street, clearly trying to provoke a fight. You cautiously walk away, never turning your back. The aggressor follows you, graduating from insults and taunts and threats of bodily harm to brandishing a piece of pipe. As the aggressor continues his rant, a reasonable person knows that the time for possible self-defense is at hand. Rather than pull your legally concealed handgun, you reach for your chemical weapon, in the hopes of ending the fight. You should also have taught yourself how to dial 911 on your cellular telephone by feel. Do that with the other hand and call for the cops.

Damascus is the name in sap gloves, the knuckles loaded with powdered lead. Sap gloves can be used as a glove to deliver a punch, a backhanded slap or used held in the hand like a blackjack. Sap gloves are quite likely illegal for wear on the street in your locale, their use highly specialized. These look like G.I. mule hide gloves.

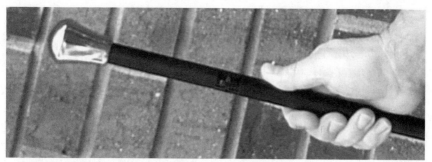

One of the sword canes from Cold Steel, this "City Stick" is made from eleven layers of fiberglass and is, essentially, unbreakable.

Only if the chemical weapon neither discourages nor deters the aggression and no opportunity to escape presents itself should you move to the next level of response.

If you must use force to deter aggression, do so vigorously, but cease as soon as it is apparent that you have defeated your opponent or you are able to get away. If you seriously injure your attacker or you think you might have killed your attacker, when you call 911, make certain to express your concern for your attacker's physical condition, urgently requesting medical assistance. Also, accurately describe how the person attacked you, how you tried to get away, how you were forced to use your chemical spray. Describe how the attack went on and, in fear for your life because of your attacker's menacing gun or knife, you drew your firearm. Explain how you warned him that you would shoot if he didn't leave you alone. Explain how you finally, as he pressed his attack, were left with no alternative but to fire your legally carried weapon.

Describe your appearance, how you are dressed, etc., so that when the cops arrive they will know you are the good guy. Stay on with 911 until the cops do arrive.

Aside from all this being practical at the moment, that 911 call that was recorded is the best evidence you have to prove you're not a bloodthirsty vigilante avenger, but just someone trying to live his life unmolested, a humane person who regrets having had to take violent action to defend himself against attack.

Stock Photo

BODY LANGUAGE

Chapter Six

Women probably have this experience more often than men: just looking at someone and getting the creeps. Body language can, in fact, project a great deal of information – as well as disinformation – concerning someone's state of mind, health, etc. The end result can be positive or negative, but it matters in everyday life, nonetheless. But body language is also an important factor in going armed and in determining whether or not someone else might be armed.

The body language issue is a two-edged sword, as it were. If you master the appropriate techniques to disguise the fact that you are armed, someone equally or more skilled may read these techniques and deduce that you are armed. If you don't practice these body language techniques, however, you will make it obvious to almost anyone who cares to notice that you are, indeed, carrying a weapon. The idea of caring to notice bears some exploration. These days, even persons who aren't armed have bulges under their clothes – and I'm not alluding to over-eaters. Most of us carry cellular telephones and/or other electronic devices, often holstered at waist level or just stuffed into a pocket; these make bulges.

When we had our holster making business some years ago, by far, we were best known for our front pocket holsters. Setting modesty aside for a moment, they were really terrific. We made them for handguns as small as NAA mini revolvers all the way up to Glock 26s and 27s. Potential customers – especially those interested in carrying the larger guns – would sometimes ask me, "With your holster, will the gun show at all?" I explained, politely, that we were holster makers, not magicians. The idea, when carrying a gun on-body, is not to have it appear that you have been poured into your clothing and there are no bulges. Bulges are natural. It is what these bulges suggest to the observer that is important. Because of the electronic gear so many of us take along on a regular basis, even trained observers actually have a more difficult time determining whether or not someone is armed. This makes body language even more important.

I often make the observation that persons who never carry a weapon, perhaps don't even own a weapon, would be well-advised to learn the body language associated with weapons carriage. In that way, even if you are unable and/or unwilling to use a weapon to defend yourself or an innocent, you may well be able to alert someone who has the means by which to respond to a potential threat. In a post 9-11 world, reading body language is more important than ever before, and not just for spotting possible guns.

> *People who never carry a weapon would be well-advised to learn the body language of weapons carry.*

The guy at the mall who seems oddly nervous and carries a shopping bag in such a manner that it would appear to be the most important thing in his life could just be an eccentric or could be a bomber with a sack of explosives or could be carrying an illegally altered automatic weapon and a bunch of magazines he plans to expend on human targets of opportunity. Read a person's moves and mannerisms. If they look like there's something just not right, in this ever more hazardous world, it won't hurt to mention the person to armed security. If you are legally armed and just happen to notice our fellow with the shopping bag and, while debating about telling security, you see him pull out a weapon, you're that much ahead of the curve. It never hurts to be observant. And don't be paranoid about being paranoid!

The late Jeff Cooper promulgated what has come to be called by some the Color Code of Awareness. White meant that you were perfectly at ease in what was assumed to be a perfectly safe environment. Yellow meant that you were cautious. Orange meant that you perceived actual danger. Red meant that you were in a threatening situation, which triggered the fight or flight response. As any rational person would agree, one should never really be in white. Yellow should be standard operational condition. Remember what I said about not feeling paranoid about being paranoid? I carry a gun whenever it is legal to do so, and this includes having a handgun on the desk as I write this and having a gun on my person even just hanging around the house. Think I'm a little

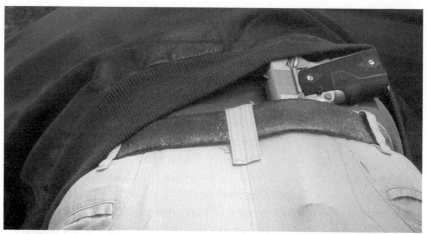

With a gun carried in the small of the back, not only will the gunbutt sometimes show, but with lighter weight pants what is below the waist may also profile.

over the edge when it comes to security? One of my oldest and best friends, a man whose wisdom I trust and whose experience is priceless, goes so far as to take a revolver sealed inside a Ziploc bag into the shower with him, just in case (one would never use a semi-automatic pistol in such a context, because the confines of the bag would, more than likely, cause a feeding related failure and/or jam the slide with pieces of the plastic).

Reading body language will help to enable you to shift from yellow to orange and back again as circumstances dictate.

Here's the body language you will want to master if you go armed and know how to recognize the armed condition in others, whether you are armed or not. Think of this skill like learning to read "tells" in a poker game. But, winning in this context could be considerably more important.

For this example, you are wearing a handgun the size of a Glock 22 or Kimber full-size or Commander-size 1911 in a properly designed FBI Cant strongside belt holster. Your covering garment is a bomber jacket. You reach for anything at shoulder level or above with your right hand and, if it wasn't showing already, the muzzle end of the holster shows below the bottom of your coat. Watch people as they reach for something, anything.

If you are the person with the full-size pistol in a belt holster, either wear a longer coat or switch to an inside waistband holster or some other type of holster.

You are wearing that same gun and holster combination. This time, you're wearing a sportcoat or something of similar length. It is appropriate for you to be wearing a coat (i.e., it's not the middle of August in Georgia or Florida). You're in the grocery store and you want some of that terrific Progresso New

England Clam Chowder out of the top of the display. You reach well over the level of your shoulder. The coat does not pull up and expose the bottom of the holster. Instead, the action of reaching with your right arm draws your sportcoat tightly across your back and tightly across your gun and holster combination, particularly the butt of the weapon.

To counter this, if you are carrying the weapon on your right side, always reach for things at shoulder level or above with your left arm. As you do this, something quite naturally occurs. As you raise your left shoulder and extend your arm, your right shoulder will drop slightly lower. The entire left side of your body will lean into the action of reaching. This lowering of the right shoulder and slight raising and bending of the left side of the body into the reach causes the right hip to move slightly left and the covering garment – your sportcoat – to fall away from the body. Your gun is better concealed than it normally would be.

You are still attired as in the previous scenario. You drop your keys to the floor or the ground. You bend over to pick them up. Your sportcoat pulls

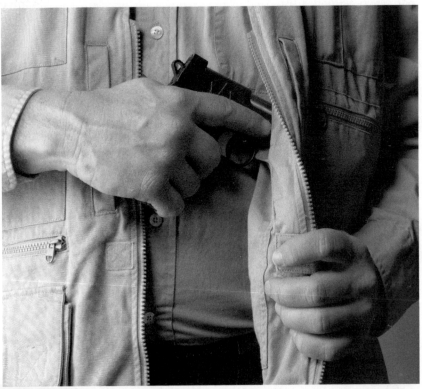

If a coat isn't going to be closed – and, if a tight fit, it shouldn't be – keep spare ammunition or some other heavy object in the pocket to keep the coat in place.

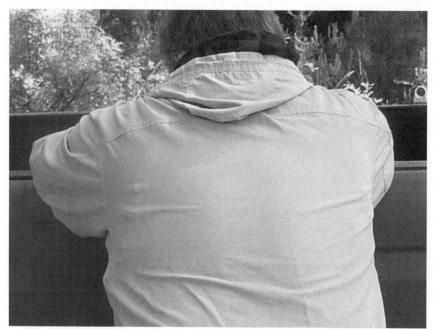
If you look really closely, you'll see a gun and holster profiled under the left shoulder.

tightly across the butt of your gun and anyone with a half an ounce of visual acuity and the brains to go with it realizes that you are armed. Now, try the same thing while wearing your bomber jacket or windbreaker. The coat may pull up so high that the entire gun and holster combination is exposed. You can always tug down on the bomber jacket's waistband, which looks extremely suspicious.

The remedy for either of these scenarios is to do something besides bending over. Pretend you are doing calisthenics. Do a deep knee bend and try to keep your back straight. The covering garment you are wearing will cover just as much. If you have sore knees, bending at the knee rather than the back can be painful; so be careful, of course.

It's a windy day outside and you are wearing your sportcoat again with your full-size pistol in a strongside belt holster. If you constantly tug at your clothing to keep your jacket under control against the wind, you could be telegraphing the fact that you have something to hide under it. Buttoning a jacket over a large concealed weapon invites profiling under the fabric. Either shove your hands in your pockets, making certain not to push the pockets forward and draw the fabric tightly over the gunbutt, or weight your pockets. Weighting the pockets with speedloaders or spare magazines serves two purposes: the weight helps keep your sportcoat down and the extra reloads can never hurt.

You are at a restaurant with your wife or girl and you are wearing that sportcoat again (hopefully, it's been dry cleaned) and your full size pistol and holster. Do you want a booth or a table? Which side do you sit on?

A booth is always better, when available, if you are armed at waist level. When possible, following Wild Bill's habit, the disregard for which cost him his life that one time in Deadwood, try to face the most likely direction(s) of ingress. Ideally, you should be able to observe all or most of the room and occupy the last booth toward the wall, this so that no one can sit behind you. Unless you want to constantly think more about showing that you are armed than the enjoyment of your companion and the cuisine, sit so that your armed side is facing the interior of the booth rather than the rest of the diners. There's another advantage to sitting in this orientation. If someone tries to jump you, you can get your back against the wall of the booth and your strongside is furthest away from the attacker as you make your draw. Such a scenario, by the way, is another example of why it is good to learn to shoot from a variety of positions and why, when possible, Crimson Trace LaserGrips (or some other laser system) can be a lifesaver. If you sit with your armed side exposed and you are attacked, it is vastly easier for an opponent to pin or disable your gun arm so that you cannot use your weapon.

Unconscious movement is what most often betrays our weapons.

Sticking with a restaurant scenario for a moment, if you carry your money in a money clip rather than your wallet, the money clip will usually be in the strongside front pocket. As you go to pay (assuming you use money rather than plastic), sweeping your coat back to access the pocket can reveal your gun and, if you are standing across the counter from a cashier with an open register, that could prove awkward. Instead of pushing your coat back, raise your sportcoat just slightly as you dip under the bottom edge of the garment and slide your hand into your pocket. Practice this so that you can do it smoothly, without drawing attention to yourself.

If you're a man and you pay with plastic or carry your money in your wallet, the wallet is likely in your left hip pocket. If you're right handed, reaching for the wallet should be no problem. If you are left handed, you will expose your gun when you sweep your coat back. Use the same technique of slightly raising the bottom of the garment and bringing your hand toward the pocket from underneath. As you do this, lower your left shoulder slightly, so the coat falls away from your left side, thus giving added concealability.

Photo courtesy of Crimson Trace.

Crimson Trace LaserGrips can be a lifesaver when shooting from an awkward position.

Unconscious movement is what most often betrays our weapons. Strive to be conscious of your movements in public.

To obviate the problems presented by the butt of a strongside carried pistol profiling under a covering garment, try the deep cross draw position. The butt of the weapon cannot profile rearward because it is pointing to the front. Your gun will also be more easily reached when seated. If you are right handed and adopt this carry, remember that reaching for a hip pocket carried wallet might betray your gun and holster combination, as just mentioned. Use the same technique the left handed person must use and you should be fine.

If you start sneezing – I'm a serial sneezer, letting howlers go to the tune of a dozen and a half or more at a set – and grab for a handkerchief in a hurry, don't forget that you could be showing your gun. People who suffer from allergies, etc., should practice making a fast draw with a handkerchief without flashing the gun. Sneezing will already draw attention to you; don't give people a look at your gun.

Any kind of waist level carry imposes certain parameters if you are going to use a public restroom and plan to sit down. What do you do with your waist level carried handgun? There are hooks on the insides of most stall doors for men or women to hang jackets and women to hang purses. Many more modern ladies restrooms, Sharon advises, have hooks on the walls behind the toilet for a purse to be hung. Sometimes, there's a shelf provided. Door hooks historically enable thieves to steal women's purses by reaching over the top of the door, grabbing the bag and running. The same can happen to your gun if you hang it there by the trigger guard. Also, with some guns more than others, you could have an Accidental Discharge when hanging the gun on the hook or removing it from the hook.

There is a famous story about this, purportedly taking place in the men's restroom at a police station. One of the cops hung his cocked and locked 1911 on the hook, did what he had to do and made to retrieve his pistol. Sadly, the thumb safety had slipped off and his pistol's grip safety had been pinned. As he picked the pistol off the hook, the hook pressed against the trigger and a shot was fired into the ceiling, the bullet passing through the ceiling and coming up out of the floor of a room where various law enforcement personnel were tending to other types of paper work having nothing to do with bodily functions. Thankfully, no one got hurt, as the story goes.

So, what do you do with your gun when you sit down to go potty? If you carry in a shoulder rig or ankle rig or pocket holster, there's no problem. But, waist level carry demands that you draw the gun from the holster (unless you want it resting on the floor of a public restroom, something no one in his or her right mind should even consider). After the gun is drawn, if there is no safe place to set or hang it, place it on your thigh and keep your finger well away from the trigger. When you are through, the gun can be clamped under your arm for a moment while you pull up your pants, then returned to its holster.

Some very knowledgeable people advise that a man should never use a urinal in a public restroom, because inherent to its use is the practice of turning one's back to the rest of the restroom. I see the point. If you habituate the worst possible neighborhoods or are being followed by killers eagerly waiting for you to lower your guard for a split second, follow this advice. If not, a small gun worn in a crotch holster (more about these holsters in a subsequent chapter) is one possible suggestion: you can draw the gun even more rapidly than usual because your fly is already open!

Although shoulder holsters are considerably more convenient when using the rest room, they also have other virtues – and shortcomings. Mike Hammer, James Bond and Dirty Harry notwithstanding, shoulder holsters do not render handguns essentially invisible. Although they will be discussed at length in a subsequent chapter, remember that any holstered firearm worn under a covering garment can profile, thus betraying your armed condition, certainly to the practiced eye, often to anyone who bothers to look. Among professional gunny people, true concealment with a shoulder rig can involve some interesting – in at least one case, drastic – techniques. This was especially true when almost all shoulder holsters were straight vertical rigs and hiding the butt of the gun and the entire gun's bulk alongside the wearer's rib cage – even under heavy suit jackets or sport coats – would be tackled with "alterations." A man's suit could be tailored so that the side of the jacket where no gun would be present was built up, structured to match the side of the jacket which was relieved and opened up to accommodate the shoulder rig and the gun. When one looked at the man so attired, he might seem a bit more broad chested than the typical fellow, but there wouldn't be a noticeable bulge.

When we go to drastic, however, we're talking DRASTIC. What some few persons would do – hopefully, very few indeed – was to have themselves surgically altered. I'm not talking about "Bob" going to Sweden or Switzerland and the new "Bobbie" needing a different picture for "her" driver's license. This procedure in question entailed having muscle mass removed from the side of the chest beside which the gun would be worn, thus forming a natural pouch, achieving the same effect as the tailored suit.

You have to make certain that, as you bend or lean forward, the holster unit and the gun in it do not swing forward, pendulum fashion, and make an unscheduled appearance outside the confines of your covering garment.

The shoulder holster always employs a harness. In decades gone by, a strap might encircle the chest, the strap supporting the harness portion that suspended the gun from the shoulder. The strap had to be hidden under a necktie and a buttoned suit coat. Since something almost always had to augment the portion of the harness from which the firearm was actually suspended, people got in the habit of looking for some sort of strap visible in outline as it passed over or across the back. One hears stories about hookers and bar girls gauging whether a prospective "john" was "john law" by rubbing the prospective client's back between the shoulder blades. If she felt something that didn't feel like suspenders, the gentleman in question was quite possibly a cop.

Here's what to remember if you are wearing a shoulder holster for your concealed weapon. Let's assume a full-size handgun again, our Glock 22 in .40 or our Kimber in .45 ACP. If the holster unit itself is anchored to the belt as well as being suspended from the shoulder – not a practice I recommend with most shoulder holsters – every time you raise your gunside shoulder, you'll be hiking up your pants on that side. If the holster is not anchored – best with most shoulder holster types – you have to make certain that, as you bend or lean forward, the holster unit and the gun in it do not swing forward, pendulum fashion, and make an unscheduled appearance outside the confines of your covering garment.

Assuming you have this problem licked, when you are getting out of a vehicle, climbing around on equipment, etc., the holster and gun can slide forward and be seen or actually swing away from the body and bang into something – possibly with an audible thud.

When you bend over or reach for something, your coat will be drawn more tightly across your back. With a leather bomber jacket, that's not a problem. With most fabrics, you will be profiling the back of your shoulder holster's harness and, with certain types of holsters, the muzzle end of the gun/holster combination may very likely profile quite noticeably.

Flashing your gun is a violation that could cost you your concealed carry permit.

When you reach for something at shoulder height or above, you will want to drop the gunside shoulder and reach with the off-gunside arm. In this manner, as your entire body moves in the direction of your reaching arm, your coat draws tightly over the off-gunside and falls away from the gunside. This aids in maintaining concealment. The only potential problem arises from whatever you might be wearing on the side opposite the shoulder holstered handgun. There might be magazine or speedloader pouches actually attached to the shoulder harness, or separate units worn on the belt. There might even be a strongside carried backup handgun.

There is one important thing to remember when wearing a lot of "stuff," even just things like cellular phones or PDAs, in addition to a shoulder holster with pouches for spare loads. The lower end of the pouch will bump into the top end of the stuff on the belt, possibly making noise, certainly getting on your nerves, most likely creating a bulge.

The windy day scenario applies with shoulder rigs, too, but not as often, since the holster is higher up. As with the strongside carried handgun, however, closing the covering garment in order to prevent the garment from blowing open and revealing that you are armed won't work. With most shoulder holsters, unless a coat is specifically tailored for use with it, the suitcoat or sportcoat should not be buttoned closed. Almost assuredly, the handgun/holster combination will egregiously profile.

Akin to body language as concerns weapons concealment is the idea of not dressing oddly in order to disguise the presence of a weapon. I've mentioned that in this work before and likely will again, because the wrong attire is a dead giveaway for being armed.

The next carry to consider in the context of body language is ankle carry. Ankle holsters will be covered in greater detail in a subsequent chapter, but the body language issues bear addressing here. Body language concerns are clothing related, as with waist level and shoulder carry. The principal body language issues with ankle carry derive from carelessness.

Here's a scenario. You are right handed and properly carrying a Walther PPK or J-Frame Smith & Wesson in a holster on the inside of your left ankle, butt rearward. You have been driving and are about to exit your vehicle. Your left trouser leg has pulled up and reveals the lower portion of the holster and much of the band supporting the holster. You try to tug your trouser leg down. As you finish standing, your trouser leg – a little too tight and a little too short – catches on the butt of your gun. You have to bend over to tug the trouser leg down.

Here's another scenario. You sit down, forgetting momentarily about the ankle holster and the gun it carries. You cross your left leg over your right. Or, you stretch your legs out. Or, you sit on a bar stool instead of a regular chair.

The solution to most of these difficulties is to select your pants carefully when they will be paired with an ankle holster. The bottom of the trouser leg should be able to break over the top of your shoe, so that the length, when standing, allows the lower edge of the trouser leg to reach to the mid-point at least of the bones on either side of your ankle. Ankle holsters were a natural when slightly flared trouser legs were in vogue. Be that as it may, the trouser leg should be wide enough that it isn't drawn tightly around the ankle holstered handgun. Trousers of the width associated with a conventional business suit or, for that matter, a tuxedo, are of the appropriate width.

The idea of carrying a concealed weapon is to be discreetly armed in the event circumstances dictate weapon use. If you flash your gun, aside from this being socially awkward, it is technically a violation of most concealed carry statutes and can cost you your permit or worse. Plus, it's impolite because there are and always will be (as long as someone armed is there to protect them) people who fall into a panic at the sight of a weapon. We have an obligation to comport ourselves as civilized people.

Body language issues have been written about extensively over the years. Some news analysis incorporates considering body language and facial and eye movement. If someone is extremely nervous appearing, there's a reason for it, a reason as simple as shyness or as nefarious as terrorism. If someone looks odd, moves strangely or gets too close to you, it is not at all paranoid to prepare to take action.

You are in the bank waiting to cash a check or make a deposit and the person in front of you in line, who has seemed a little edgy in his movements, keeps tugging down the bottom edge of his waist length jacket. And, maybe it's a little warm outside, so why is this guy wearing a jacket in the first place?

Body language and other physical clues are just that – clues. You add up the clues and consider the sum. But, remember, someone may very well be watching you and doing the same.

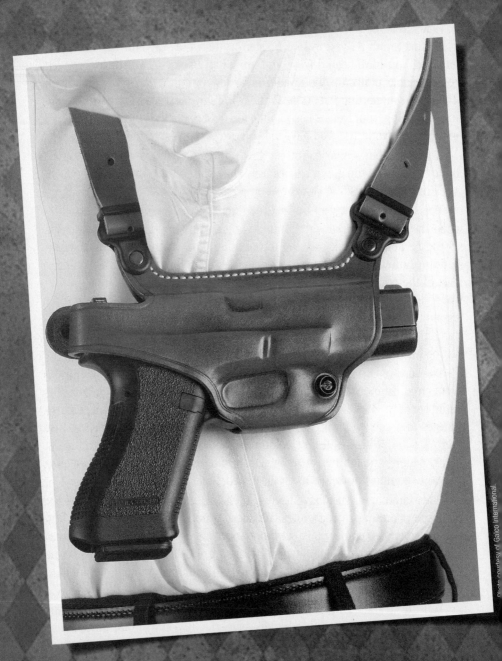

Photo courtesy of Galco International.

SHOULDER HOLSTERS

Chapter Seven

Shoulder holsters, as a generic type, have many applications. Among these are those designed for military use, field holsters for hunting handguns and even cowboy holsters. Although he most certainly did not invent it, probably the most famous real-life early shoulder holster user was gunfighter John Wesley Hardin with a rig made for him by saddle and holster maker Sam "Tio" Myers. It must be remembered that, after his long prison term, Wes Hardin practiced law, studying for and winning his degree while incarcerated. As an officer of the court, Hardin would have dressed like a civilized "townie" much of the time, a shoulder holster under a suitcoat quite a bit more socially acceptable for an attorney on the streets of El Paso, Texas.

Hardin's shoulder rig was a simple affair, but a good design. If we can judge from the modern versions offered by various makers, it was a holster much like a conventional belt holster of the period, but suspended from a two piece, U-shaped harness. The two pieces would have been sewn together at the height of the shoulder; otherwise, if a solid piece were used, the harness would not lie flat. The holster and harness were mated – at least judging by the modern versions – by means of leather thongs securing through matching holes in the holster unit and the U-shaped harness half. This also allowed adjustment for height. The classic modern version of the Hardin holster employs a crossover strap which passes from the top of the U-shaped harness half across the shoulder and down the opposite shoulder and along the front of the body. The crossover strap's end would secure to the front of the trouser belt. The original may have used some other arrangement, perhaps a chest strap.

The most famous fictional early shoulder holster user was the Val Kilmer characterization of Doc Holliday, in the marvelously well-done Tombstone. Dr. John Henry Holliday, my personal all-time favorite historical westerner, was most certainly real and Kilmer's portrayal of Holliday was memorable in the extreme, as was Kirk Douglas's portrayal of the consumptive gun-fighting dentist decades earlier. Both actors were truly outstanding as Doc. What is likely fictional is that really cool looking double shoulder rig with the attached knife sheath that Mr. Kilmer wore in the later film. Rigs such

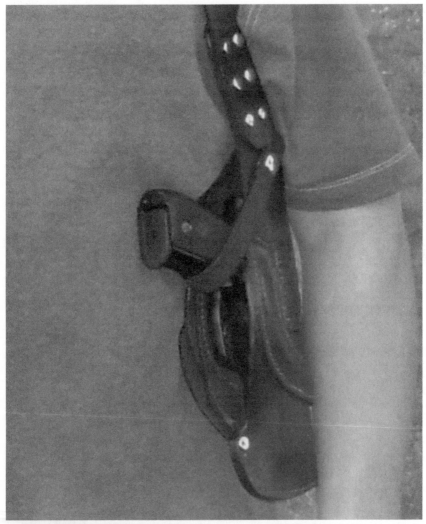

The tactical shoulder holster from Lawman Leather is shown here with the Taurus 809B, a really superb pistol.

as this — more or less — likely existed in the old west and Doc may have had one, but there is nothing to suggest that he did. In the film *Tombstone*, Doc carries two nickel-plated Colt-style revolvers with ivory grips. The inimitable Mr. Douglas carried a similarly flashy gun for most of the 1957 film *Gunfight At O.K. Corral*. According to The Peacemakers — Arms and Adventure in The American West, by R. L. Wilson (Chartwell Books, Inc., Edison, N.J., 1992), Doc Holliday presented his nephew with the gun he carried most of the time on the frontier. It was a standard looking 7-½-inch barrel Single Action Army .45 with one-piece wooden grips, with most or all of the bluing gone and the cylinder badly "ringed" by the bolt. Doc's claims concerning the gun were, supposedly, a deathbed statement. It is unlikely that he carried this gun in a shoulder rig.

As the 19th century turned to the 20th century, the shoulder holster's popularity seriously increased. But, where did the shoulder holster concept begin? Or, at least how did it begin?

I have always felt that the shoulder holster traces its roots to the weapon belt being worn as an impromptu baldric, the sword belt which traverses the right-handed person's chest from right shoulder to left hip. I theorize that someone who tired of wearing a firearm at the waist shifted the belt around and wore it like a baldric, but only with a holstered handgun rather than a sword. Eventually, someone had such a holster built that was designed for this kind of carry. As concealment became an issue, the shoulder holster started to become popular.

By the interim period at the end of the 19th century and the beginning of the 20th, wearing of weapons openly had taken a hit. Apparently, as we get more "civilized," we are supposed to pretend that we do not need to be armed and, accordingly, hide the fact that we are. This is not just a western phenomenon. In Japan, in 1876, the Haitorei Edict banned the wearing of weapons — swords or guns — in public. This forced many Samurai to dismantle their swords, removing the Fuchi (the sleeve-like haft) from the blade of their Katana and having a Saya (sheath) built which resembled a walking staff, replacing the original Fuchi with a matching piece. Voile! A sword cane!

In the United States, ever since the 1880s, many an armed man would utilize a "town carry," as it was sometimes called. This was a fancy term for stuffing one's sixgun holsterless into one's pants under a coat. Bat Masterson went back East and became a well-respected sports writer. He was concealing his Single Action Army in a "town carry" in New York City in 1902 and was arrested for carrying a concealed weapon. Sadly, this book had not yet been written to aid him in his concealment technique — and if that isn't a conceited remark on my part, I don't know what is!

Revolvers don't really conceal too well when stuffed inside the pants. The Hip-Grip didn't yet exist and would never be made for a Single Action Army, at any event. A trick of the old timers was to leave the old Colt's loading gate open, the gate serving as a hook extending over the waistband and belt.

We were coming into the age of organized crime, which had its roots, some would argue, in the southwest. But organized crime in Eastern cities not only demanded being armed, but being armed discreetly. It was customary, in those old days, to "knock off" a rival or someone who was to be made an example of as a group effort. Several assassins armed with revolvers all in the same caliber would ring the intended victim and all would shoot him, rather like a firing squad. In this case, however, everyone had live ammo (in many firing squads, the rifles of all but one of the participants are loaded with a blank cartridge, so no one of the squad knows whose bullet actually made the kill). It was lucky for the gangsters that most of their handguns were probably under-powered .32s or something similar; otherwise, their bullets might have passed through their victim and the killers would have killed each other, as well! This technique had some advantages. Crime scene investigation was such, in those days that little more than telling the caliber of a recovered bullet could be regularly expected. So, if the guys who did the killing were arrested, one could not "rat out" the other, claiming his own innocence, since there was no way to tell whose bullets had done what.

By the early decades of the 20th century, the character of the firearms used by good guys and bad guys alike had radically changed. 1905 saw the introduction by FN of John Moses Browning's first .25 auto and the firearms design genius had already released a larger .32, the Colt 1903 Pocket Model. In 1905, that same gun emerged as a .380, again from Colt. The 1905 .25 was eventually replaced by the Baby Browning, but the .32 and .380 served as undercover and General Officers' pistols through World War II. Colt introduced the Police Positive Special revolver in 1908, the short barreled version known as the Detective Special in 1927. The real Eliot Ness carried one of these. And, of course, even though the 1911 was originally hard to get, it quickly caught on with civilians, both good and bad. Cowboy guns and underpowered Remington derringers no longer comprised the bulk of defensive handguns.

My maternal grandfather, Hunting Colfax Morrell, a consummate rifle marksman by all reports, kept a .32 Smith & Wesson caliber Hopkins & Allen revolver with folding hammer spur for occasional pocket carry. But, getting much beyond the little Colt autos and the FN .25 and similar small guns, it was a matter of stuffing the gun in the trouser band – the guys in the classic Warner Bros. gangster flicks did that a lot – or getting a holster. Often, this was a shoulder holster. The George Lawrence #7, a "snap draw" vertical shoulder rig with springs set between layers of leather, holding the gun in the holster until it was "snapped" out, and similar holsters were made for the Colt and Smith & Wesson revolvers and the 1911s and war-trophy and commercial Lugers which comprised the bulk of larger caliber, larger sized handguns. Often, too, the Colt 1903 and 1905 pistols were carried in shoulder holsters. A rather innovative shoulder holster for the 1903 .32 was issued to some American OSS (Office of Strategic Services) personnel during World War II, a skeletonized vertical design.

Vertical Shoulder Holster

The vertical shoulder rig – quite similar to the Wes Hardin rig – could be made in several different ways. In those early days and into the early 1960s, shoulder holsters were frequently made with a strap that supported the U-shaped harness piece from which the actual holster and the gun within it were carried. That strap passed around the back and around the chest and was hidden by the wide ties of the era, or the vests found with many suits. One of my first shoulder holsters was like this. But, I had the advantage of knowing better. I cut a slit in the harness a little above where the crossover strap was attached and doubled the strap back, thus converting this old J.M. Bucheimer unit into a more modern vertical rig.

> *Some guns are simply too big for shoulder holster applications.*

When donning this sort of rig, the right handed person slips the U-shaped piece over the left side shoulder and puts the right arm through the crossover loop which goes across the back, under the right armpit and back across the shoulder a little below the shirt collar. It's like putting on a vest. Some shoulder harnesses are even more like that, with identical U-shaped harness halves on both sides. These look cool; but, they are a little much, in my experience.

The discussion of shoulder holsters is a great time to mention the concept of too much holster for too little gun. We encountered this when we had our holster business. People would ask for shoulder rigs for ultra tiny guns, where the amount of leather was way over the amount of iron it held. Although shoulder holsters are under discussion here, a good example of the leather to gun ratio can be found as well with the ankle holster. Ankle holsters are best worn with guns of the general size of a Walther PP series semi-automatic or a S&W J-Frame revolver. Carrying a .25 automatic or similar sized .32 or .380 in an ankle holster is absurd.

A shoulder holster, by its very nature, is designed to be discreet – at least

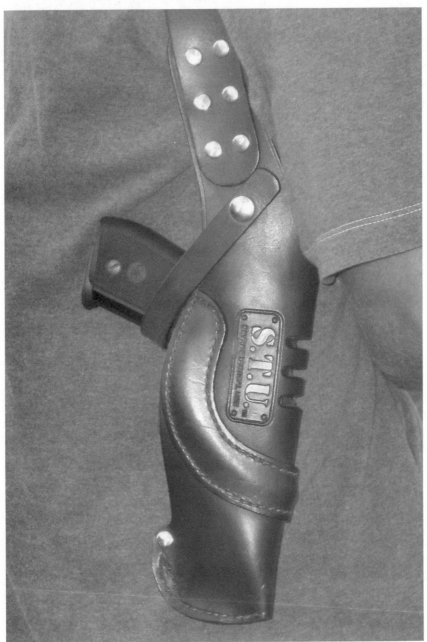

This Lawman Leather holster is a tactical shoulder rig and not really designed for concealment, but can be used in that regard in a pinch. The curious thing about this holster, its rugged construction aside, is that a proprietary method for holster sizing was used to produce this well fitting holster for the Taurus 809B by using only a couple for photos and the pistol's dimensions. Lawman Leather, it will be remembered, is the home of the Original Dirty Harry Shoulder Holster.

those not intended for open use in the military or hunting context. Some guns are too big for certain shoulder holster applications. Take, for example, the fictional character of James Bond as he is portrayed in films. In the original movies, with Sean Connery, through George Lazenby and Roger Moore, the British agent carried a Walther PPK (Connery carried a PP in the first film and Moore carried a P-5 in *Octopussy*). Bond used a much more practical shoulder rig with an upside-down carry for his PPK in the two excellent Timothy Dalton films. Pierce Brosnan used a PPK in the Bond films, up until switching to a Walther P-99 in 1997's *Tomorrow Never Dies.* A fine gun to be sure, but trying to conceal a high capacity 9mm police/military Walther P-99 pistol under a tuxedo, as Mr. Brosnan's Bond does in subsequent films, is ridiculous. Most times, a spy or secret agent wouldn't use a shoulder holster, simply because the holster and the gun it carried might have to be ditched to avoid detection, discarded for possible future retrieval.

The gun and holster combination you use must be in line with the way you dress. That P-99 would be great in a shoulder rig worn under a bomber jacket or maybe even under a heavy woolen sportcoat – but not a dinner jacket.

Sticking with movie use of shoulder holsters for a bit longer, the big guns can be concealable even in vertical shoulder rigs, with the right clothing and the right body shape and size. Take the film *The Girl Hunters,* which happened to star Mickey Spillane as his own character of Mike Hammer. Spillane was a powerfully built, barrel chested man. When his Mike Hammer dons a vertical shoulder rig and puts his 1911 into it, then slips into his suit jacket, it works. And, of course, Mike Hammer very frequently wore that trench coat, which could have hidden an MP-5 or an Uzi within its folds – or maybe even a Thompson.

Probably the most famous vertical shoulder holster of all time is the Dirty Harry Shoulder Holster. Popularized in the movies, everyone with a Model 29 wanted one. The holster was a combination of real shoulder holster elements made specifically for the films. Jerry Ardolino, of the original and the new Lawman Leather, acquired the original dies and patterns and produced this holster for a wide range of guns. An author and businessman, as well as an ex-cop, Jerry returned to holstermaking in 2008; the Dirty Harry Shoulder Holster is now made for any handgun, old or new, that someone might wish to carry in this classic rig. The Dirty Harry is one of the few holsters people actually collect. For carrying a big handgun under the right conditions, one couldn't ask for better.

Upside–down Shoulder Holster

The vertical shoulder holsters, as used in so many films and in real life,

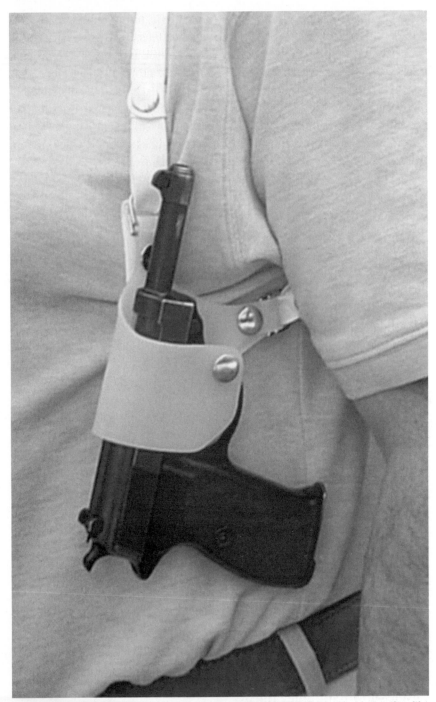

This K.L. Null shoulder rig carries the weapon upside down and is very fast into action. It's worn here with a Walther P-38, a very serviceable antique.

certainly throughout the end of the 19th century and for most of the 20th century, had serious shortcomings if the handgun had too long a grip frame or the man wearing it was too thin framed. The gunbutt profiled under the covering garment, not to mention the harness outlining, too. In the 1930s, the Berns-Martin company came along with the first truly unique shoulder holster to see wide currency. It was the Triple Draw Lightnin', as it was called. A snubby revolver was worn in the holster, either carried on the waist belt for a strong side draw on the right or left side of the body or upside down as a shoulder rig beneath the right or left arm. This holster design, like the George Lawrence #7, also incorporated spring steel sandwiched between two layers of leather. Rather than the spring opening, allowing the underside of the weapon – the trigger guard side – to come out first, because of the inverted carry, the

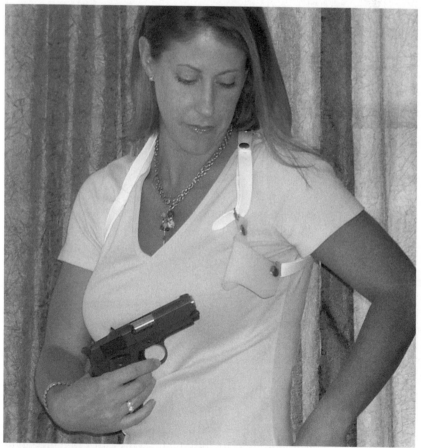

A Detonics USA (Pendergrass) CombatMaster in the rare Detonics black finish is shown here with a Null upside down shoulder rig. This is an ideal holster for man or woman. It can be concealed under a loose fitting sweater, etc.

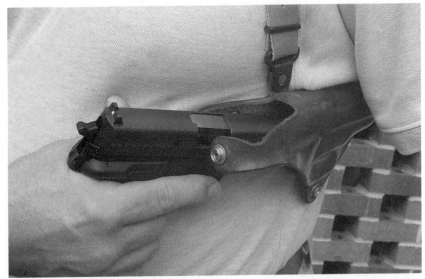

A proper draw from a diagonal shoulder rig, the gun a SIG-Sauer P229, the holster an old, original Galco Miami Classic.

revolver was grasped quite naturally and the frame top strap was the first portion of the weapon to exit the holster. When worn as a belt holster, the presentation was at once fast and natural. Grasp the gunbutt as one normally would and push the frame top strap out of the holster between those spring reinforced lips. Bianchi acquired the Berns-Martin brand, modified its own Agent 9R upside down rig to match the Berns-Martin holster and sold it for a number of years. I actually liked the original Bianchi one better as a shoulder rig, although it could not be used as a belt holster. Clint Eastwood wore one of the Bianchi Berns-Martin holsters in his film *The Gauntlet* and Steve Mc-Queen wore Safariland's elastic gusset upside rig in *Bullitt*.

Almost no one makes an upside-down shoulder holster these days because of worries over liability and because the once ubiquitous revolver has been partially – but substantially – replaced by the semi-automatic pistol. The typical upside-down rig requires the concave curve which is formed as the root of the trigger guard flows into the grip frame front strap of a revolver. There is nothing corresponding to this in the typical semi-automatic pistol. The only person I know of who is still making upside-down shoulder holsters is that genius, that master of the uniquely functional, Ken Null. Null not only makes upside down holsters for small revolvers, but also for semi-automatics. I have an excellent example in horsehide that I use sometimes with a Detonics Com-batMaster. I had one years ago for a Walther PPK/S I used to carry. They are fast and reliable and concealable.

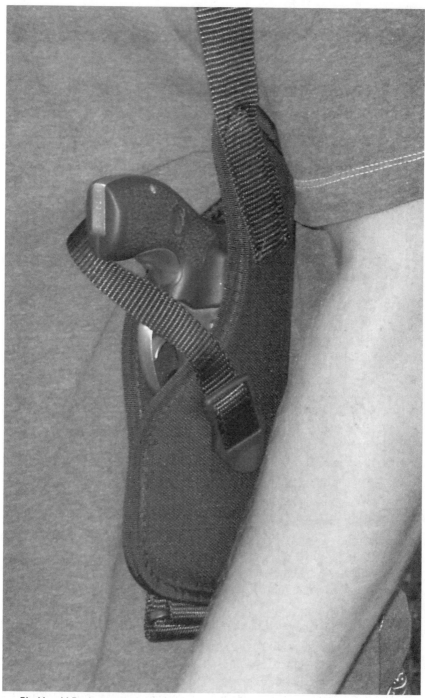

Blackhawk! Products makes this vertical shoulder holster for 2-inch and 3-inch revolvers. It is easily and quickly adjustable through the innovative coupler featured in the harness.

Balanced Shoulder Holster

Although I cannot say who made the first "balanced" shoulder holster, I can tell you who made it the dominant style of shoulder holster in the United States and much of the rest of the world. That was "The Famous Jackass Leather Company" of Waukegan, Illinois, which soon thereafter became Galco International of Phoenix, Arizona. Galco still offers the Jackass rig, but is more famous for its later variant, the Miami Classic. The original Miami Classic, as worn by Don Johnson on television's *Miami Vice* and the DeSantis New York City Classic, as worn by Bruce Willis in the *Die Hard* films, are my personal favorites of this type.

> **The idea with a balanced system is that it floats on the wearer's body.**

The balanced shoulder harness brought the shoulder holster into the modern age. For the right handed man or woman wearing an auto (many are made for revolvers), the pistol is holstered under the left arm while (usually) two spare magazines are worn under the right arm, thus balancing out much of the gun weight. Cuff cases can be attached beneath the offside magazine pouches or speedloader pouches on the Galco Miami Classic. Custom holster maker *par excellence* Sam Andrews makes a variant that packs three or more magazines on the off-gun side and can be set up to carry a boot knife for an inverted draw between the magazine pouch and the body. He made the first one like that a number of years ago for a fellow who was going to Beirut on business. Galco has gone that one better still with a four magazine pouch for the offside. I have one for my Glock 22, which is 15+1. Add on four 15-round magazines as spares and you have 76 rounds available to you. That's enough for a fast gunfight in an adventure movie!

In the balanced system, the harness halves are the same on either side and they are joined by some sort of coupler which should, ideally, hit between the shoulder blades, over the spine, about three man's fingers' distance below the shirt collar. Rick Gallagher, the man behind Galco and Jackass before it, personally taught Sharon and me how to fit and set up such a holster rig.

The idea with a balanced system is that it floats on the wearer's body; when adjusted and worn properly, there is – most of the time – no need to secure either or both sides of the rig to the belt. I never do, as it generally defeats the purpose of the rig.

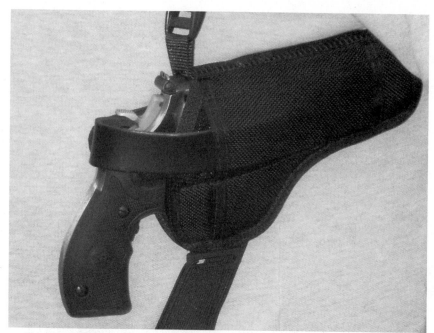

This fabric diagonal shoulder holster from DeSantis works quite well with a 4-inch L-Frame Smith & Wesson. The harness is adjustable and tie downs are provided.

What was also radical with this design was the angle at which the actual holster was worn. Neither straight vertical nor inverted (upside-down), the gun was to be worn diagonally. Length of the weapon could be compensated for by increasing the angle of the holster. Let's explore that a bit. My old friend Chet, an Illinois cop, wore a Walther PPK/S in an original Jackass rig. This was many years ago. He carried the gun at a sharp angle and never once could Sharon or I spot it, even though this was the age of the double knit sport coat and we knew he was wearing the gun. When Rick Gallagher was demonstrating the Jackass rig to gun dealers in those early days, he would walk into the shop – the staff knew he was coming, of course – wearing a six and one-half-inch blue Smith & Wesson Model 29 under a tweed sportcoat. He'd have the gun at the steepest angle possible, because of its length, the .44's muzzle right by the rear of his armpit, the heel of the gunbutt close to his belt. Whether it was Chet or Rick, either could reach under his coat, pop the thumb break and the gun came right into the hand, ready to go.

Many people carry diagonal shoulder holsters with the holsters essentially horizontal. With a small gun, that can work satisfactorily, although I would never recommend it. With a larger gun – even a compact auto like the SIG 229, for example – carrying horizontally will allow the muzzle of the gun to

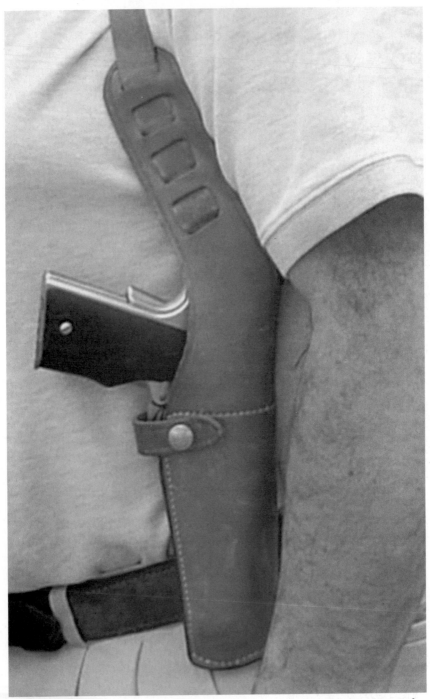

Vertical shoulder holsters are among the least concealable shoulder rigs, but can serve for casual carry quite nicely.

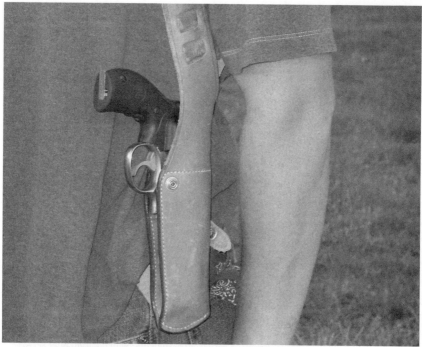

The Bianchi X-15 is one of those holsters that is so versatile that it is almost silly not to have one. It is shown here with a Model 686 four inch revolver.

profile or print under the coat, whereas, were the holster worn properly, that would be obviated.

Wearing Shoulder Holsters

As this is written, a staple for many of our brave men and women in the war zones is the shoulder holster. Many of these holsters are what we would consider concealment rigs, but worn openly. The shoulder holster, when worn openly, offers unique control potential to the wearer. If someone is too close, but not so close that the gun will be drawn, the gun can be clamped down under the arm. When the gun is worn in wet terrain, the shoulder holstered weapon can stay above the wet grass or snow drifts. When worn in dusty conditions, the weapon can be sheltered within a field jacket or under a BDU blouse.

I use shoulder holsters, at times. These include an original Galco Miami Classic with a SIG 229. I use a very well-worn Bianchi X-15 vertical rig that can carry a full-size .45 such as a Detonics Model 9-11-01 or a four-inch L-Frame like the S&W Model 686 or any number of other similar handguns (but I don't carry this rig concealed because it is a vertical style). I use a DeSantis New York City Classic with a Detonics Model 9-11-01. I use a Ken Null up-

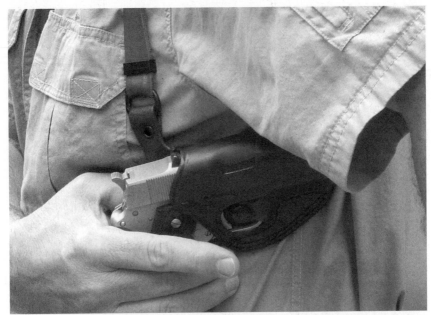

Truly one of the best shoulder rigs on the planet, the Alessi Bodyguard is concealable, fast and comfortable. Note the pull through snap which closes through the trigger guard. This design will not work with certain guns, of course, but is excellent with the right gun.

Early Alessi Bodyguard rigs featured a single magazine pouch worn horizontally, the magazine held with a magnetic strip. A more conventional snap closure double inverted magazine pouch is currently produced.

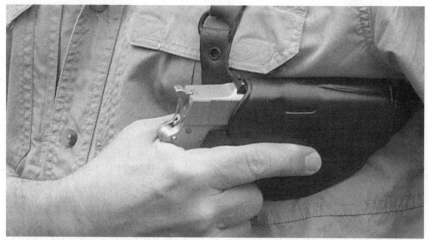

Merely obtain a full combat grip and jerk the gun free of the holster, the snap popping open as you pull. This is a fast system.

side down horsehide shoulder rig for a Detonics CombatMaster .45. I use an Original Dirty Harry Shoulder Holster with a 7-½-inch Cimarron Arms single action, if I carry the gun afield.

In our Survivalist series of novels, the main character, John Rourke, always carried his "twin stainless Detonics .45s" in a "double Alessi shoulder rig." Diagonals, they utilized a pull-through snap closing through the trigger guard, rather than a more standard thumb break. Tugging the gun from the leather broke open the snap. These are fast and concealable and comfortable. Alessi has always made good gear. In those days, I actually carried twin stainless Detonics CombatMasters in a double Alessi shoulder holster – sometimes.

John Rourke and Jerry Ahern usually wore the double rig under a leather bomber jacket, beneath which the two Walther PP-sized .45s concealed quite nicely. Some shoulder holsters – with small handguns – can be worn concealed quite effectively, underneath a bulky sweater or a sweatshirt. Certain persons contend that a full-sized pistol can be worn underneath a loose fitting shirt. There may be some who can do this, but most of us cannot and few of us really should. Certainly, if the shirt is worn as a jacket, that can be fine. If the shirt is worn as a shirt, the gun will almost certainly protrude from beneath it, the harness will reveal itself as the fabric drapes over it and, in order to draw, one will have to either rip the shirt open or have a shirt which utilizes hook and loop fasteners under fake buttons. There are firms which offer such shirts, specifically made for hiding a gun. And, they can work. The ordinary shirt doesn't cut it with a shoulder holster, in my opinion.

The problem with a shoulder holster is clothing related. You have to wear something over the shoulder holster in order to keep your weapon concealed. There is no choice. That means you may very well encounter awkward social situations. Let's say you're wearing my original Galco Miami Classic with my SIG 229 under a corduroy sportcoat. It's late fall and lovely weather. You go inside a building and some idiot's running the heat. Every man in sight has his jacket off. If you remove yours, everyone sees your gun. If you leave your jacket on, people may become suspicious that you are armed. And, you'll be uncomfortable.

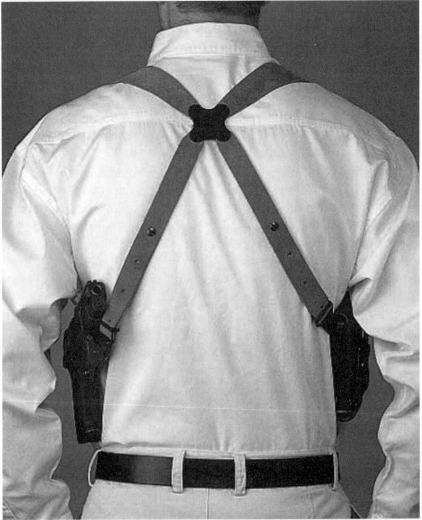

Note how flat the harness is against the back. This makes for good concealment.

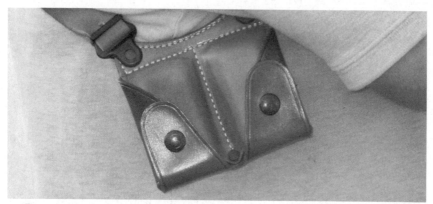

The ammo carrier side of this Galco Miami Classic for a revolver. This is one extremely good holster.

What do you do? Well if you really practice this a lot, you can take your coat off and roll the lapels slightly inward, catching the harness halves at the front and folding the holster rig into the coat, being careful, if you succeed in doing this, not to have the gun fall from inside the coat after the coat is removed. If you decide to master this technique, it must be practiced with an empty gun, while observing all other safety considerations, of course.

You may see this as a lot of bother, or you may see this as practical. If I still lived in the North, where there isn't a period of five or six months of merciless summer every year, I'd probably use a shoulder rig much more than I do. They are convenient in the extreme when seated, when behind the wheel, when sitting down to use a toilet, etc. They can be really fast into action. They can be hidden when you open your coat by sweeping the coat around the holster and offside unit and pushing the rig rearward. If you elect to wear two identical handguns, it's actually easier to conceal the double rig than a single rig, since both sides are perfectly balanced in size and weight.

It is well to remember, however, that shoulder holsters are not a cloaking device out of a science fiction movie, rendering the gun invisible to the naked eye. When you see the shoulder holster wearing hero of an action movie wearing a coat in a scene where no gun is produced, chances are very good the actor is not wearing the shoulder holstered handgun and that's a principal reason why you can't see any sign of it.

The balanced shoulder rig has an advantage generally shared only by the police duty rig or the cowboy rig: when you throw the rig on, you have your gun and your spare ammo in one package that goes on fast. You can hang it off the bedpost and be ready to go in a heartbeat at three in the morning – if you need to.

WAIST LEVEL POSITIONS

Chapter Eight

Discounting pocket-size pistols, the most natural position for carrying a handgun on body is at the waist. Even with the ultra-tiny handguns, there are always some who want a holster that will allow waist level carry on the belt and not even inside the waistband. The origins of this carry style have nothing to do with firearms and pre-date all modern civilizations. Long before firearms were ever conceived of or gun powder even known, weapons were slung at the waist. These weapons were, of course, edged. From ancient Egyptian times with beaten bronze sidearms to the Renaissance with hard armoured knights strapping on a crusader hilt sword to young men studying in the schools of defense and practicing the rapier and *main-gauche,* it was always the blade. Granted, the cross-body carry of a sword suspended from dominant side shoulder to offside hip on what was called a "baldric" enjoyed great currency and was, indeed, the inspiration for the Sam Browne belt, wherein the baldric was combined with a waist belt. But, baldric use, however much currency it enjoyed, was specialized.

In the United States, the favored close range serious personal defense weapons long into the 19th century were swords and large knives. This, for example, accounts for the tremendous popularity of the Bowie knife up until the Civil War era. With a single shot pistol, in close combat, there was no time to reload. Multiple pistols were carried whenever possible. Fire a ball at an attacker, miss a vital organ or only graze him and he still had plenty of fight left. Simply grasp your pistol by the barrel and use the butt of the weapon as a bludgeon (which is why so many of these fine old single shot pistols have such elaborate metal butt caps) and you'll crack his skull, possibly rendering him unconscious or dead.

Then there was the reliability factor. The powder charge was damp – remember the old aphorism about keeping your powder dry? – and there was no shot fired. Maybe the powder in the pan just produced a "flash in the pan" and nothing more when the trigger was pulled. Even into the age of the percussion cap, firearms were still not the most reliable things in the world and reloading was still terribly time consuming. During the American Civil War, confederate cavalrymen were well known for closing to saber distance and using multiple percussion revolvers, shooting out one cylinder full and drawing another pistol in order to continue firing. Sometimes, a truly prepared individual would have additional loaded cylinders, belt carried and ready to replace the spent cylinder.

The technique of multiple pistol use has never been better exemplified than in the classic western *The Outlaw Josey Wales*. Eventually, though, no matter how many firearms one carries, it's necessary to reload.

But a blade!

A blade will never jam or run out of ammunition!

The Bowie Knife – whatever it looked like – was always thought to be big and intimidating and, regardless of design, didn't have to be reloaded. In those days or these days, one fact is indisputable as concerns a well-made fixed blade knife, short sword or full-length sword. It will neither jam nor run out of ammunition; therefore, if it is so well-made and well-tempered that it will not break, it will never fail you. You cannot say that about any firearm. When I was running the Detonics operation in Pendergrass, Georgia, for example, we put 31,000 rounds through one of our full-size pistols in only five days. That the gun had no malfunctions, despite running a little slow because of powder residue build-up (it was never more than wiped off, never cleaned), showed it to be remarkably reliable. Yet, had it failed and locked up, the pistol would have been reduced to a club.

Such knives as the Bowie and the double edged Arkansas Toothpick were almost invariably carried at the waist. I've seen shoulder holsters for knives, even worn one once or twice, but they are rare, popping up on occasion and never really enjoying widespread use. Some big knives were worn in boot tops, of course, but too big a knife was impractical in such a carry

And then, we have the sword. If it were not carried slung at the waist or from a baldric, it was relegated to being concealed within a cane. Sword canes are tremendously useful weapons, even to this day, and had considerable wide-spread popularity well into the 20th century.

Normally, though, a weapon was carried at the waist. As firearms became more reliable and more readily reloadable, the world changed. Some might argue not for the better. But change it did. Even the best schooled and consistently trained man with a sword or knife – unless reasonably close – could be bested by an average man or woman who was alert, had nerve and could shoot straight with a reliable firearm. At close range, an agile person armed with a knife and possessed of deadly intent cannot be bested by a handgun or any firearm, because of reaction time. Stretch that distance a bit with a sword and a skilled man or woman behind it. The key to quick use of the sword is the draw. In Japan, for example, many fights involving the Katana were settled without any exchange of blows; the man whose steel flashed first would cut his opponent from abdomen to shoulder in one deadly move.

Sword canes employ various methods – whether friction fit alone or a catch or something else – for staying sheathed until intentionally withdrawn. Hence, sword canes can be terribly fast or not fast enough.

This heritage of the personal sidearm being worn at the waist had already transitioned into firearms long before anything close to the modern handgun was developed. At first, unlike the sword, even knives were often worn just tucked into the belt or sash. This practice likely resulted in some extremely nasty surprise cuts. It was natural for pistols to be carried this way, also. Wild Bill Hickok, possibly the deadliest man with a handgun who ever walked the earth, often carried his 1851 Navy Colts thrust into his sash, one on either side, butt forward.

But, well before Wild Bill or his contemporaries on the American Frontier, the holster came along, likely evolved from the scabbards made to accommodate the ultra-large handguns like the .58 caliber Model 1855 Harper's Ferry Horse Pistol. Although these 12-inch rifled barrel pistols could be mounted to a shoulder stock, the weapons were generally used for what the name implied. If you shot the horse out from under an enemy trooper, that man was no longer an effective combatant. Often, these large, heavy firearms were carried in holsters mounted to either side of the saddle. The practice of carrying large handguns holstered to the saddle had been going on for decades. Early holsters that could be worn on body likely derived from these.

Military, paramilitary and/or (these days) police requirements dictate the major trends in most weapons and weapons accessories developments. As the military started to use on-body holstering, eventually moving into the new-fangled multi-shot handguns called revolvers, this spread to the civilian sphere. Initially, on the American frontier, many civilian holsters were made from modified, full-flap military holsters, the chief modification being excision of the flap. Old boot tops were also quite commonly used. Eventually, saddle makers and even amateur craftsmen simply making something for personal requirements were making holsters. The image in western movies notwithstanding, most men working from horseback did not carry a sixgun slung from the hip. They carried crossdraw. This kept the revolver out of harm's way – brush, steer horns, etc. – and provided rapid access when seated in the saddle.

Military holsters for revolvers were designed to present the weapon butt forward to a left handed crossdraw. The reasoning behind this was quite solid. The saber was still a viable weapon and could only be drawn crossdraw, of course. It had to be accessed with the right hand. The revolver, conversely, was short enough – even the Colt Cavalry variant with 7-½-inch barrel and the earlier 1860 Army, etc. – to be drawn with a reverse or twist draw, often called a "cavalry" draw. In theory, at least, an officer skilled in equitation and the saber could guide his mount with knees and heels and fight with his saber in the right hand and his revolver in the left; this likely was little if ever practiced in actual combat.

Most probably, the earliest holsters featured crossdraw presentation. All other holster styles evolved from this.

Waist level carry can be accomplished either on the belt or inside the trouser band (this latter and quite important variation will be covered in a subsequent chapter).

Waist level carry is divided into several positions. Strongside carry places the firearm on the same side of the body as the dominant hand, the butt of the weapon usually pointed rearward, thus obviating the need to twist the hand and make a cavalry/reverse draw. Wild Bill's 1851 Navy Colts were worn butt forward and usually accessed twist draw, history tells us.

A twist draw is accomplished literally by twisting the hands. The hands are turned thumb rearward, palm outward. The guns – Wild Bill carried two, remember – are grasped with the last three fingers and jerked from the sash or holster, the muzzles swept across the body – not a safe practice, generally. The trigger fingers enter the guards and the hammers are thumbed back as the muzzles come on line and shots are fired.

The twist draw is almost never employed as primary means of access in the context of concealed carry at the waist. However, when a gun is worn crossdraw, should the dominant hand become disabled, the weapon can be accessed with the other hand by means of a twist draw. Twist draw is also used with some pocket holsters (hip pocket) and certain variations of small-of-the-back carry.

Traditional strongside allows the dominant hand to reach to the dominant side, grasp the butt of the gun and withdraw the gun from its holster. In the context of concealed carry, the gun would be worn so that the butt of the weapon is higher than the wearer's trouser belt line, sometimes considerably higher.

For a time in the closing decades of the 20th century, it was fashionable to construct holsters so that the butt of the gun would ride radically higher. With high waisted persons and most women, drawing the gun practically required double jointedness. The idea behind this carry was to pitch the gunbutt so far above the waist that the bulkier (for some) part of the body nearer to the chest would enhance masking of the firearm's presence, especially, some thought, when one bent over, sat, etc., because the gunbutt was well above the part of the body that flexed with such movement. Certain holsters were designed with multiple sets of slots for attachment so that height could be varied, as well as angle.

Typically, in modern times, this overly high positioning for strongside carry has gone the way of the double knit leisure suit. Today, the rear face of an automatic pistol's slide would be about level with the upper edge of the belt. The height issue reconciled, however, angle becomes of paramount importance.

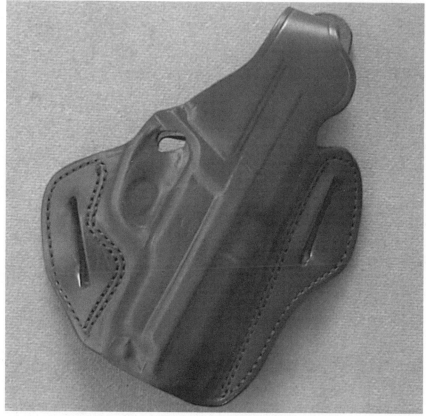

Gene DeSantis was asked to build a holster for federal agents that would be easily concealed, yet allow added security when the holstered weapon was removed. This DeSantis holster for the SIG-Sauer 229 features a hole through the trigger guard area that allows an agent's cuffs to be slipped through, thus locking the gun safely in the holster.

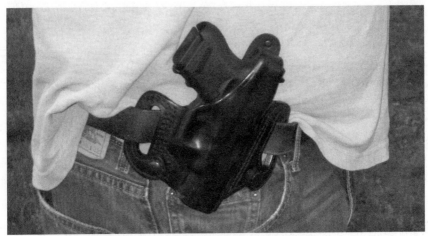

This two slot belt holster for the Glock is from Blackhawk! Products.

When a handgun was worn openly in a strongside carry back in the days of the old west, it was normally positioned straight vertically; in other words, the line made by the barrel of the wearer's "smokewagon" was parallel to – but not necessarily coincident with – the side seam of the "britches." A straight vertical carry is still used these days with cowboy holsters, some field holsters and many police duty holsters. It was found, however, and widely promulgated by the FBI, that for concealed carry, it was better to tilt the muzzle of the weapon so that it angled rearward. This drew the gunbutt more in line with the body plane. This carry became known as the "FBI Cant."

With an FBI Cant, we can once again use the principle of parallel lines. This time, however, the line of the barrel is out of the picture. Instead, an imaginary line is drawn between the toe of the handgun's butt and the lowest point on the muzzle of the weapon. It is this line that should be parallel to the trouser side seam.

Does this mean that the gun should be worn smack over the hip so that these two lines – the butt to muzzle line and the side seam line – are positioned one over the other? Not a bit. Parallel means parallel and nothing more. More than likely, for comfort and concealability, the holster will be positioned slightly behind the hip bone, in proximity to the kidney. Concealment issues aside, this style of carry presents the gunbutt at a convenient angle to enhance the draw by making the grasping of the weapon more natural while, at the same time, lowering the front of the holster, thus enhancing the muzzle's clearing of the front edge of the holster top.

Some terminology seems in order before returning to the discussion of positions. That "edge of the holster top" is more properly called the "lip." The

The Glock 22 is a full-sized gun, but can be worn by a woman at waist level in a belt holster. A better choice in the caliber would be the Glock 23 or even smaller Glock 27. Note the way too narrow belt. For women particularly, belt width is an important consideration. Using this Serpa Sportster paddle holster from Blackhawk, belt structure is not a problem.

With Galco Side Snap models like this one, the holster goes on and off without having to do anything with the wearer's belt. The gun is a Detonics USA (Pendergrass) Model 9-11-01 .45 in Detonics Black.

actual portion of the holster which holds the gun is called the "body." The bottom of the holster body is generally referred to as the "muzzle" or "muzzle end." The holster attaches to the belt – usually – by means of a "single tunnel loop," two or more "belt slots" or a combination of single tunnel loop and a single slot. Failing any of these attachment methods, a paddle can be used. The paddle is slipped over the belt so that the effect is much like that of a single tunnel loop. The paddle is often fitted with hook-like appendages which catch against the lower edge of the belt so that the holster stays in place when the gun is drawn. I met a Chicago Police detective about 45 years ago, as this written, who wore a holster the likes of which I have never seen since. It was a belt holster with a heavy duty pinch clip, rather like something used on a clip board, but much heavier. He clipped his holster on and off his belt with this device. He used this holster crossdraw with a Colt Detective Special (he championed the Colt, claiming that even though it was less accurate than a Smith & Wesson, it was less fragile if dropped in an alley).

The single tunnel loop is clearly derivative of the belt holsters of the past centuries. Even the fancier cowboy rigs – buscaderos and Hollywoods – had to incorporate a tunnel loop. Either a belt was directly passed through the loop,

Shown here is a two-slot belt holster from El Paso Saddlery with a Crimson Trace LaserGripped SIG-Sauer Model 229. El Paso is one of America's oldest holster making entities. It has been in the McNellis family for decades.

as in traditional cowboy rigs, or the loop was opened, then slipped through a horizontal slot in the belt, as with the less basic cowboy rigs. This loop, in the context of a cowboy-style holster, can be called a "drop loop" or "shank." The length of the drop loop determined the height at which the holster was worn in relation to the belt. But, there always had to be a loop.

The trouble with a loop, when concealment is at issue, is that the front to rear measurement would have to be unnecessarily huge in order to span sufficient belt distance to keep the rear of the holster, hence the gunbutt, tucked close to the body.

Along came slots – not the machines which eat coins in Las Vegas, but slots cut into the leather which skirts the actual holster body. The belt is passed through the slots, which can be and are positioned widely enough apart that the holster is hugged to the torso of the wearer. This makes for a wonderful arrangement. Sometimes, combining a single tunnel loop on the body side of the holster with only a single slot at the rear of the holster can be just as good or even better.

Continuing with terminology, belt holsters and other types of holsters will often employ some sort of safety device. In the old west, some holsters – not most, and certainly not all – employed a hammer loop, the intent of which was to keep the gun in the holster when one was moving about vigorously. As holsters developed into the early 20th century, some holsters employed screw

This Galco Halo belt holster is unique in that it allows the wearer to have a weapon light in place. This Glock 22 has a SureFire X300 WeaponLight mounted.

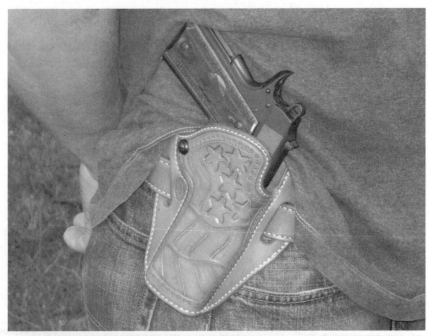

This holster is a very unique one from El Paso Saddlery, the carving on it a patriotic motif featuring the American flag. The pistol is a Detonics.

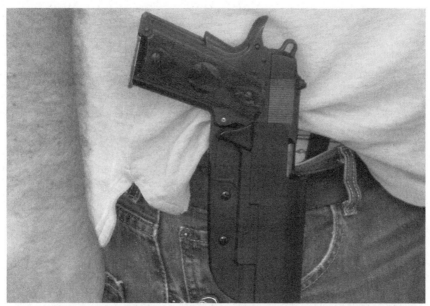

5-11 Tactical's belt holster for the full sized 1911 pistol is a bare bones affair that fits very well. 5-11 Tactical first got started by making pants for rock climbers and gradually branched off into a wide range of tactical gear.

tension devices which could be loosened or tightened to provide a "custom" fit. These are really unnecessary in many of the holsters employing them, but also harmless in most holsters. If the holster is designed properly and fitted to the gun, there is usually no need for tension screws with all but the most esoteric designs. Some people – including some makers – think they look good and, therefore, they are still sometimes in demand. If you acquire a typical leather holster from a major maker and it has a tension screw, that screw is almost certainly as superfluous as the proverbial screen door on a submarine, even though it can be tightened or loosened. But, as stated already, with an otherwise finely made holster, a tension screw is not a detriment.

At first, after the hammer loop and the military style full-flap (and half-flap variations) there was the "snap closure safety strap," which works wonderfully well when speed is not at issue. The system works with a strap that is secured to the holster side of the single tunnel loop, which, in duty rigs and field rigs, sometimes served as a drop loop. The gun was placed in the holster and the safety strap was folded over the gun, then snapped to the holster body. The strap incorporated the female snap and the male snap was set on the body. Unless the male snap was backed with some protective material or the holster body was a laminate of some kind, the snap could and would contact the weapon surface and scratch the finish.

This DeSantis three slot belt holster was specially designed for federal agents for their SIG 229s, with a hole on each side of the holster through the trigger guard area, so an agent could handcuff his gun into the holster. You will notice the typical DeSantis quality and how well the gun and holster combination hug the body.

With a revolver, the safety strap would most frequently pass below and behind the hammer spur, where the at-rest (fully lowered) hammer emerges from the frame. With autoloaders, this same arrangement could be used or, in the case of single action semi-autos, which might be carried "cocked and locked" (hammer fully raised and manual/thumb safety set in the "on" position), the safety strap might be designed to pass between the cocked hammer and the rear face of the slide, thus forming a shield should the hammer somehow fall, preventing contact between the hammer face and the firing pin.

Greater speed and less unnecessary motion could be had with the "thumb break safety strap," a system wherein the safety strap does not open and close by attaching or detaching the end of a long strap mounted with a female snap to a spot on the holster set with a male snap. Instead, both ends of the strap were fixed, sewn in place or cut as part of the holster body. Near where the older style strap would have crossed behind the hammer or in front of the hammer, a female snap was set on the body side of the holster and a male snap on the side away from the body. Precisely designed for length, the male side strap folds over and closes to the female snap. In most cases, such thumb breaks are designed to pass directly over the hammer spur when used with a double action semi-automatic or revolver and to pass directly over the rear face of the slide with a single action semi-automatic worn cocked and locked. Persons who are admittedly eccentric, such as I, and enjoy carrying single action semi-autos of 1911-ish format (the John Moses Browning designed Colt Government Model, usually in .45 ACP), hammer down, often have a considerable amount of thumb break safety strap stretching to do in order to close the strap over the hammer spur of one of these pistols. And, yes, I know this practice is frowned upon by a great many aficionados of the .45.

In order to make these thumb breaks work reliably, it is often necessary and prudent to place a metal reinforcement behind the leather on the body side of the female snap strap. This is held in place with the snap shank itself and a rivet. To prevent scratching of the firearm's surface, it is often wise to have still another layer of leather or a manufactured plastic piece which will form a shield that will serve to keep the flange on the female snap out of contact with the firearm surface. It is essential that the male snap's back be protected with a layer of leather or, these days, a plastic insert, which snaps into the back of the male snap. Again, this guards against scratching. Continuing with the discussion of positions, we return to the FBI Cant. More concealable, faster and more comfortable, there is a group of people who cannot employ this carry and, when wearing strongside, must wear the gun/holster combination straight up and down. These are people who suffer from carpel tunnel syndrome. Bending the wrist downward in order to grasp the gun butt doesn't work for persons so afflicted.

But there are other carries at the waist. Working from right to left, assuming a right-handed individual, the next carry position is one of the fastest, one of the least concealable and is known by at least two names: "appendix forward carry" or "felony carry," especially when the gun is worn holsterless. I personally prefer the latter name, since it has a much nicer ring to it. And, oddly, this felony carry, with a holster, was a favored carry of New York City Police plainclothes officers in years gone by.

The other name – appendix forward – although less colorful, is perfectly descriptive. The right-handed person would carry the weapon butt pointing outward to the right, positioned roughly over the appendix, between the navel and the right hip bone. Keeping a coat closed over this carry does little to conceal the weapon. When men wore their trousers with very high waistbands, a snubby (two-inch barrel) .38 Special revolver in a single tunnel loop belt holster would have been comfortable enough. But, go to more modern trousers, a more modern holster and something larger than a snubby and that weapon muzzle will gouge into the wearer's groin. The carry works fine under casual clothes when standing or walking, even with full-size guns such as the 1911

An appendix forward carry, sometimes called a "Felony Carry," was a popular position with New York City Detectives years back. The gun is a full-size 1911 with Crimson Trace LaserGrips, the holster made from Kydex by Grandfather Oak.

or the Beretta Model 92. This carry is often accomplished holsterless. And, as with other holsterless carries, the wearer must be cautious that the firearm doesn't slide up and out over the belt line or slip down below the belt line and exit along the trouser leg.

No cocked and locked carry should ever be attempted holsterless, movies not withstanding.

The next carry is quite controversial and quite effective, one of my personal favorites. It is "crossdraw" (the gun is worn between the navel and the left hip bone, the butt of the gun still pointing toward the right). Crossdraw has been branded as a "widow maker" by some trainers. Here's why. With the gun positioned in the classic crossdraw carry, the butt of the gun is not only accessible to the wearer, but can be accessible to an opponent. Bad guy grabs gun, bad guy shoots good guy with gun, hence "widow maker." Certainly, that can happen. However, with modern weapons retention training, it is less and less likely.

Of further consideration when viewing the crossdraw option is common sense. If you let a potential opponent penetrate so deeply into your private space that he can grab your gun without you being able to shove him away, step back or, if necessary, brandish your weapon, you're already in serious trouble.

At any event, I'm not suggesting open carry in the crossdraw position for uniformed police officers, etc.; but, for concealed carry, crossdraw offers a number of advantages. As with the cow punchers of old, accessing a gun from the crossdraw position is vastly easier when seated than accessing from strongside. This is especially true in the modern context. These days, strongside carry pitches the gun considerably higher than an old west style cowboy rig. Accessing a strongside carried firearm when seat-belted behind the wheel of an automobile (or, like as not, when strapped into the pilot's seat of an aircraft) is extremely difficult because of the lap and shoulder restraints themselves, the construction of the seat itself and the sheer awkwardness of getting the upper arm, elbow and forearm enough clearance to get at the gun butt for the draw. This is compounded when thumb breaks need to be opened. The gun may well be – at least partially – between your body and the seat itself. Such a carry isn't wildly comfortable when seated, either.

One of the finest and strangest crossdraw rigs ever made illustrates my point. Consummate holster craftsman Ken Null of Resaca, Georgia, makes a holster called the "Vam." The Vam was designed for Royal Canadian Mounted Police security personnel to use while chauffeuring dignitaries. It is part of the subset of holsters referred to as "driving holsters" (holsters meant to be worn while seated behind the wheel in preparation for possible carjacking or executive protection duties). Many driving holsters are not practical to wear while standing or moving about. The Vam is. It is also quite possibly the fastest holster available for concealable handguns. The gun is worn in the standard crossdraw location, but positioned completely horizontally. When seated, grasp the gunbutt and jerk slightly upward to break open the snap closure which serves as a safety device. This snap closure device is a version of what is called a "pull-through snap" (the action of the draw causes the gun itself to push between the two strap/snap sections, breaking them apart).

When standing, simply grasp the gun and jerk it free and you have presentation. The fastest way with this is the old "belly roll draw" (assuming a right-hander, as the gun is to be drawn, the left hip is slung forward – the midsection rolled – as the right hand reaches for the gun butt; once the gun is grasped, the action is reversed). The result of a properly executed belly roll draw is that the gun is moved toward the hand as the hand is moved toward the gun, then the holster pulled away from the gun as the gun is pulled away from the holster.

Yet, drawing guns worn in the standard crossdraw position is not easy for the off-hand. If you wish access with either hand, you must go to what I label "deep crossdraw" (the gun is positioned on the left side, behind the left hip bone, butt forward). In deep crossdraw, if your arms are long enough, you can handily reach the gun with your right hand, stretching just a bit. You can also draw the gun with your left hand, using a reverse or cavalry style draw. Accessing with the right hand is slower than a standard crossdraw when one is standing, but being able to grasp one's primary ordnance with either hand can prove advantageous under many circumstances.

The next normal waist level position is "small-of-the-back carry" (the firearm is positioned over the kidney or over the spine, accessed by reaching behind the back). The virtues of this carry are vastly overblown. If you are standing perfectly erect, this is an extremely concealable carry position. If you are bending over, you will either flash (actually expose the firearm from beneath the supposedly covering garment) the gun or it will profile (the shape of the gun is revealed as the covering garment is drawn tightly across it) under your clothes. Concealment is out the window.

Carrying the gun in this position is hard on the back, could possibly bring about spinal damage or kidney damage in the event of a fall. and is uncomfortable. Add to this, when the gun is drawn, if the slightest mistake is made – i.e., you sweep the muzzle across your own body plane and actually trigger a shot for one reason or another – you might very well shoot yourself in the posterior, the kidney, the hip, the thigh or the abdomen, to name a few obvious targets for a stray bullet.

The issue of shooting yourself by accident is no laughing matter. Anytime the muzzle of a weapon pans across something, if a bullet were to be discharged, something could be hit. If that something is yourself, you are doing your attacker's work for him.

The small-of-the-back carry is actually two separate handgun orientations. The most common of these positions involves the gunbutt facing outward – right for the right handed – and being grasped by the hand with the palm outward and the hand interposing itself between the gunbutt and the body. The least common of these involves the gunbutt pointing left and up and the hand oriented palm

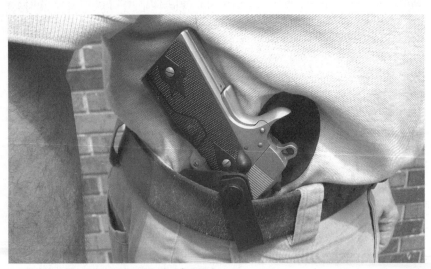

A strongside carry worn somewhat forward.

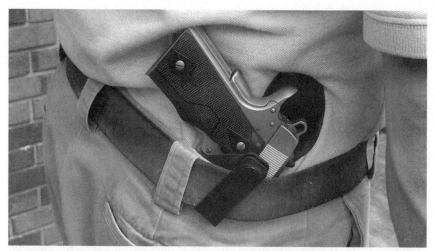

A strongside carry worn rearward, a better choice for many applications.

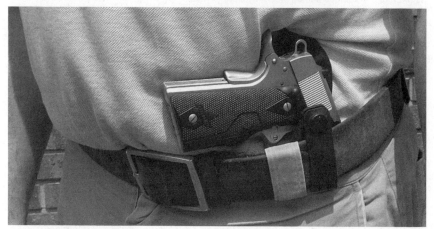

A conventional crossdraw.

inward, as in a normal strongside draw, but simply reaching way, way back. This is not something I'd recommend at all. In either event, the gun's muzzle passes across your body plane, unless you practice the correct technique. And, who is to say that, under the stress of a life or death situation, you will execute your draw to perfection and not trigger a shot prematurely?

I don't know how James Butler Hickok ("Wild Bill" was a sort-of generic nickname for a young fellow who was considered cool, etc.) did his cavalry draw, but my idea of a draw from either small-of-the-back position or any butt forward carry is what is known as a "twist draw" (whereby the gun is grasped and drawn, twisted, then presented). Here's how to do a properly executed twist draw while minimizing the potential for shooting yourself.

A left-handed twist draw from the deep crossdraw position. Another advantage of this carry is the fact that the gun can be drawn with either hand.

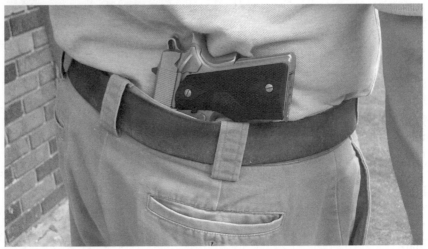

A small-of-the-back carry over the kidney with the butt positioned for a twist draw.

Turn the right hand one hundred eighty degrees to the left so that the palm is facing outward. Close the last three fingers and the thumb around the butt of the weapon as you would normally with a full combat grip. Keep the trigger finger out of the trigger guard and, as the weapon emerges from the carry, the trigger finger should come alongside the trigger guard, but never enter the trigger guard. Consider the action of a piston. A piston moves straight up and moves straight down. Once you have properly fisted your weapon, your trigger finger outside the trigger guard, you piston the weapon upward and out of the carry – hopefully, a holster.

A deep crossdraw, the gun behind the offside hip bone, butt forward, for a draw with either hand.

As soon as the muzzle is clear of the carry, your trigger finger still outside the trigger guard, you pivot your forearm on your elbow, just enough to have the muzzle of your weapon clear of your body and pointing at the ground or floor. Your trigger finger is still clear of the trigger guard, but likely alongside it. To "aim" the muzzle at the ground or floor, it is necessary to accomplish a slight downward motion, the backstroke of the piston. As you are doing this, but only when the muzzle is clear and pointed downward, you twist your wrist to the right one hundred eighty degrees. Only then, as you raise the handgun into its firing position, do you begin to allow your trigger finger to assume the normal position it would have as you present.

With practice, this draw can be accomplished with good speed, but not blindingly fast. And, because it is rather complicated, there is a very good chance that it will be done improperly in the heat of a life or death situation. If a handgun is drawn from one of the small-of-the-back carries in such a manner as to allow the muzzle of the weapon to cross the body plane, there is danger. I would never carry a cocked and locked single action semi-auto this way.

Waist level carry, regardless of the position chosen, demands a belt which is built to accommodate the weight of a gun and has enough body not to deform. Good belts like this will last and last. I have several Alessi and several Milt Sparks belts which I have been wearing for 25 years or so. Lined belts are generally the best, but one of the Milt Sparks belts I use a great deal is unlined and still works remarkably well. Major makers like Galco, DeSantis, Bianchi, Mitch Rosen and others can be counted on for excellent quality belts as well as holsters. The quality of the belt cannot be overestimated, even if one carries holsterless. But that's another story that we'll touch on later.

Photo courtesy of Galco International.

INSIDE WAISTBAND CARRY

Chapter Nine

For sheer concealment convenience, no waist level carry tops inside carry. Second only to pocket holsters and ankle holsters, it is the most concealable of all conventional carries and – for many of us – is wonderfully convenient. My first handgun was a two-inch barrel Model 36 Chiefs Special in blue. My first carry system for that gun was one of the old, heavy leather Bucheimer-Clark inside holsters with a really stout nickel-plated spring steel clip (Lawman Leather, of Dirty Harry Shoulder Holster fame, is the successor company to Bucheimer-Clark, and plans, as this is written, to reintroduce these terrific old holsters). Eventually, I moved away from this carry for the J-Frame Smith & Wesson and, for decades, used a Barami Hip-Grip. With other guns, I continued to use inside waistband holsters and, to this day, still do.

When one carries a holster on the belt at waist level, there are two concealment problems presented. First, the holster must conceal the gun, of course. But, how do you conceal the holster? That may sound illogical, but consider the following scenario to get the idea. You're wearing a bomber jacket. The bomber jacket covers the butt of your gun quite nicely. The bottom edge of the bomber jacket hits a little below the lower edge of your belt. What about those extra inches of holster that extend below the lower edge of your belt? The answer is either to wear a longer jacket – not that much of a problem if you wear a suit and tie – or to do away with worrying about the bottom of the holster. I usually opt for the latter.

With an inside waistband holster, the lower portion of the holster is hidden by whatever garment is covering the lower half of your body. Problem solved – or, at least, almost.

Inside waistband carry has its origins in the earliest of handgun carries and, really, in the carry of short edged weapons before that. Although I'm an enthusiastic proponent of inside waistband carry, I've never been taken with the idea of carrying a fixed blade knife without a sheath. That is dangerous in the extreme.

As single-shot pistols were reduced in size from weapons so large that they needed to be carried attached to one's saddle, the natural thing was to stuff the pistols into one's belt or sash. Since the pistols were single shots and took some time to reload, it became de rigueur to carry more than one pistol – sometimes three or four. Even after the development of revolvers, multiple handgun carrying with one or more of those handguns being worn stuffed holsterless under the waistband or under the belt was often encountered. During the Civil War, some Southern Cavalrymen would ride into saber range with their Northern counterparts, pull their 1851 Navy Colts, or whatever less well-known model was available, and blast away until all their handguns were empty or they had run out of Union cavalry at whom to shoot. The carriage of extra weapons, on body, when battle loomed, often necessitated holsterless carry.

The most famous gunfighter of the Old West, James Butler Hickok, most often carried his brace of 1851 Navy Colts butt forward, tucked into his sash,

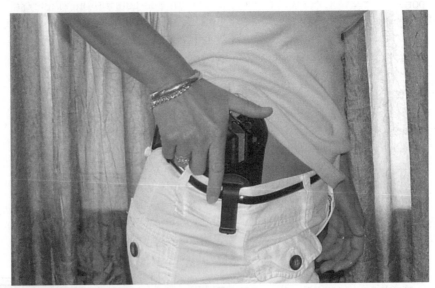

Inside waistband carry can make good sense for a man or woman, especially with a semi-auto, the gun a Walther PP in .32 ACP. The holster is a fabric model from Blackhawk!.

without holsters. The judgment of history is such that Wild Bill Hickok seems to have done okay using that carry technique.

As cartridge revolvers became more widely available, the "Town Carry" came into vogue, Wyatt Earp and Bat Masterson and others using this carry when going openly armed was socially unacceptable or legally dubious. Town Carry merely meant that the gun was stuffed into the trousers, holsterless, covered by the coat. Bat Masterson got arrested for a Sullivan Law violation in New York City while carrying this way. One way in which single action Colts were carried holsterless inside the waistband of the trousers was, at once, quite simple and quite ingenious. The Colt's loading gate would be left open and the loading gate – almost like a 19th century version of the Barami Hip-Grip – kept the revolver from sliding down through the trouser leg.

As automatic pistols became ever more popular, inside waistband carry, with a holster or without, was even easier. Semi-autos were flatter, hence more comfortable and, in many applications, more concealable. While the cylinder of a revolver lent itself to the gun sliding out of position when carrying holsterless and making a bulge when used with a holster, semi-autos seemed made for concealed carry. Carrying a 1911 without a holster was sometimes called a "Mexican Carry." Certain practitioners of this carry method would even remove the grip plates from a 1911, in order to make it still flatter.

The more one learns about inside waistband carry, the more one becomes convinced that flatness – with or without a holster – is among the most important things to consider. Notice, I'm not using the word "thin," just "flat." A SIG 229, with Crimson Trace LaserGrips, is not a skinny handgun, not thin. But, the SIG is flat. Flatness – within reason – is more of a consideration in concealment than whether or not a gun has achieved maximum thinness. Removing the grips from a 1911 for some largely imagined concealment benefit detracts from the gun's overall shootability.

The little Detonics CombatMaster .45s of which I am so fond are, often times, the subject of a quest for skinny grips. I've never understood this since the thickness of standard 1911 grip plates – the CombatMaster grips are just shorter, neither fatter nor thinner – isn't much at all. But, as Sly and the Family Stone so beautifully put it, "Different strokes..."

As the 20th century wore on and holster making became a business for large concerns and custom makers, holsters themselves became more diverse and widely available.

The inside waistband holster filled a niche, although some persons cannot abide them. These persons argue that the holster and gun are somehow invasive, get in their personal space because the holster and gun are partially inside their clothing rather than on the outside. I'm sure this is a real concern

This extremely well-made inside waistband holster for a full-size 1911 is from master craftsman Sam Andrews, whose son also makes holsters, their work at times hard to tell apart.

and I respect it, although I've never experienced it. Persons who are exceedingly thin or exceedingly not-thin may have trouble with an inside carry. The exceedingly thin person may be so thin that the waist area isn't wide enough to accommodate a gun and holster worn inside. And, even if the gun and holster combination can be worn, they won't conceal worth a flip. The solution for this type of person is a smaller gun or a different carry. Most shoulder and regular belt holsters won't do this person much good, either.

The not-thin person will probably be fine with an inside waistband carry, unless that person's mid-section is so large that a fat roll will roll over the gun and holster. Again, this latter person may have no better luck with a traditional belt holster, either. This person may well be able to use a shoulder holster quite nicely, unless girth is such that reaching across the body to the area below the opposite arm is difficult. A crossdraw holster may work quite well, though, because the gun butt is facing forward.

Joe Average is the ideal candidate for any type of holstering, and especially so with the inside waistband carry. Muscular and well-built — as most men see themselves when looking in the mirror, regardless of reality — there is just the right amount of body thickness and musculature that a firearm of normal size works great in this carry.

Inside waistband holsters go on in a number of ways. The really solid clip of the type used on that old Bucheimer-Clark holster I used to wear was both strong and durable. As everyone knows, there will always be somebody who

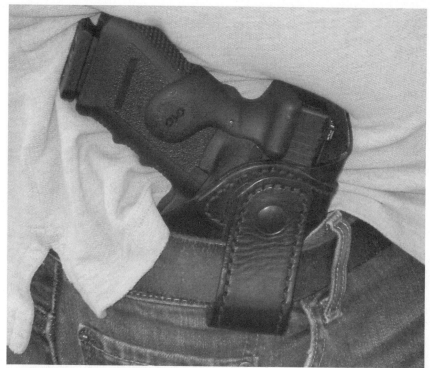

This inside waistband holster for the Glock 22 conceals quite well. It is from Blackhawk! Products.

will find a way to save three and one-half cents by cheapening a product. That is exactly what happened with some lower end brands of inside waistband holsters during the 1970s. Cheaper clips were produced, clips from brittle steels. The result was that all inside waistband holsters featuring a clip suffered. These cheap clips – none of the better companies used them – would break as the holster was put on or taken off. This rendered the holster useless, except as something with which you could accidentally slice yourself or your clothing. Where the clip broke could be as sharp as a jagged razor blade.

Most spring steel clips these days – at least on holsters made in the USA – come from one or the other of two primary sources, both concerned with high quality.

But, there are other ways in which the inside waistband holster can be attached. Principal among these are those utilizing one or two wrap-around leather straps or tongues. When I started carrying a gun more than 40 years ago, Sharon and I visited a shoe repair shop where we met a one-armed American Indian. If I ever was told his name, I don't remember it. He made a holster for me out of what was probably a six ounce leather. It featured two

The Galco Trident Kydex inside waistband holster is typical of Galco quality, even in this medium other than leather. A Glock 27 was used in this Glock 22 holster to take advantage of the shorter grip frame for added concealability.

comparatively narrow leather straps, sewn to the holster lip. You slid the holster into your pants, slipping one of the straps behind your belt and closing it with a snap to the second strap which passed over the belt. I got Sam Andrews to make me one like it a few years back, but for a different gun, of course. That little holster and the gun it carried went everywhere with Sharon and me. Eventually, I sold the gun and holster to an old friend. Later, I bought the gun back from him, but the little holster had been stolen.

My point is that an innovative and well-crafted inside waistband holster can be a marvelous carry solution. That one-armed American Indian shoe repairman's holster making skills would compare favorably with some of today's best makers.

The one problem with an inside waistband holster is that the portion of the gun that is above the belt line still shows. Even that holster the American Indian made for me allowed a little of the gun butt to peek up over the waistband.

One of the first people to successfully attack that problem was firearms writer and all-around gun guy Dave Workman. Mitch Rosen made the holster and called it "The Workman." The means of attachment to the belt is quite ingenious. Rather than the means of attachment being at or near the holster lip, a leather piece is sewn to the bottom of the holster. You secure the holster around the belt, as usual, with a snap closure. Picture a "V" formed between

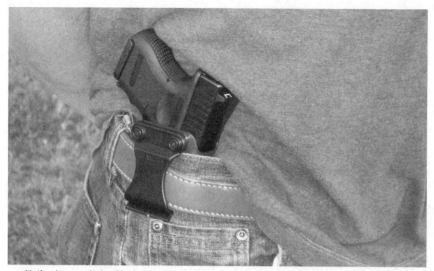

Notice how well the Glock 27 with the Galco Trident inside waistband holster conceals.

the attachment snap and the holster, the two legs of the "V" meeting at the bottom of the holster. You tuck your shirt in between the two legs of the "V" and no one sees the gun butt or holster. There is provision to get the holster so nothing shows on the outside at all, the leather piece not coming up over the waistband, but securing inside the waistband with Velcro instead. You'd just have to have matching Velcro placed inside whatever different pairs of pants you might wear when using the holster.

The Galco "SkyOps" holster attacks this problem from a different perspective. Utilizing what is called a "Y Hook" that takes the place of a piece of leather coming up from the bottom of the holster, the two legs of the inverted "Y Hook" pass behind the belt and catch the lower edge of the belt. The shirt tucks in, covering everything. All anyone might notice – if he or she had good eyes and really knew holsters – would be the very small portions of the "Y Hook" legs which show near the lower edge of the belt. The holster and the "Y Hook" are black and it is recommended that this unit be used with a black belt. A special version, with a tensioning device, is made for federal law enforcement use with the SIG Sauer P-229.

More than ever, today we must make certain that anyone from the legally armed citizen going about his daily business to the Sky Marshal who may be a fellow passenger on your next plane trip can be effectively armed with a gun of sufficient capacity, power, reliability and accuracy to take down an assailant, whether criminal or terrorist, when circumstances leave no other option. The inside holster is a fine equipment choice toward that goal.

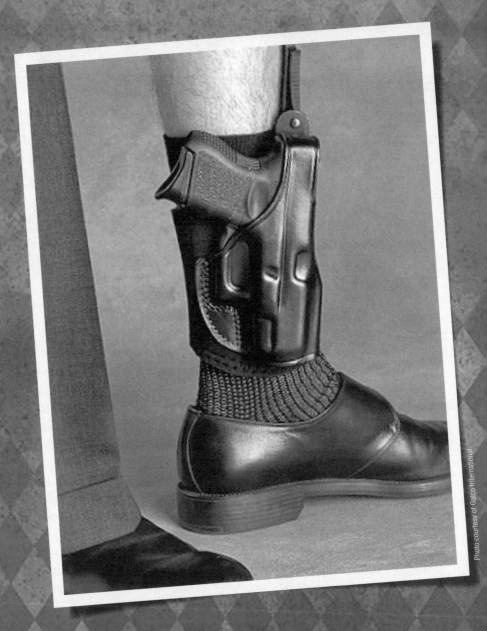

Photo courtesy of Galco International

ANKLE AND LEG CARRY

Chapter Ten

Carrying a weapon on one's leg or ankle is nothing new. Frontiersmen would sheath a knife in a boot top and, likely, the concept goes back even further. It must be remembered that, when this practice was initially undertaken, concealment was almost never an issue. You were a mountain man and you carried a knife in a boot top. Who cared who noticed it?

For women, ankle and leg carry was another matter entirely. A well-dressed woman typically wouldn't have been wearing pants for anything but manual labor until well into the 1960s or 1970s. In the 19th century, her skirts were long enough and full enough that a knife or a gun or both could be well hidden on her thigh or her calf. She certainly would have looked odd with a gunbelt strapped to her hourglass waist. The knife would likely be some sort of stiletto, the gun most likely a Remington over/under derringer. If she were foolish enough to carry either just tucked into a garter, she would soon enough have come to regret the practice when the weapon slipped from under the garter and fell to the floor. Were it a knife that slipped from beneath her garter , she might have stabbed herself. Were it the Remington o/u derringer, a fall against the floor or hard ground could have precipitated an unintended discharge – more than an embarrassment.

Although ankle holsters for men may have come into fashion in major metropolitan areas sometime in the late 19th century, it's doubtful. Most men were wearing boots or shoes that came up over the ankle. Later, men wore spats. For women, with their high buttoned shoes, the ankle holster wouldn't have worked, either.

Fobus is a well-respected name in holsters. This ankle holster carried a J-Frame well. The J-Frame sized revolver, whether from Smith & Wesson or someone else, is just about ideal for ankle holster carry, unless you're in an area where climate can figure in and the more enclosed construction of a semi-automatic makes a more sensible solution.

If men were wearing boots, a derringer or one of the smaller revolvers, like one of those from Hopkins & Allen could have been tucked inside the boot top. If someone wore such a gun habitually, he could have his boots made with a built-in holster, or have a holster sewn into commercially available boots.

Ankle Holsters

Although I can discern no supportive data, I'm guessing true ankle holsters started seeing more currency by the 1920s or 1930s, although ankle holsters have never been exactly super popular or common. The modern interest in ankle holsters – by no means a groundswell of demand – picked up momentum when Gene Hackman starred as "Popeye" Doyle in the 1971 film The French Connection. "Popeye" Doyle was based on the real New York cop turned actor and technical consultant Eddie "Popeye" Egan. I don't know whether the late Mr. Egan used an ankle holster the way it was used in the film. But an ankle rig should not be worn on the outside of the strong side ankle, as Mr. Hack-

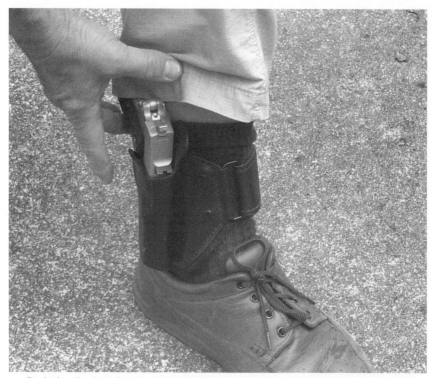

Beginning the draw from the Alessi Ankle Holster. Usually, an ankle holster is better with a physically smaller and lighter gun, something like a J-Frame Smith & Wesson or the Taurus 709 Slim ideal for the application.

man does in the film. Perhaps it was more visual for movie-making purposes, but that film has confused novice ankle holster wearers ever since. As a right handed man, on those occasions when I wear an ankle holster, it is worn on the inside of my left ankle. Were I left handed and I wished to get the gun with my dominant hand, I'd wear the ankle holster on the inside of my right ankle. If I were right handed and had some sort of joint or tendon problem which made wearing an ankle rig on my left leg uncomfortable or unsupportably painful, then I would wear my right handed ankle holster on the inside of my right ankle, butt forward. Were I a left handed person so afflicted, I would wear my left handed ankle rig on the inside of my left ankle, butt forward.

Under no circumstances, you may notice, would I wear an ankle holster on the outside of my ankle, right or left. Why? Aside from considerably decreased concealability, every time I was close to something or someone, I would run the serious risk of banging the gun and holster combination into said inanimate object or person. Bad for the gun, certainly, it's also potentially noisy to go banging your hidden handgun into things.

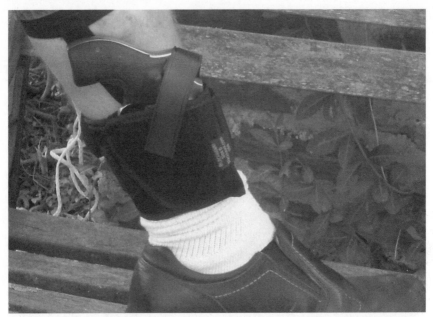

Nylon can be the perfect material for an ankle holster. Light weight and rugged, it's even more easily cleaned than leather. This holster, with supporting T-strap/calf strap, is from Blackhawk! Products, the gun a J-Frame S&W.

Some writers make much of the draw problems with an ankle holster. Indeed, there are problems. You either have to drop to one knee – the strongside knee – or drop onto your butt in a partial roll or stand on one foot while you raise the offside leg so you'll be able to reach the gun. Or, you can just bend over. All of these draw positions leave you more than a little vulnerable to a close range attack, none of them holding the potential for real speed.

I always view the ankle holster a little differently. I see it for backup, for carrying a second handgun or a third one. That said, although rapidity and fluidity of the draw must still be considered, I don't expect my access to an ankle gun to be anywhere near as easy as with more conventional carries.

Handguns worn on the ankle have size limitations, in both directions. An old friend of ours named Hal, thirty years ago, was a really big guy. A little overweight, granted, but not that much. He had an enormous chest and shoulders and was reasonably tall. He was extremely strong. Hal used to ride a motorcycle quite a bit. When he wasn't working one of his numerous jobs, he was a part-time deputy. A wheelgun person – in those days most of us were, to one degree or another – he carried a four-inch barrel Smith & Wesson Model 27 .357 Magnum. When it didn't ride on his right side in a pancake style holster, it rode on the inside of his left ankle.

This Alessi ankle rig is made for the Detonics USA (Pendergrass) CombatMaster, a large gun for ankle carry, but it works. Classic construction for an ankle rig is evident in the photograph. A band encircles the ankle, slips through a buckle at the front and folds back onto itself, securing with hook and loop fastener.

A four-inch N-frame revolver is well outside the norm for ankle holster carry, both from a standpoint of weight and size. Hal was a really big guy. The largest gun I've ever carried on an ankle rig is a Detonics CombatMaster .45 and that's pushing it for most people.

Similarly, we've all seen ankle holsters made for guns the size of a See-camp .32 or a Beretta 950BS .25 or even something the size of a mini-revolver. Why would one carry such a fine gun in such an awfully questionable way? There's nothing wrong with those guns and there's nothing wrong with ankle holsters. But, put them together, and it's a choice I would not make. Putting an ankle holster together with a gun that is best carried in a pocket violates the Leather to Gun Ratio. If you've got more leather in your concealment holster than you have gun to conceal, you're usually doing things wrong. Think of it like getting ready for an overnight stay at a hotel. You're going to drive. As a guy, what you need is a little more limited than what a woman might typically bring along; but, let's assume that, whether a man or a woman, you're a sensible packer. What you need for an overnight stay can certainly be packed in a small suitcase. Hence the term "overnight bag." Instead of packing in such a sensibly sized bag, you get out an old steamer trunk, something that is big enough in which to hide a corpse. Then, you can't fit it in your car, of course, so you rent a trailer to haul it. Sound ridiculous? It certainly does. Having a wide band wrap around your ankle with an enveloping holster attached to it – with, of course, a thumb break or pull-through likely included – for a gun not that much bigger than a package of cigarettes makes about as much sense.

Actually, there's a relatively limited range of practical ankle holster handguns. The original medium frame revolvers in .32 ACP or .380 ACP work great, as do the snub-nosed .38 Special revolvers. I typically advise people to go to a stainless steel snubby .38, and to inspect the weapon for proper functionality

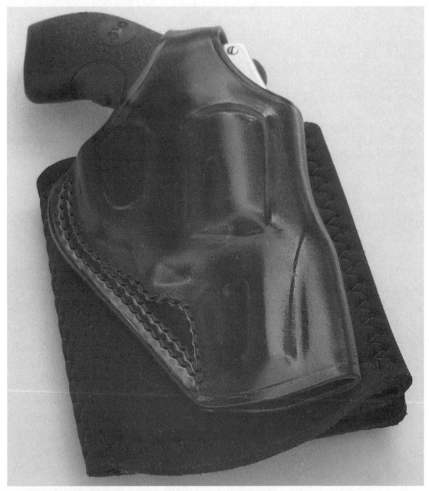

One of the best ankle holster and handgun combinations is this Galco Ankle Glove with a 2-inch J-Frame Smith & Wesson revolver. The Ankle Glove is shown sans calf strap, a useful item to stabilize the holster when worn.

This Galco Ankle Glove holds an old-style S&W Model 640 .38 Special. The Model 640 was produced only between 1990 and 1995 as an all stainless steel .38 Special. It's an outstanding gun and mated to the Galco Ankle Glove it makes a terrific carry.

more regularly than a gun carried on the belt, under the shoulder, etc. Why? Worn on the ankle, the gun is less protected than guns worn elsewhere, more subject to dust and debris getting into the action, etc.

One of my very best friends carried an ankle gun as a third gun for several decades. The gun he carried was at the outside extreme of size – a SIG P-230 .380 – but had an alloy frame to keep down the weight. Over the last 40+ years of carrying a handgun concealed, the only three guns I have ever carried on any more than an occasional basis in an ankle holster are a Walther PPK/S .380 (years ago) and a Detonics CombatMaster (nearly as long ago) and a J-frame Smith & Wesson .38. This latter gun would have more than one incarnation – years ago a Model 60, more recently Model 640.

The Galco Ankle Glove is a fine example of an ankle holster. It's available with a safety strap or a tension screw as the means of retention. I chose a thumb break strap, reinforced of course. It's not quite usual, in that the 640 has an enclosed hammer. The holster body itself is black leather. The strap that secures around the leg is neoprene and the closure is Velcro hook and loop. On the body side of the holster/band combination is a pad made from sheepskin, to cushion the ankle bone. An optional, adjustable T-strap or calf-

This K.L. Null ankle rig is a left-handed model, made for the Glock 27 and designed to carry a hidden cuff key as well. For the right handed person, carrying a handgun as if one were left-handed could be a tactical advantage.

strap can be added to the Ankle Glove. I recommend it to keep the holster from slipping down on the ankle as it is worn. This improves comfort and concealment.

I've seen it recommended to draw one's sock up around the ankle holster for further concealment. I would find this arrangement uncomfortable, with the ankle band against my bare skin. I suppose you could wear two socks! But I wouldn't.

The ankle holster, if properly designed, will have a cant, rather than being straight up and down, this to keep as much of the handgun and, particularly, its grip frame within the outline of the leg as possible. The bulk of the gun – this, of course, so important with a revolver's cylinder – should be above the ankle bone, in the properly designed ankle holster.

When you're wearing it, you need a trouser leg that is cut to break on the shoe, and wide enough not to draw tightly over the gun and holster combination. Getting out of a truck or SUV, climbing a ladder, taking a seat in bleachers – any of these things can betray the ankle carried gun, if you are not careful. Just crossing your legs will do it. We attended a rather high profile criminal trial at a federal courthouse about ten years ago, to hear a friend's key testimony. The court room was loaded with federal agents and state and local plainclothes people. Their ankle holsters empty because of where they were, Sharon and I amused ourselves by spotting the empty holsters as a good many of the plain clothes lawmen casually crossed their legs, their handguns out of holster and out of mind, it seemed.

Leg Holsters

But, when it comes to leg holsters – and there aren't that many of them – it's a totally different situation. Decades back, Bianchi International made its Number Eleven Leg Holster. This was a rare type of holster designed to be worn on the calf, one strap circumferencing the leg above the calf muscle, the other below the muscle. It was made for guns no larger than a snubby .38 or an old medium frame auto like the Walther PPK. I had one that fit a wide range of .25 automatics. It would have worked with a Seecamp or NAA Guardian .32.

It was designed to be worn by someone wearing cowboy boots, the boot's upper masking the bulk of the holster and the gun under the trouser leg. Like an ankle holster, a right handed person wore the holster on the inside of the left leg. A use perhaps never envisioned for the holster would be for a woman, wearing a long dress or skirt. That would have worked as well. The holster is no longer catalogued and hasn't been for a very long time.

For wear on the leg, an option that only women and traditionally dressed Scotsmen might utilize is the thigh holster. These were/are generally made for small frame autos, medium frame autos (.32 and .380) and J-Frame-sized revolvers. Again, a right handed person would wear the gun and holster combination on the left thigh. Typically, the unit consists of a belt – hook and loop closure is best – worn around the waist just above the hips. This supports the weight of the gun and holster. The holster is then banded around the thigh, the gun worn between the thighs. Some women find this arrangement comfortable; many would not. The thigh holster demands being worn under a reasonably loose skirt or dress and I wouldn't think it would work under even the most baggy slacks. Kilt-wearers could probably get away with it, a sporran further masking the presence of the gun. In Robert Heinlein's fine novel *Methuselah's Children,* a story set far in the future, men apparently wear kilts and carry their "blasters" holstered beneath their folds. What can I say?

Except in the case of a woman who can carry a gun in no other way because of attire considerations – and that's increasingly more rare in these times – carry in a thigh holster would be an exceptional carry for most. A leg holster would have to be designed and made by a custom leather craftsman, an experienced holster maker. Otherwise, unless you find an old Bianchi Number Eleven on eBay or somewhere like that, you're out of luck. Clearly, the

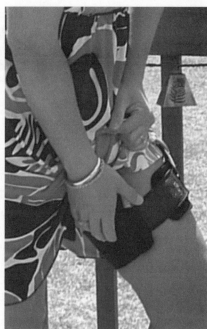

A North American Arms Guardian .32 in an old Galco thigh holster. The holster features a slender belt which goes around the waist, under the dress, and an adjustable length drop shank. The holster is Velcro secured around the leg.

Detail of the Guardian .32 in the thigh holster. Some women rave about this carry, while others cannot abide it.

only regularly available leg carry system is the ankle holster. Ankle holsters will never be as widely used as belt holsters or perhaps even as popular as shoulder rigs. But, every serious male concealed weapons carrier should have one and the gun to go with it. For women, the weight factor and the size of the gun versus smaller bones might mitigate against this. But, with the right gun and holster, an ankle rig can be a real plus for a woman's battery, as well.

CLOTHING AND CARRYING

Chapter Eleven

Clothing concerns cannot be over-emphasized when it concerns carrying concealed weapons. Historically, clothing was frequently more a concern of female concealed carriers, because women's clothing is usually made from lighter weight materials and is more form fitting. That still is true, of course, but men no longer wear heavy woolen suit jackets or even windbreakers; leather bomber jackets aren't seen as often as they once were, as this is written. Heavier clothing – made from wool suiting, for example – allows a handgun to print less easily under clothing.

To counter the problems present day men's and women's fashions present the concealed handgun carrier, specialty clothing manufacturers have arisen, offering unique tailoring solutions which address many of the classic concealment issues. These usually devolve to really loose shirts, vests, outerwear and – for women – over-large tops or jackets. There are also specially constructed undershirts for men and women which incorporate a holster positioned along the rib cage under the offside armpit and even men's compression boxer-type underpants which incorporate a built-in holster.

I have, over the years, meticulously avoided special concealed carry garments – for the most part, at least. Yet I have found some interesting and effective items of late. The reason I avoid special concealment wear is because all those of us in the gun field are exposed to it. Consequently, the aware gun-knowledgeable person will very likely recognize it. Although the more obvious concealed carry wear will fool the uninitiated, I started my concealed carry career having to look out for all sorts of observers, some of whom would be the firearms informed.

A small .45 automatic conceals easily in the breast pocket of the Woolrich Elite Series Tactical Algerian Field Jacket. A gun the size of a Detonics CombatMaster .45, or a 2-inch J-Frame Smith & Wesson, etc., conceals quite effectively and carries quite comfortably in the Algerian Field Jacket's many pockets – thirteen in all!

The classic example is the "photographer's vest," or whatever one wishes to call it. If you don't care that gun-knowledgeable people will assume you're armed, by all means wear one. But don't make the mistake of wearing such a vest when everyone around you is almost ready to pass out from heat prostration – unless you can safely assume that everyone around you is relatively ignorant of the basics of firearms concealment, stupid or just doesn't care. If these conditions exist, make yourself more comfortable and pull your shirt over the gun and take off the vest. If you're an off-duty cop or Fed and everyone with whom you interact knows it, a photographer's vest is just fine. It covers the gun and you're not brandishing your weapon. In northeast Georgia, where Sharon and I live, cops in plainclothes generally seem to wear their badge on their belt and everybody gets to see that along with their Glock and their cuffs. Sharon and I are always happy to be in a restaurant, etc., with an openly armed plainclothes cop. The officer's presence makes for a safer environment and a more relaxing meal. And, considering that Georgia averages between five and six months of summer-like weather each year, it's quite practical for those officers.

We civilians, however, can get in trouble if we "flash" a gun. We have to hide it. The regulations accompanying our concealed carry permits demand that the gun is hidden.

Back to clothing. I have discovered some serendipitous sartorial solutions. Let's take a fine example, namely the Woolrich Elite Series Tactical Algerian Field Jacket. Okay. It could use a shorter name. I know. The jacket has thirteen pockets, last time I counted, many of these on the inside of the jacket, some outside pockets situated behind outside pockets. The outside breast pockets, namely, are flap pockets, capable of holding all sorts of ordinary stuff. Work the zipper open on the inner (breastbone side) of either of these pockets – or both, if you wish – and you can easily hide a serious handgun. I will routinely slip my Detonics CombatMaster .45 into one of these pockets when I'm walking Honey the Wonderdog on cooler evenings. My snubby .38 Special S&W Model 640 revolver or my .32 ACP Century International Arms Walther PP fits in there just as well. If I really thought it were going to be likely I'd need to pull a gun and I were silly enough to go outside only armed with a medium sized handgun, I can put the gun in one of the two large side pockets and seal the flap in the open position. If I want to be sneaky, I can take my trusty old Seecamp .32 and carry that in the pocket on the upper left sleeve.

> *Cargo pocketed pants have been around for a long time and likely will remain in vogue.*

But propriety demands wearing clothing on the lower half of the body, as well. I have several interesting choices there, too. Again, from Woolrich, I have some of their "Operator" pants. Sharon joked that telephone operators wear them. They probably don't. Operator pants, by any other name, would be "tactical" pants. There are two general classifications, namely those which are obviously tactical pants and those that have extra pockets, extra reinforcement at stress points, etc., but don't look like you're heading out on a mission. Woolrich Lightweight Operator Pants are the kind of pants that look to be mission-ready, and they are. Some of the many pockets have elastic bands within them for accommodating AR-15 (or similar-sized) magazines. Smaller magazines can be well-carried in these pockets, also, of course.

Tactical pants tend to have more capacious pockets and their more careful construction will support weight better than regular pants. One pair of tactical

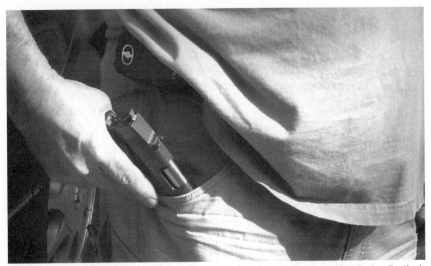

A Detonics CombatMaster .45 in the pocket of a pair of Woolrich Elite Series Tactical Lightweight Operator Pants. The pockets are deep enough and sturdy enough to handle a gun this size for an occasional impromptu hide.

pants I really like comes from Blackhawk. Called the "TNT" for Tactical-Non-Tactical, the pants only have two additional pockets – suitable for a pistol magazine or a folding knife, perhaps – beyond the usual front/side pockets and the hip pockets. These latter are fitted with flaps that can be closed on the outside or inside of the pocket, sealing with magnets. Yes, magnets. Sharon and our adult daughter, Samantha, both asked me to throw myself against the refrigerator to see if I'd stick. I didn't try it. Extremely durable, but equally light in weight, these Blackhawk Tactical-Non-Tactical TNT Pants are very comfortable and dressy enough for anything from the office to a golf outing (if I played golf) to pairing with a corduroy sportcoat or similar.

The nice thing about tactical pants, however very tactical or slightly tactical they look, is that tactical looking pants and shorts are popular with the general population, as this is written, and one of the keys to successful concealment is blending in. Woolrich, indeed, makes tactical shorts. I'm wearing a pair as I write this. They have large hip pockets, smaller hook and loop closure pockets superimposed over these, capacious front/side pockets and hook and loop closure flap pockets further down on both legs. These flap closure pockets are ideal for holding magazines and other gear and also work great for a wallet. The main front/side pockets are deep enough to easily handle a pocket holstered pistol. As I write this, my Crimson Trace LaserGripped North American Arms Guardian .380 in its Grandfather Oak Kydex pocket holster is in the right front/side pocket, and there's room to spare.

All the tactical pants I've seen or worn – including the shorts – have belt loops wide enough to take a substantial belt of at least one and three-quarter-inch width, this also a real plus when carrying a belt holstered concealed weapon.

Are tactical pants from Blackhawk, Woolrich and others like the photographer's vest? At this point, they are not. Cargo pocketed pants have been around for a long time and likely will remain in vogue. As to the Algerian Field Jacket, this simply looks like good old manly outerwear with a little bit of a military appearance. You wouldn't even be likely to offend someone at a peace demonstration (if you cared about that), since, oddly enough, military looking outwear was always fashionable for people who couldn't stand the military.

There are some basic considerations when part of getting dressed each day includes wearing a gun.

Most of us cannot carry a full-sized handgun in a shoulder rig under a shirt. Even if the gun were not spotted – which I sincerely believe would be the exception rather than the rule – dressing in a super baggy shirt of heavier material, so the gun and holster cannot be seen beneath it either by bulge or as a dark shadowy object, and then wearing a T-shirt or similar garment under the rig so that the shoulder holster isn't sitting on your bare skin would be intolerable for me under most temperature and humidity conditions. I genuinely feel sorry for cops wearing body armor when it's hot outside. They're tougher than I am. I'd dissolve. The other problem with the shirt alone approach can be appearance. But, if this carry works for you, by all means use it.

If you're a guy and you don't wear your pants insanely tightly at the waist, you'll probably not have to follow the advice given in some quarters to buy your pants and belts one waist size larger if you'll be carrying a gun in an inside waistband holster. I'll tell you a true story concerning this. When Sharon and I first got married in 1968, like a lot of young just-marrieds, we weren't rolling in dough. I'd lost a little weight in the summer of 1967 and I had this pair of trousers I really liked, but they were too big in the waist. Rather than spend the money to get them taken in – not something Sharon could have done on a home sewing machine – or give them away, I always carried my old Model 36 S&W in a heavy leather Bucheimer-Clark inside waistband holster. That added enough bulk that I could keep my pants up. But, unless you're carrying a revolver in a holster made from exceedingly thick leather, you'll not need to get a size larger at the waist. Any handgun I own will slip inside the waistband of my trousers and would do so in a proper holster, too.

One of the most important clothing considerations involves selection of a belt designed to support the weight of a gun. Women's belts are generally so ill-suited to supporting handgun weight that they cannot even be considered.

Using a pair of Blackie Collins Toters and a well worn Milt Sparks belt as background, this is just some of the gear that can easily be carried in these specially designed pants. From top left a North American Guardian .32 in a hip pocket holster, an old style Smith & Wesson Model 640 .38 Special with Crimson Trace LaserGrips, a Detonics USA (Pendergrass) CombatMaster .45, a Benchmade Presidio Axis Auto, then from left again a North American Arms 1-5/8-inch .22 Magnum Mini Revolver and a Seecamp .32 in a front pocket holster.

Some of the high fashion men's belts, although they have more body, aren't really much better for holding up a gun. Although I use belt holsters infrequently, the quality of one's belt is a consideration with inside waistband holsters and even if you just carry holsterless at waist level. You need to support the weight of the gun. The effect is more dramatic with a belt holster.

I have belts from Alessi, Milt Sparks, Galco, Mitch Rosen, Dillon Leather By Mitch Rosen and a couple of beautifully hand carved belts made for me years ago by El Paso Saddlery. These belts are so good that they don't wear out! The women in the family probably wish some of them would. For example, I have a Garrison width single ply brown belt made for me by Milt Sparks. I've been wearing this brown belt for more than twenty years. It looks like that, I suppose, but it is as reliable as the day I first wore it and wonderfully comfortable. That is what you want in a belt to hold your pants up.

POCKET CARRY

Chapter Twelve

As alluded to at various times in this book, to legally carry a concealed weapon, the weapon must be actually concealed. Yet, how does one do this – day-in and day-out – when one considers everything from frigid winters to steamy hot summers that impose inescapable clothing demands? For a great many of us, the answer is the pocket holster.

To the best of my knowledge, my paternal grandfather – a serious shooter, occasional hunter and fisherman and a gunny guy – only owned one handgun. It was a nickel plated .32 S&W revolver. I doubt he ever had a holster for it. The very size of the little Hopkins & Allen revolver and its folding hammer spur would have made it just perfect to drop into the side pocket of his suit jacket or, in colder weather, the pocket of his overcoat.

Art tends to imitate life. If you're watching films shot in the 1930s, the plain clothes cops and private detectives carried their handguns in the side pocket of a suit coat or the back pocket of their pants. Movie people probably got the idea from real cops and real detectives. But a great many of us wear a sport coat or suit only on rare occasions. And no longer are men's suit jackets wide-lapeled or double breasted; no longer are men's trousers extraordinarily wide in the leg. And in those days, wool was just about the only suit fabric used.

With no jacket at all, more form-fitting clothing and lighter-weight fabrics, just dropping a gun in your pocket doesn't work for serious concealment. Remember the late Mae West's famous question to Cary Grant? "Is that a gun in your pocket, or are you just glad to see me?" As with many of the inimitable Miss West's quotes, this one incorporates a great deal of wisdom – once you get past the obvious sexual innuendo. A gun carried loose in a front/side

The North American Arms Guardian .380, the .32, a 1 5/8-inch .22 Magnum Mini-Revolver and a Mini-Revolver in .22 Long Rifle with one and 1 1/8-inch barrel. NAA is known for ultra-concealable handguns of the highest quality, which look good as well.

pocket will bottom out because of weight, which will frequently get the muzzle poking forward. Whether the bulge reminds an observer of a particular portion of the anatomy or not, it'll be recognized as what it is: a gun.

In order for front/side pocket carry to work as one of the most efficient and convenient carry methods, one vital ingredient is needed. That is a well-designed pocket holster. By well-designed, I mean that the holster must not only help to disguise the shape of the gun when the pocket material draws tightly over it, but must also hold the gun in proper position for the draw and – extremely important – yield the gun when the draw is made. For about fifteen years, I carried my trusty Seecamp .32 in a leather pocket holster, a Pocket Natural. That same holster carries that Seecamp still today, and more efficiently than ever. And I'm not talking about another holster of the exact same type. I'm talking about the same holster. My Seecamp went in and out of that holster so often, the slickness of the draw was unmatched. A little lift from the middle finger against the pistol's grip front strap and the Seecamp all

The Covert Carrier replacement grip is identical to the grips that are original on the Seecamp, except for the clip which allows the Covert Carrier, like a Hip-Grip, to keep the pistol from sliding down from the waistband. This is a terrific accessory for bare bones concealment of one of the finest hideout handguns ever made.

but sprang into my hand. These days, I alternate between that same Seecamp in the Pocket Natural holster and a North American Arms Guardian .380 with Crimson Trace LaserGrips, this carried in a Grandfather Oak Kydex pocket holster. This holster works really well, too.

In my same pocket with the holstered gun, I usually carry my money clip. That further helps to break up any outline of the gun. Now, you may be thinking, "Doesn't that make a bulge?" A little bit, sure, but the bulge doesn't look like a gun. That's the important thing. As I've often pointed out to people who were worried that a pocket holster would "print" and reveal the armed condition, men carry "stuff" in their pockets. We're talking about concealing a weapon, not doing a disappearing trick in a magic show.

Years ago, a man told me that his father, who worked construction, carried a Beretta 92F in his front pocket every day (talk about literally having deep pockets!). Nevertheless, the usual upper limit for front/side pocket carry is a five-shot or six-shot revolver with a nominal two-inch barrel or an automatic the size of a Glock 26 or Glock 27. Not only is size important but so is weight. If a handgun weighs too much in the pocket, it will cause the trousers or shorts to sag on the side with the gun. For some men, it would prove necessary to constantly tug up their pants or to wear suspenders.

Another virtue of the front/side pocket carry is access to the handgun. It is a normal thing for a man to casually thrust one or both hands into his pockets. Unless one is particularly paranoid for good reason – like the brave men and women of the United States Secret Service when they are working a crowd with a presidential candidate – you won't think the person with his hand in a front/side pocket is necessarily reaching for anything. If you are carrying a handgun in a front/side pocket, you can have your gun hand right beside the pistol. If things start looking promising – in a bad way – you can grip the pistol. If things look ready to deteriorate almost instantly, you can have the gun partially or completely free of the holster, but still hidden in the pocket. If the proverbial pizza hits the fan or the balloon goes up (or whatever expression you prefer), just clear the pocket and do what you have to do. More likely, nothing will happen and you can slip the gun back into the holster and, after a little bit, take your hand out of your pocket. With no other concealed carry – none – can you be that ready without revealing that you are armed. Another reason why it's likely that nothing will go down is that your body language will convey alertness and preparedness. Most criminals are not suicidal. If you somehow subconsciously convey the fact that you are armed and ready, the potential mugger or tough guy looking for a fight will take his intentions somewhere else. If he doesn't, you're ready.

> ## *Lasers stretch the effective reach of smaller pistols.*

Remember, though, we're talking about ordinary criminal situations. If, instead, we have a terrorist in play, or a wannabe killer looking for suicide by cop, it's a different story altogether. These people really don't care if they get killed, just as long as they can kill plenty of other people in the process. Such people may also be wearing body armor. Given the choice, leave such people to professional law enforcement who have the training and the equipment. If you have no choice but to engage in order to defend your life or the life of an innocent and all you have is the handgun in your front/side pocket, you've got bigger problems than you might imagine. The only possible remedy I can suggest – and, it's a long shot – is giving yourself the capability of making just that – a long(er) shot.

Now that pistols small enough to be carried in one's front/side pocket can be fitted with lasers, their effective reach is stretched. Typically, smaller handguns have smaller sights. Some have no sights. With Crimson Trace Laser-Grips on the North American Arms Guardian .380 – they are sighted for fifty feet by Crimson Trace and easily adjustable – I can reliably reach out with an accurate shot to a greater distance than I can with the iron sights.

I wish I had some additional advice that would help, but I don't. Be armed with your front/side pocket handgun wherever legally possible and keep your cellular telephone handy. Be observant.

> **Remember that a reverse draw heightens the potential for shooting yourself.**

Guns can be carried in almost any pocket, of course, but perhaps the most common carry beside holstering in your front/side pocket is the back/hip pocket. I am not, by the way, talking about wallet holsters of the shoot-through variety. When combined with the gun for which they are made, these are considered an "any other weapon" by ATFE. It doesn't cost a fortune to get a federal license for a shoot-through, but I fail to see why anyone would want to. North American Arms had an excellent shoot-through wallet holster designed for them a number of years ago. We had our holster business then and were commissioned to manufacture these for North American Arms. Not long afterward, what was then known as the BATF made an "any other weapon" ruling concerning the NAA wallet holster and they could no longer be sold domestically. This wallet holster actually worked and worked well. That was because the holster was made for a revolver and there were cut-outs for the cylinder so there would be free rotation.

With a semi-automatic pistol, that's a totally different story. Typically, a shoot-through wallet holster can be relied upon to handle one shot from a semi-auto. After that, it's a gamble. The reason is that the sides of the holster – the wallet part – are close to the slide flats. All the holster has to do is retard slide movement ever so slightly and the chance for a jam seriously increases. Add to that the potential for ejection to be interfered with and it's as if you wanted the gun to malfunction. Except for those that were made to work with the NAA guns or any shoot-through made to work with a derringer, legality aside, using a shoot-through is asking for trouble.

The type of back/hip pocket carry to which I refer has nothing to do with a shoot-through wallet. It's merely a hip pocket holster. These are typically flat on one side, a molded holster on the other side. The idea is that the flat side will profile like a wallet in the wearer's hip pocket, while the molded holster will hold the gun. To get to the gun, since the flat part of the holster is worn away from the body, and it would be rather difficult to wedge one's finger between the flat wallet side and the butt of the pistol – and these only work with automatics, derringers or mini-revolvers – turn the hand palm outward

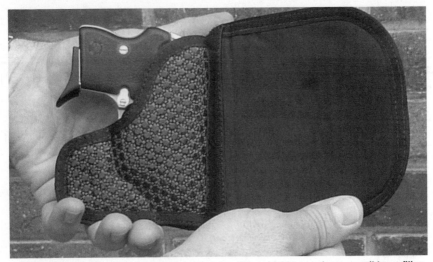

The DeSantis Superfly is a front pocket holster with a shield to mask any possible profiling through the clothes. The pistol is a Guardian .32 from NAA.

and slide the hand between your butt and the butt of the gun. This is a reverse draw. It may be remembered that a reverse draw heightens the potential for shooting yourself as you start to present the gun, since it is very likely the muzzle will cross your body plane unless you are extremely careful. Add to the potential for plugging yourself that you'll be sitting on the gun part of the time and the advantages to back/hip pocket carry over front/side pocket carry keep adding up. People like hip pocket holsters and they aren't any more illegal than any other carry position and, if you practice your draw, you'll hopefully do it safely. As for me, I prefer to take a right-handed hip pocket holster and wear it in the inside left breast pocket of a sport coat or the outside right hand pocket of whatever outerwear I might be using.

Front/side pocket carry for women is usually more complicated and the potential more limited. It's discussed in the chapter particularly devoted to women's concealment issues.

If you do carry in your front/side pocket – it works with most jeans, with shorts, etc. – you have to have something beside elastic at the waist. A belt is best, but a drawstring as found on some athletic wear will do unless the handgun is too heavy for it. Front/side pocket carry affords you the opportunity to be armed almost regardless of what you're wearing without having to let the handgun dictate how you dress. If you are new to concealed weapons carry, you'll soon learn just how important that versatility can be. Front/side pocket carry is the most liberating concealed carry option. After a while, you forget the gun is even there.

WOMEN AND CONCEALMENT

Chapter Thirteen

More and more women are buying guns and carrying them as concealed weapons. This is something to cheer about! For centuries, women suffered oppression because of upper body strength inferiority. Granting various degrees of difficulty, most men could physically subdue most women most of the time. Many women in many cultures – from Renaissance Europe to the glory days of the samurai in Japan – were taught and mastered the use of arms. But using a pike or a katana in "man on man" combat was not all skill, considerable strength still being required at times. When it comes to upper body strength, a woman was and is, typically, at a disadvantage.

The advent of conveniently sized, reliable firearms radically altered that equation, however. One of the finest "marksmen" who ever lived was a woman whom Sitting Bull called "Little Sure Shot" when they both worked as performers with Buffalo Bill Cody. Annie Oakley was among the best of the best and her sex did have something to do with it. Women generally have better hand-eye co-ordination and fine motor skills. Women tend to fight recoil less, moving with it, thus handling it better. In short, the typical woman has a congenital advantage over the typical man when it comes to shooting skills.

All that said, a woman's firearms needs may be somewhat different from those of a man. Regardless of gender, we all want a weapon that stops an attacker as quickly as possible, once it is deployed. And we all want a weapon that we can handle confidently. Therein lies the rub. We're back to strength, but not the upper body kind. Rather, we're dealing with hand strength. Lots of women, regardless of size can handle racking the slide of a .45 automatic with the best of them. Yet lots of women, regardless of size, cannot handle racking the slide of a 9mm Parabellum, let alone a .45.

The Glock 22 with Crimson Trace LaserGrips.

Arming a person with a firearm which that person cannot manipulate with confidence, reliable competence and smooth rapidity is a terrible mistake. As more and more women become proficient with firearms and at least participate in acquiring their own weapons, this problem will be less and less prevalent. As this is written, it is still widespread, however. Giving your wife or daughter or girlfriend a pistol she cannot reliably rack will intimidate her, not an attacker. The late Bill Jordan, lawman and gunman par excellence, is credited as originating the line, "A hit with a .22 is better than a miss with a .44 Magnum." Obviously, that's correct. But, extrapolating on that concept, we should note that carrying a .22 which can be reliably operated is better than packing a .45 automatic the slide of which is impossible to rack half the time.

For novice female shooters especially, but also for women generally, I recommend a two-inch barrel .38 Special revolver, and for several compelling reasons. Most women carry their concealed handgun inside a purse, along with everything else women habitually carry. I know that's not the best way to carry a handgun, but it beats not carrying at all. We'll return to the purse

A Fobus paddle holster with the Walther PP.

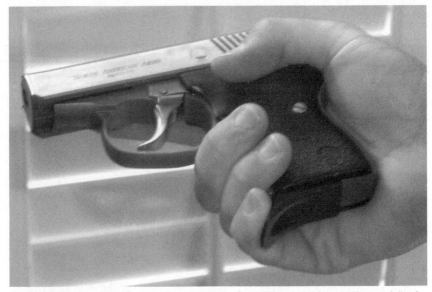

North American Arms Guardians aren't usually hand-filling, but this one allows a full grip for a small hand.

issue, but something rarely mentioned is the safety concern when a woman puts her purse down. When Sharon and I go to our son and daughter-in-law's house, for example, since they have four children ranging widely in age, Sharon takes her gun out of her purse and leaves it in the car. The reason is that she'll be putting her purse down when she gets inside their house. The kids are very good and we're certain the younger ones would never go exploring in Sharon's purse, but why take any sort of chance at all? We don't. When we visit our daughter and son-in-law and their little girl, Sharon can place her purse well out of reach or she just leaves it in the car. I'm always armed, anyway.

The safety issue with a revolver is this. If there is no place to leave the gun or the purse holding it and there is no place that the purse with the gun in it can be put that is impossible for a child to reach, you can easily remove the gun from the purse, take the cartridges out of the cylinder and put the empty revolver, cylinder rolled out, somewhere in view, yet out of the way. If a child or other unauthorized person reaches for it, you can see what's happening and see that the gun is empty. If you're inclined toward being even more careful, unload the gun as before, keeping the cartridges separate from it, and put an ordinary combination lock – the kind you may have used on your locker in high school – around the frame top strap. The most curious kid or unauthorized adult in the world isn't going to get the lock off the gun – unless the person in question is a talented "box man" – and the cylinder won't close with the lock in place. Problem solved. Cops would use a bracelet from their handcuffs to achieve the same effect with a revolver.

The revolver is easier to load and unload, unmistakably looks like a handgun as opposed to a chemical spray or some other device and hand strength is not an issue in readying the gun to fire.

By now, some readers may be wildly upset. "Just a puny .38 Special!" Wouldn't it be fun to see how many of those upset readers would volunteer to be shot with one?

The tip-up barrel Beretta autos and Taurus autos are also easy to load and unload. Take the gun from your purse, remove the magazine and activate the barrel lever, tipping up the barrel. Pluck out the chambered round. That's it. Sadly, what I feel was the best .25 auto to be had – if you don't mind a .25 ACP, that is – has vanished from the scene. That's the single action Beretta Model 950BS. These days, of course, most people want something more than a .25 auto. Lots of women are given .25s by well-meaning men, men who would feel grossly under-gunned with only a .25 to protect themselves. Why give one to a woman, then? Go figure!

The ultimate reason why most women who carry a concealed weapon carry the gun in a purse is that women's clothing generally does not lend itself to hiding guns. Some will argue that a woman can wear a blazer to cover up a belt holster or shoulder holster. Okay. Maybe. But not every day, right? A woman can carry a gun in an ankle holster. All right. If a woman always wears the exact same kind of clothing – which most women don't want to do – that in itself is suspicious, hence draws attention to her and may get some people looking to spot her handgun.

Certain things don't work for women with certain carries. Let's go back to the idea of a woman carrying a gun in a diagonal shoulder holster under a blazer. A woman's shoulder span is narrower than that of a man. The holstered gun doesn't interact with a woman's torso as it would with a man's. A man's greater shoulder span – even if he is overweight and has a serious potbelly – is going to be wider side to side than his torso. Because of this, the shoulder holster handgun will hang either straight down or actually angle the butt in toward the body. Because a woman's shoulders don't have a greater side to side length than any other part of her body, the upper portion of the torso may actually push outwardly against the gun and holster combination. This not only leads to poor concealment, but can also cause discomfort. The butt of the gun can hit against her waist or even her pelvis and the rear of the slide may well rub against her breast. Depending on how amply endowed she may be, the gun and holster combination may actually press against her breast.

Even with this wonderful, all-concealing blazer, the fabric is likely not as heavy as would be used in a similar male garment, so there is greater chance the shoulder holster's harness will profile under that blazer. The harness straps will be a second or third set of straps – depending on her taste in underwear – with which her body must contend.

How about the belt holster? Hip-hugging jeans would make the gun and holster combination stick way out, impossible to conceal. If whatever she wears has its waist at her waist, then we have other concerns. If she goes to a high ride holster, she'll have a tough time drawing the gun in a hurry unless she's a contortionist. Depending on how high-waisted a woman is and the overall length of her chosen firearm, she might have to get her elbow up as high as her shoulder in order for the muzzle of her weapon to clear the holster. If she opts for a holster that will provide an easier draw, the holster will ride lower, which means it must be specially designed to let the gun butt stay slightly away from her waist so the muzzle of the gun will not flare outward with her hips, this pushing the butt of the gun toward her waist. The result can be poor concealment and possible physical discomfort.

Okay! We put the lady in an ankle holster! Well, the trouble is that women tend to have smaller bones than men and even that snubby .38 Special revolver may be way too big for her smaller ankle with its reduced circumference.

Bra holster? What man would think it practical to have to partially disrobe in order to get to his gun?

Thigh holster? Nothing bigger than a snubby or medium frame auto will usually work, such a holster only works under a skirt or dress and, after discussing this subject with a number of female concealed weapons carriers, what I had suspected would be the case seems to prove out. Namely, some women handle a thigh holster without any discomfort. For others, such a holster feels grossly uncomfortable and invasive.

Although things are changing, typically a woman – unless packing a gun is job related – will be worse than a guy when it comes to finding an excuse to leave the gun at home or in the glove compartment or the trunk. Even the lightest firearm is heavier than most women like when carrying it. Men tend to look for disasters to occur, critical needs having to be met and dire consequences. At least I do. Unless a woman lives in a high crime rate area or is just naturally paranoid – a good way to be – when she realizes she has to run out to the store for a dozen eggs or some baby formula or some milk or a six pack, she'll probably figure all she needs is her wallet and keys. Maybe her cellular telephone. The gun won't come into the store with her and might not even leave the house.

Since a great many women will find any excuse possible not to take a gun along, in the final analysis, carrying a handgun in a handbag is the best com-

Photos courtesy of Galco International.

In the final analysis, most fashion conscious women will usually stick with purse carry for a personal protection handgun. This holster handbag is from what is an ultimate source for style and quality in women's holstering, Galco International.

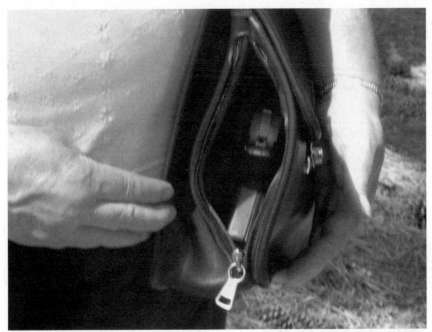

A pistol concealed in this Galco shoulder bag, the gun securely holstered in the center compartment until needed.

promise under the circumstances. Sure, the draw can be slow, unless the purse is designed for gun carrying; but, it's better than no draw at all. Yes, if the purse gets snatched, the bad guy has just snatched the gun, too. There's nothing that can be done to counter that except to carry a purse hugged to the body suspended from the shoulder and make yourself ready to draw the moment a potential threat is identified. There were some special holster handbags that featured a small strap that went around the butt of the weapon, the other end around the wearer's wrist. If somebody grabbed the purse, the very action of tearing the purse away freed the gun.

It is well to remember that if someone steals your purse and you still have your gun, firing at him is everything from reckless endangerment to attempted manslaughter, not to mention the civil actions that can come at you depending upon where your bullet or bullets go.

Holster purses – purses specifically designed to carry a handgun – can be terrific looking purses. Several decades ago, when holster purses were first coming into the market, some of them looked like carelessly crafted saddle bags, the interiors roughly finished, the sort of thing a woman who had any kind of fashion sense would run away from. Today, of course, there are a great many fine holster purses on the market, as beautifully crafted as any woman

This Blackhawk! Products shoulder bag – like a musette bag – can double as a spot to carry a handgun, the weapon here a full-size .45.

could want. A name that instantly comes to mind for this type of holstering is Galco.

Galco holster purses are as beautifully crafted and finely finished outside and inside as any super high end purse one could find in the most fashionable shops. Galco offers a wide selection of styles, too. Sharon, like most women, has definite likes and dislikes in purses and she likes the offerings from Galco.

Typically, these days, a holster purse may consist of two separate pouches sewn together. A cavity is left between them. One end of the cavity is usually sewn shut, while the other end is closed with hook and loop fasteners. There is a holster with hook material on its outside which attaches to loop material

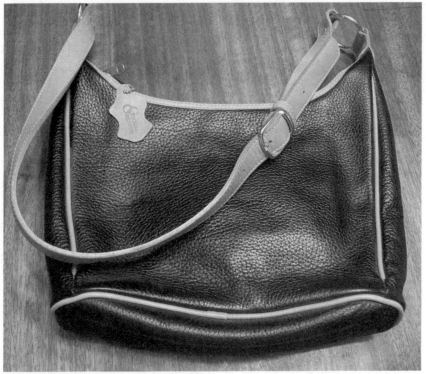

This holster bag is from Gould & Goodrich.

lining part of the purse's cavity. This allows different holster sizes or different positioning. When trouble looms, you merely tear open the end that closes with hook and loop and draw the handgun. There are other arrangements, of course. For example, there may not be a holster within the cavity. Some purses open as normally, but have a hidden compartment inside, or a holster that can fasten with hook and loop.

The nice thing with modern holster purses from the top manufacturers is that they function well not only as holsters, but as purses.

Sometimes, however, the best carry for a woman may be what is often the best carry for a man. I'm referencing front pocket carry, which was covered in greater detail in a previous chapter. Suffice it to say at this juncture that a woman may have to be a bit more pro-active for pocket carry to work, since women, having smaller hands, frequently have shallower or narrower pockets in their clothing than men have in their clothing. And, if the pocket is of the sack type, the fabric itself may be too flimsy. If size or flimsiness of the pocket is a concern, a woman who's handy at hand sewing, using a sewing machine or finding someone who is can replace the original sack that formed

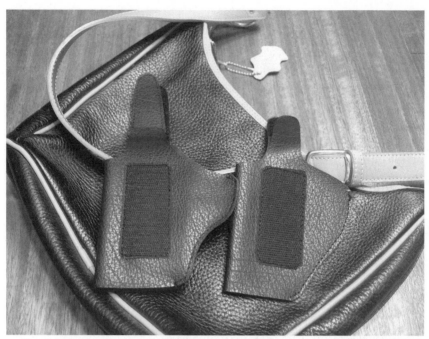

Two holsters for the Gould & Goodrich bag, the holsters able to be secured within the purse using hook and loop fastener, holding the handgun securely until needed. Most holster purses feature a center compartment, between the two halves of the purse. This compartment closes with hook and loop fastener strips. While the purse is slung from the shoulder, the compartment is pulled open and the wearer reaches into the compartment and draws the gun. Some holster purses actually have a band which can be slipped around the purse side wrist so, in the event the purse is "snatched," the gun will pull out and be attached to the wearer.

the pocket lining with something larger and more sturdy, so long as entry to the pocket will be adequate for the gun and the hand.

With pocket carry, a woman must be even more careful than her male counterpart concerning gun selection, since size and weight will factor in more so for her than for an individual who is larger. Also, unlike male clothing, many more women's clothing items have elastic waistbands. Without the help of a belt or, at the very least, draw strings in addition to the elastic, any gun heavier than the smallest North American Arms mini-revolver will draw the garment down. This will betray the fact that there is something heavier than a handkerchief or a lipstick in that pocket and could make the wearer constantly have to tug the garment upward.

Pocket carry for a woman will only work, of course, if whatever she's wearing has front/side pockets. Many women's garments don't include any pockets at all. And, only a loose fitting skirt or loose fitting slacks would allow pocket carry; otherwise, the garment will outline the gun for everyone to see.

If you are a woman who must carry concealed in a particular way, at least while on the job, but you have some latitude in equipment, here are a few suggestions. If you must wear a concealable belt holster, make certain it is actually designed for a woman's use. Normally speaking, a man's concealable belt holster will not work for a woman who must conceal a weapon. For a woman, the means of a belt attachment – whether a loop, slots or a combination thereof – must be offset to provide for an inwardly curving waist and outwardly curving hips. The only other belt holster option is to use a holster that rides extremely high. This makes the draw horribly awkward. Some women avoid both situations by wearing a gun in the small of the back. This can be uncomfortable and may lead to kidney or spinal complications, especially if you take a fall or bump into something hard. And, of course, this kind of carry doesn't really conceal too well.

> ### *Normally speaking, a man's concealable belt holster will not work for a woman who must conceal a weapon.*

If you have a relatively flat abdomen, however, you'll find that an appendix forward or "felony carry" can work quite well for a woman under a loose top. A crossdraw carry can work this way, too.

As most readers know, Sharon and I have written a significant number of novels. In one limited series of books, sold as *The Defender,* the main female character is a police officer – or, at least, starts out that way before getting involved with a group of patriots fighting a government gone bad. She carried a J-Frame Smith & Wesson .38 Special in a Ken Null City Slicker shoulder holster. It's an upside-down rig, the holster a translucent white plastic and the shoulder harness and crossover piece very white synthetic and very narrow. We had her wear the rig under a loose pullover of some sort and, in the books, she shortened the length of the adjustable crossover strap so it wouldn't have to attach at her waist, but instead crossed in front of her offside shoulder and secured to the band of her bra. The business of attaching the crossover strap to the bra might be problematic for a lot of women, but then just attach it to the waistband of your pants or skirt. There's an alligator clip, like those found on suspenders, so a belt is unnecessary. This is about as lightweight and inconspicuous as a shoulder holster can get, except for Null's skeletonized SMZ holster which is not a full coverage holster. It, too, works extremely well. Null, by the way, makes some of the finest horsehide holsters around, too.

In the final analysis, most female gun carriers will use a purse of some sort. If the purse is not one designed for gun carrying – a holster purse – there can be a serious concealment concern. When a woman opens her purse to dig through it and find something, especially with larger guns, the gun may be noticed by a store clerk or a companion or someone standing nearby. And, from a practical access standpoint, with a smaller gun, it may, at times, be a chore to actually find the gun with any degree of efficiency.

Women will, often times, do the classic "gun moll" bit. A gun moll was a gangster's girl friend who would keep his "gat" in her purse so that, if the cops rousted him, they couldn't get him for packing heat. Decades ago, when Sharon and I would be in a part of the country where carrying a handgun was illegal, but common sense dictated otherwise, Sharon would keep my gun in her purse. Women are less likely to be suspect – or, at least, were and sometimes still are – and searching a woman was a little dicey for a male cop. If the woman carries her own gun and then adds her husband's or boyfriend's gun, we start getting into some serious weight issues for the purse and the woman carrying it.

Some of the best concealed weapons for women are not necessarily handguns. Non-firearm weapons are covered at great length in another chapter, of course, but it's well to remember that a woman's special self-protection needs can often be well-served with a knife.

I can think of no more ideal non-gun concealed weapon for a woman than a push knife. If a guy assaults you because he wants to get up close and really personal, a small push knife carried somewhere in the clothes – maybe in the pocket of a coat or sweater or inside an outside pouch on a purse – can really ruin somebody's plans for the evening. Sharon used to carry a single edged push knife in her purse, and still does, on occasion.

The important thing is to be armed, no matter what, and whatever physical inconvenience might result be damned. Just don't become a statistic in a crime report.

Stock Photo

OFF–BODY AND OPEN CARRY

Chapter Fourteen

When off-body concealment comes into the picture, the possibilities for weapon size and volume increase dramatically. If you happen to be one of the few people in the world who has never seen the James Bond film *From Russia, With Love,* Bond is issued an original Armalite AR-7 dismountable rifle (as this is written, an improved version is available from Henry Repeating Arms). He carries the rifle in his flat attaché case. One of the flattest attaché-style cases to be had was the Samsonite Slim-Line. I still have an old one around the house and carried these cases for years. On a few occasions, I actually concealed one of these rifles in one of these cases. Does that mean I wanted to play superspy? Not really. I've also carried a six-inch barreled Model 629 S&W revolver in a long, thin brown bag, muzzle up. Does that mean I wanted to look like a wino? No, but a friend in law enforcement, when I mentioned this off-body technique, recounted that one of the guys on stake-out duty with him had used that same technique while watching the alley exit their subject might use.

When our kids were little and disposable diapers were a new novelty, Sharon and I would carry a gun in the bottom of a diaper bag. Nobody in his or her right mind is going to go searching the inside of a bag containing wet and/or "poopy" diapers. Sharon and I would, routinely, carry guns in and out of the house inside the old brown paper grocery bags, along with the groceries.

Hollowed out books – which can be great for storing guns and other items, such as jewelry, in the home – can be carried under one's arm or in one's hand. Books look innocuous, even if you know there's a gun inside the book. Usually, something no larger than a two-inch J-frame, a Walther PP or one of the small Glocks will work in this application. With the diaper bag, wine bag or grocery bag, virtually any size handgun short of the old Remington XP-100

Here's the muzzle of the single action .45, held in the fist.

or the Century Arms Draco AK-47 pistol will work. And with a big enough diaper bag or old-fashioned grocery bag, the sky's the limit!

Years ago, we had the opportunity of examining one of the special MAC attaché cases. I believe the subgun inside it was a MAC-11, not a MAC-10 – but, that was about a quarter century ago, as this is written. For the purposes of this chapter, we're not concerned with disguised weapons which can be fired while in "stealth mode," but, rather, with hiding conventional weapons off-body.

Women have it much tougher than men in a lot of ways, and concealing weapons on body is one of those ways. However, women can carry the most outlandishly sized purses and no one gives it a second thought. Sharon was doing some journalistic work once with the rather short-lived Illinois Bureau of Investigation. One of the female agents had a Model 19 2-1/2-incher in her purse, along with a couple of other guns, spare ammo and cuffs and all the regular things women carry in purses, like hair brushes and lipsticks.

The key to successful off-body concealment is subtlety. By way of illustration, consider the following. People are conditioned to see things in certain ways, and that includes guns. If you carry all the time, unless somewhere legally prohibited, you may, from time to time, find yourself carrying a pistol or revolver openly in the hand for a short distance. People expect to see a handgun carried with the muzzle of the weapon pointed away from the person who is holding it. What I do is simple. Let's say the firearm is a full-sized 1911. Rather than holding it in the conventional way, I'll turn the gun muzzle rearward and butt downward. So, my four fingers will curl around the pistol's grip backstrap – with a 1911, the mainspring housing and grip safety – my

With the gun in the bag, muzzle up, it looks like a bottle of wine. If the gun is needed, rip the bag away. A right handed man might be best holding the "wine bottle" in the left hand. This is an extreme hide technique used on stakeouts and what have you. The moral is that looks are oft times deceiving, as the phrase goes, and what you see may not be what you think you see.

little finger closest to the concave radius of the grip safety, the fleshy part of the hand, just behind the thumb, brushing against the underside of the trigger guard. The slide and dust cover are pressed against the interior of my forearm. Just look nonchalant and you'll likely get away with it.

If subtlety is the key to successful off-body carry, imagination allows you to use that key.

Consider common objects – other than a woman's purse – that people carry with them. A newspaper folded in half will handily carry almost any handgun. Large format magazines aren't really around that much anymore, but a standard sized magazine – of the same size as *Gun World* magazine, for example – will hide a typical, modestly sized handgun. As with the newspaper, fold the magazine in half, with the gun in the center and your hand clutched

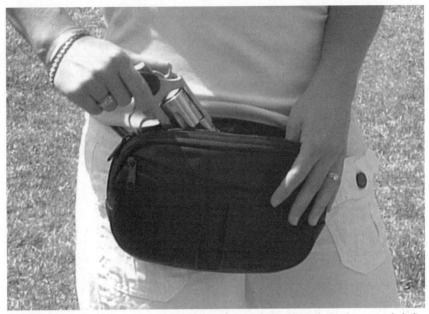

This beautifully made leather Bianchi fanny pack is designed to slip on the wearer's belt. The gun is an old style Smith & Wesson Model 640 all steel .38 Special.

below the fold. The gun is best carried upside down, with the frame topstrap or the slide topstrap against the fold and the grip rearward. The right handed person can hand-carry a gun in such a fashion in the left hand. For getting the gun into action quickly, just invert the left hand and grip the pistol as normally in the right hand. Easy. If the gun fails or you run out of ammo, the magazine or newspaper, when rolled up, makes an excellent thrusting weapon against soft targets, such as the solar plexus, the Adam's Apple or the face.

Probably the most well-known open carry, although not strictly off-body, is the ubiquitous fanny pack. Giving credit where credit is due, the fanny pack holster was pioneered by Gene DeSantis and copied by everyone else; that said, many of the copies have included some outstanding innovations and are of very fine quality. Today, most major manufacturers offer fanny pack holsters in nylon and/or in leather, in a wide range of colors and styles, from inexpensive to those made from the finest leathers. The problem with a fanny pack, of course, is that almost anybody who's into guns knows about fanny pack holsters and assumes, when seeing anyone wearing a fanny pack, there's a handgun in it. The fanny pack as a sign of being armed is only surpassed by the photographer's vest worn in extremely warm weather.

Sword canes and sword umbrellas – even the collapsible kind – allow one to go about one's business carrying a weapon essentially openly and ready to

This Galco fanny pack holster is comfortable and smooth into action.

hand. The blades concealed within these objects would be generally classifiable as rapiers, although most times shorter in length. A properly made version of a sword cane or sword umbrella will afford the user a handy device for parrying an opponent's blade, etc., that device being the very scabbard from which the blade was drawn: the scabbard is rigid and can actually be used as an impact or thrusting weapon before the blade is drawn or used in conjunction with the blade. Two weapons in one!

Off body carry of a handgun can be as simple as slipping a pistol or revolver into a large pocket of a raincoat or heavy winter jacket, the outerwear folded over your arm. Years back, I carried a revolver and fifty rounds of ammunition in the bottom of my briefcase. The revolver was in a holster that I could don or doff quite quickly. Off body carry solutions can be quite obvious. Who, reading this, hasn't stashed a handgun in the glove compartment of an automobile a time or two or three?

Of course, there are weapons and then there are weapons. The growing trend of constructing high quality writing instruments to be strong enough to serve such purposes as shattering automotive glass to save a life or be used as a yarawa stick to fend off an attack is a fine example of open and obvious carry. When Georgia is not locked in the relentless heat of the long summer that almost everyone else likes and I can't stand, I've been wearing one of the Woolrich Elite Series Tactical Algerian Field Jackets. Among the many pockets tailored into these coats is a left sleeve pocket for a writing instrument.

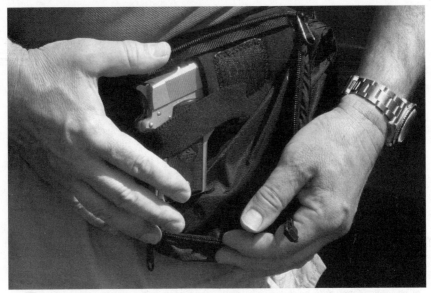

The Galco fanny pack's dual zippers make accessing the handgun – a CombatMaster .45 in this case – easy.

Although there are other makers of such pens, I use Surefire and Benchmade models and one or the other of these goes in that sleeve pocket.

I also have tactical shirts from both Blackhawk Products and Woolrich Elite Series Tactical. These all feature a sleeve pocket for a pen. I would not care to wear one of these pens, openly or otherwise, when visiting an airport, a Federal building, or any restricted access facility, but a regular pen with a metal body will work in a sleeve pocket just as well and can serve as a writing instrument or aid in other situations.

The same can be said of many smaller tactical lights or smaller versions of police flashlights. Almost invariably, these are constructed from aircraft or similar quality aluminum. They serve the purpose of illumination and can be used in self defense. Many times, these lights are worn openly on a belt "holster" or with a pocket clip. The actual tactical lights with the higher lumen ratings, of course, can be used to temporarily interfere with an attacker's night vision just by aiming the light at your opponent's eyes.

A great many fine lockblade folding knives can be worn similarly holstered or pouched in full view on one's belt or in a pocket or trouser/skirt waistband by means of a pocket clip. In fact, a tactical folder of slim proportions can be an ideal on-body hidden weapon for man or woman when worn inside the waistband, a belt covering much of the pocket clip or a shirt/top bloused slightly over it.

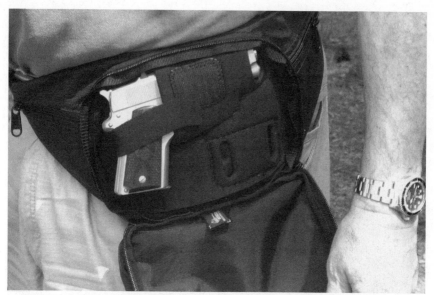

With the shell fully zipped open, the holstered pistol can be seen. The holster is sewn in place over a semi-rigid backing, a hook and loop strap securing the gun in the stretchable holster.

There is a true story my parents told me, one which arose from the early days of the Great Depression. There was a chain of banks in the Chicago area, and certain members of the family who owned these banks saw the writing on the wall for the economy and absconded to South America or somewhere with the bulk of the banking chain's assets. My mother had just deposited her most recent paycheck the day before these banks began to collapse. At any event, there was, at that time, no law in the City of Chicago which actually prohibited carrying a firearm openly. One of the hapless depositors with this chain of banks happened to be a well-known Irish gangster of the day.

Depositors were lining up at these banks, trying to withdraw their hard-earned money. The gangster walked into the bank with his handgun in one fist and his deposit book in the other. Politely, we assume, he excused himself to the head of the line. He handed the harried bank teller the deposit book, saying, "I want to close out my account," or words to that effect. A lot of the other people were screwed in whole or in part, but the openly armed Irish hood got every dime the crooked bankers owed him. Sometimes, it's good not to hide your intentions, or your weapon!

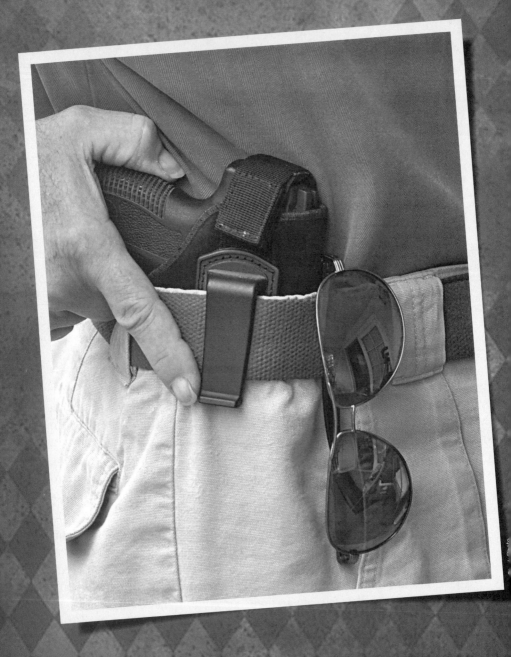

CLOSE CONCEALMENT

Chapter Fifteen

Years ago, when I was Associate Editor of *Guns* magazine and *The Shooting Industry* magazine, I got to edit some of the great firearms writers, men like Colonel Charles Askins, Bill Jordan and Major George C. Nonte (who sometimes wrote as "C. George Charles" or "W. Sterling Berdan"). I was always interested in concealed carry. I remember Nonte writing an article dealing with the various stages of concealed carry and the first time I encountered the term "close concealment" was in this excellent piece.

Indeed, as Nonte pointed out, close concealment was quite specialized. It still is. Keep in mind that this article to which I refer was written before the widespread use of metals detectors or any other electronic countermeasures designed to discover concealed weapons. The goal of close concealment then was to avoid detection by mere observation, or even during a light frisk. During the first Gulf War, A.G. Russell produced plastic versions of the World War II era lapel dagger and thumb dagger as used by Allied Agents. These plastic knives were to aid our personnel should they be captured by enemy forces, giving our Heroes a weapon that might go undetected because it couldn't be spotted with a metals detector.

The widespread use of metals detectors in this age of radical Islamic fundamentalist terrorists pretty much shoots down the old close concealment tricks. In the old days, one could hide a .25 automatic under a bandage taped to the ribcage or the leg. Nonte actually showed that. These days, however, that bandaged-over hidden firearm would be detected. I contacted a friend in the business of contraband detection equipment and he told me that Garrett Metals Detectors were the best in the security industry. The Garrett Super-

Scanner is reasonably priced and, if you've entered a secure building, you've probably seen one or been checked out with one. The scanning surface is ten inches long. From nine inches away, it can detect a handgun, a knife from six inches away and box cutters like the September 11th murderers used from three inches.

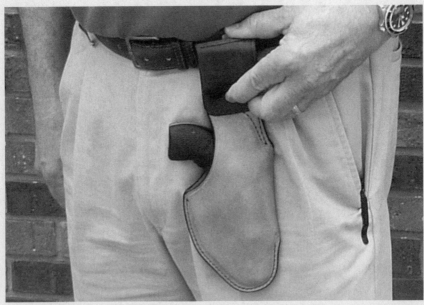

One of the most innovative holster makers on the planet, Ken Null of Resaca, Georgia, makes this crotch holster for guns as large as a two-inch J-Frame. The gun is accessed through the trouser fly. With loose fitting slacks, this carry works and is true deep concealment.

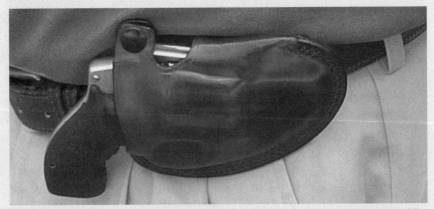

Ken Null's "Vam" is extremely fast. Originally developed for bodyguards to wear while driving a VIP, it gives perfect access when seated, but works quite well when one is moving about. Using a pull-through snap, the Vam is easy to like.

As someone who carries concealed weapons, I have mixed feelings about metal detectors. Yet in the final analysis, they are necessary. There is no way to tell how many hijackings or other terrorist activities have been foiled or abandoned merely because of the presence of a Garrett security metals detector like the SuperScanner. As I say repeatedly in the pages of this book, I am always

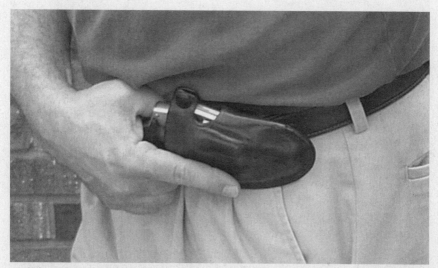

Using a belly roll draw, one moves the gunhand toward the gunbutt as one rolls the gun/ holster combination toward the hand. As fast as a full combat grip is obtained, the belly rolls away, tearing the holster from the gun at the same time as the gun is torn from the holster.

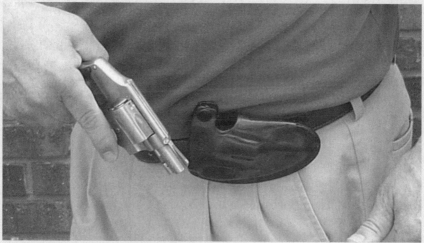

The draw with the K.L. Null Vam holster is completed, the J-Frame Smith & Wesson coming on line. With the Crimson Trace LaserGrips unit on board, the gun can easily be fired with combat accuracy from waist level, if need be.

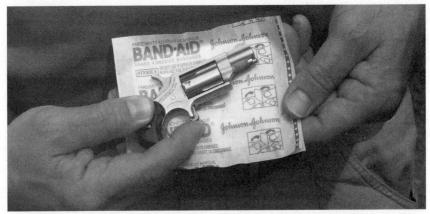

Take the grips off this North American Arms 1 1/8-inch barrel Mini-Revolver and a large bandage can cover the gun for extreme close concealment. Adhesive tape and pads will hide still larger handguns. A bandaged leg, an arm in a sling – all are ways to hide a handgun or other weapon, assuming no electronic countermeasures must be passed through.

armed, except when it is illegal to be armed. Entering a secure building like a courthouse while hiding a handgun or a knife is not only illegal, it's stupid. In the early 1990s, there were rumors of ultra-sensitive weapons detectors which could be used to scan an entire room for firearms or knives. I am assured these do not exist in the real world. There are good reasons why. If such a device were used at a cocktail party, for example, or some other social gathering, every Rolex or Omega chronometer in the place would be triggering the device. The knife used for slicing the room-temperature brie or the metal plate in somebody's head or the steel pin that's helping hold together a clavicle would give the operator of this device constant fits.

The only alternative to having buildings where weapons are not allowed would be for virtually everyone to carry a weapon, so the good guys wouldn't need protecting from the bad guys, but could protect themselves. That will not happen anytime soon. Too many people are content to let someone else protect them rather than be responsible for their own safety. It's the society we live in, and it won't change without some powerful and unanticipated social force coming along to alter that world view.

For day to day close concealment – not the sort of thing where a little Beretta's bandaged behind your bicep – we are probably talking about being in environments where weapons are neither prohibited nor appreciated. You won't want to adhesive tape a pistol to your body every day. I know that I wouldn't. So, for this modern close concealment, we'll need a modern approach.

One item you can consider, if you wear a necktie every day, is the A.G. Russell CIA Letter Opener. This non-metallic knife has been around for decades.

Except for the fact that it's not made out of steel, it's an identical duplicate to the original Sting IA boot knife. Put a little patch of industrial strength self-stick Velcro hook material on the inside of your necktie and a corresponding patch of Velcro loop or fuzz on the handle of the CIA Letter Opener and your practically weightless knife will be well hidden, but there should you need it. Do not go into secure facilities so outfitted. If you even enter an airport with one of these knives – not even trying to get through security, but just entering the building – it's a federal felony.

For one of the most discreet means by which to carry a handgun – there's a chapter devoted to the subject – front pocket carry is very, very hard to beat. With the proper front pocket holster, no one will ever know the gun is there unless or until you need it.

North American Arms at one time offered a neck chain for their excellent little mini revolvers. As this is written, North American Arms will install a tiny lanyard ring on a mini and there is a firm to which they'll refer you for the chain. You could probably get a suitable chain at a local jewelry store, if you wished. The guns are stainless steel and you can get a stainless chain, so that shouldn't be a problem.

There are a wealth of neck knives on the market, made to varying standards of quality, some truly well-crafted. The knife is worn, usually inverted in a friction fit sheath, suspended from a chain. You reach through or under your shirt or top to get to the knife, then jerk it free.

If you habitually wear something around your neck – I wear a cross that Sharon gave me as a present well more than 30 years ago – you'll probably not go for this carry, whether with a gun or a knife.

Belt Sword offers a unique close concealment product. It's an actual sword, but from a thin, flexible steel, so thin it really doesn't require sharpening to be effective, so thin that it conforms to your waist under a special belt. You put on the belt and thread the sword behind it. If you're a guy and wearing a black belt all the time doesn't interfere with your sartorial sense, you've got a sword ready for instant use, something that can be used very much like a katana or ninjato. The Belt Sword is fast into action and extremely effective as a weapon. It's found its way to the waists of lots of undercover narcotics agents and other clandestine types.

If a sword isn't required, but a serious edged weapon that's essentially impossible to spot, short of the use of electronic detection systems, is what's needed, Belt Sword also makes the Razor Dagger. Available in 9-inch and 11-inch lengths, single or double edged, fabricated from 1075 or 1095 spring steel, one-tenth thick, the Razor Dagger is worn so it contours to the wearer's body. An ideal carry spot for this is under one's normal belt. A Velcro holster

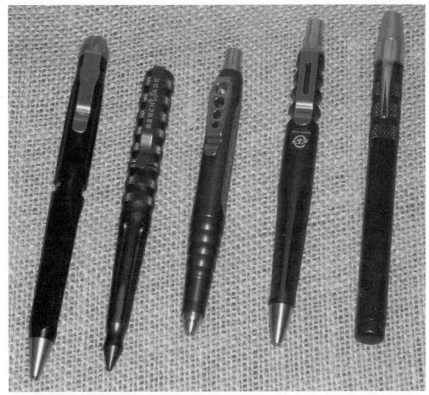

From left, a SureFire tactical pen which incorporates a stainless steel auto glass breaker, a Benchmade tactical pen that pulls apart like a fountain pen, a SureFire tactical pen which features a conventional style button on the top of the pen to release or retract the point of the refill, one of SureFire's newest retractable tactical pens (a truly comfortable writing instrument) and, lastly, what looks like a refillable grease pencil. This is actually a spike that is spring loaded and makes an excellent defensive tool. The actual pens can be used as yarawa sticks and make convenient impact weapons. As a trusted friend pointed out to me, an ordinary pen can be used as an impact weapon. I countered that these from aircraft aluminum and steel are wider bodied and easier to hold onto.

can be rigged for the Razor Dagger – the designer made one for me as Sharon and I were chatting with him at the 2009 Blade Show – and the knife can be drawn very, very quickly. This personal protection knife was created at the request of law enforcement. If a bad guy is doing a frisk, there's a good chance he'll miss it because it's so flat. It can be used to slash or, when turned blade flat down, stabbed under the ribs or into soft targets. Electronic security would catch it every time.

Bowen Knife Company produces a knife that has been around for a very long time. There are several model variations, all of them made from stainless steel, single or double edged. I'm referencing the Bowen Belt Buckle Knife, of course. It's available in sizes to go with narrow belts or Garrison width belts, the belts specially constructed to safely sheath the knife, yet keep it ready for instant action. The knife and the buckle are one piece construction. Years ago, they were even made so the handle or haft portion – the actual visible portion of the knife which serves as the buckle – could be used to open bottle caps. If you work with or hang out with people who aren't into guns and knives, no one will probably notice a Bowen Belt Buckle Knife. And they're extremely well made.

Pat Crawford and Wes Crawford make some wonderful gadgets that can generally be described as "knives," making plenty of normal knives, too. They're a terrifically talented father and son team, so trying to describe the full range of their more subtle creations would be impossible here. I'll hit on three of them. The first is called the "Crawford Credit Card Karambit" and is made from Titanium. The size of a credit card – more dangerous an implement than any knife – it features two finger holes and a slightly hooked edge. There's some knurling on the area where the thumb would rest. Just carry it in your wallet, like a credit card and no one will notice it until you need it.

The Devil Darts – these have been in various sizes over the years – are handmade, triple-edged spikes, terribly strong, made for thrusting. Pat and Wes got the inspiration for these from the sleeve daggers used by the American OSS and British SOE during World War II. There is a multiplicity of places where one of these can be hidden on body. Because of their size, they're a great choice.

Not actually a knife, the Push Pick can be used as a yarawa stick, an icepick or a push knife for stabbing. There's a four-inch long spike, a small portion of that taken up with threads. There's a four-inch long knurled handle, about the thickness of a roll of nickels. You can put the point end inside the handle so that only the threaded end protrudes and use the Push Pick as a striking instrument. Unscrew it and turn it around, re-screw it and you have an ice pick. Unscrew the spike and screw it into the threaded hole in the center of the handle and you can use it as a push knife.

The Push Pick can be dropped in pocket or purse, weighing little, taking up little room and inobvious to the casual observer, should it be noticed at all.

Close concealment isn't what it used to be, as stated earlier. Yet the creativity factor is still there and the wide range of superb clandestine knives, other edged devices and handguns is a real plus.

Remember: there's close concealment and then there's silly. Many years ago, I saw a photograph of an X-ray showing a very small handgun a man had tried smuggling by sticking it up his anus. You wonder if the guy was dumb enough to have the gun loaded; he probably was. Far be it from me to criticize someone for ingenuity, of course, but, as I said, there's close concealment and then there's silly.

CONCEALED STORAGE OF WEAPONS

Chapter Sixteen

A warning before embarking upon this chapter is in order. Some of the ideas concerning weapons storage may not be safe in a house with small children or curious weapons-ignorant adults. If people who can't be trusted to act responsibly around weapons don't normally frequent your home, just be prepared to modify what you do when great aunt Sadie and great uncle Bub come over and your brother's or sister's wild and crazy kids are on the horizon.

In Edgar Allen Poe's famous short story, "The Purloined Letter," his pioneering French detective named Dupin seeks an object of great political value. It is a letter and Dupin is the only one to reason that it may have been left in plain sight. His remarkable powers of observation lead him to the letter and Dupin saves the day – actually, the Queen of France. Now, I'm not suggesting that you leave a handgun in plain sight in a letter rack on the mantle, but there are other places to store handguns besides a locked drawer or such.

I claim no credit for the idea I've seen advanced concerning hiding handguns in cereal boxes in the pantry or cupboard. What burglar messes with breakfast cereal? It's an interesting idea. There are special storage containers from Diversion Safes made to hide valuables, such as fake shaving cream cans for hiding your Rolex, dummy wall outlets for stashing jewelry, and even working wall clocks that have a compartment behind the clock face for storing a handgun. These really work quite well. Atlanta Cutlery also offers these timely hiding places. I've seen automobile batteries that were perfectly realistic looking fakes. These would be large enough to hide more than one handgun or one pistol along with a goodly number of spare magazines.

Inside this specially altered version of a popular book by a former government official is a cutout, the cutout large enough to hide a North American Arms Guardian in .32NAA and some items of jewelry. This book is particularly well made, a number of pages at the front of the book able to be turned freely, thus enhancing this book's use should you wish to be seated somewhere reading with a handgun almost immediately to hand.

Hollowed out books are classic hiding places, but only if the nature of the book is not out of character with other books in your house or office. With a hollowed out book, you are hiding something almost in plain sight. In the James Bond novels, Ian Fleming had his character smuggle his pistol on transatlantic flights inside a hollowed out book, long before the days of modern screening.

The classic hiding place, as mentioned earlier is this book, is a book. Some years ago, there was a firm offering entire encyclopedia sets that were fused into one piece and hollowed out. You could have concealed an AR-15 or a police shotgun in one of these. Ordinary normal size hollow books are, these days at least, made from real books. I've seen hollow books made from pretend books and they don't usually look right. The best hollow books will have a quarter-inch or so of actual pages left in the front. With a typical hardbound book you will be restricted to a handgun the size of a J-frame Smith & Wesson or a Walther PP, PPKS or PPK.

When selecting a book safe or book safes, if possible, try to select titles that would be in character with other hard bound books you might have in your home. For example, if you've got a library chock full of firearms and edged weapons books, rip-roaring adventure novels and sports books, *Everything You Always Wanted to Know About Vegetarian Cooking* might seem out of place to the observant thief. Out of place draws the eye and gets the attention. Don't keep the fake shaving cream can with the fake can of beans next to the fake automobile battery in the bedroom.

If these creative hiding places protect guns and valuables from theft, that's fantastic. I'll stress again that these hiding places may not be secure at all from children and unauthorized adults.

Various sources provide attractive looking furniture pieces which are actually disguised gun safes. I've seen these as coffee tables and end tables. If you have the skills, the tools and the time – and your spouse doesn't object – ordinary furniture can be subtly altered without a great deal of effort to hide your guns, concealed weapons and sporting arms.

Got a cedar chest? Get a piece of cedar board of decent thickness from the local hardware store or lumber yard. Cut it to fit just inside the bottom of the cedar chest, making it a close fit but not so tight that you can't got it in or out without scratching the real chest. Determine how much room you want – four to six inches of depth would probably be about right – and place blocks of corresponding thickness at all four corners and spaced along the edges. Use at least one more block on each short side and at least two more on each long side. Get two pieces sixteenth-inch thick steel from a local metals shop – each piece a foot long – and have three inches bent off at a right angle. Take the long ends and plasticize or tape them so you'll have a good handle surface you can hold onto. Leave just enough gap in the false bottom that you can slide the two steel pieces in at either side. Slide the three-inch sections into the gaps and turn the long pieces just far enough away that you have clearance for your hands. Grip the handles and you can lift out the false bottom. You can use the same approach with other pieces of furniture, as well.

And there's always the toilet. Actually, the flush tank. You can hide valuables – such as handguns – and conserve water as well. Think how good you're being to the environment! The British have been doing this for years, to save on their water bills. They didn't use guns. They'd place a brick in the flush tank, which reduces the volume of water needed to elevate the ball cock to end the flush. You get a waterproof container – really extremely waterproof – with a hermetic seal and put a gun in it, close it securely and put it in the flush tank. I'd try it first with some metal object of little or no actual value, leave it for a couple of weeks and double check yourself on the waterproof qualities of the container. A professional jewel thief in a movie might check the flush tank. Most working bad guys won't.

If you try hiding weapons within your walls, keep in mind that although a thief may not get to them, humidity probably will. I had a great friend who collected Colt Single Actions. He'd kept many of the revolvers hanging on walls inside carpentered gun cabinets in a special gun room. The guns looked perfect. He took one down one day to examine it and noticed the side of the revolver toward the wall was covered in rust. Several of the guns were damaged in that same way.

If a gun safe is your choice, there are many fine examples from which to choose, and they come in sizes ranging from single handgun units to vaults that will hold a good sized collection. Prices for the Sentry safes you can buy at Home Depot are truly reasonable, but you can spend serious dollars for the larger, more high tech models. The higher end safes may provide a good deal of protection from fire, in addition to theft and tampering.

However you hide or store guns, you're walking a fine line between ready access when you need a gun, safety and loss.

CONCEALED CARRY ESSENTIALS

Chapter Seventeen

Whenever I'm wearing a handgun in a shoulder rig or a large handgun in an inside waistband holster, etc., I look at myself in the mirror quite a bit. I'm not admiring the rugged good looks of that image in the mirror – I wish I could! No, I'm trying to see whether or not my weapon shows. I'll bend over, I'll reach above my head, I'll look from the side. I have a great advantage. Sharon is sensational at spotting concealed weapons, and especially on me. She knows my body language, too. If Sharon can't spot the gun, nobody can – without the use of electronic assistance or a frisk.

> *The lighter the fabric weight,*
> *the more problematic concealment*
> *can become.*

Actually, as much as I complain about the long summers in Georgia, they're great for keeping your concealment skills sharp. With that warm weather that everyone else enjoys and I consider virtually interminable torment, one has to be especially careful when it comes to concealment. Much of the time in the summer, for example, I wear a loose fitting knit shirt and shorts. The loose fitting knit shirt is of the most breathable fabric I can find. A regular polo shirt is something I almost never wear in the "dead of summer" because such shirts are just too warm. Loose clothes hide handguns better than tight clothes; but, the lighter the fabric weight, the more problematic concealment can become. And, knit fabrics are generally poorer for concealment because they tend to

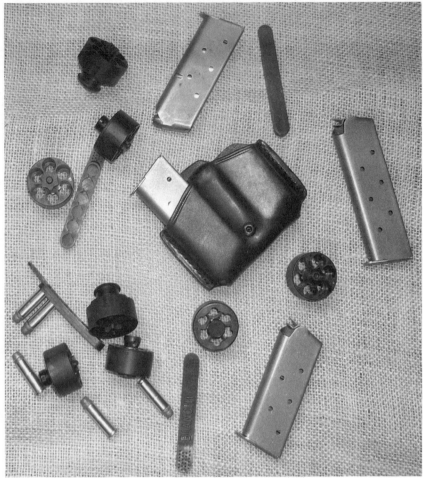

Automatic pistol magazines, some loose ammunition, Safariland Speedloaders and Bianchi Speedstrips – depending on your choice of weapons, you'll want plenty of spare ammunition delivery systems, all that these items are.

conform to what they cover and they tend to cling to checkered wooden, rubber or synthetic grips – the sharper the checking, the more the fabric clings.

When it's not summer, I have much greater latitude in what I can carry and where I can carry it.

To keep your skills up to the level they need to be, you must practice. This is true with any activity and certainly applies to carrying concealed weapons. Try this with your spouse or significant other. Carefully unload several of your handguns. Remember, even though you know they're unloaded, treat them as though they weren't when you perform this exercise, especially making certain to never let the weapon's muzzle drift over anything you don't want to see shot.

Take a couple of handguns and a couple of knives. If you only own one or two handguns and one or two knives, you can enhance the exercise with common objects. For example, a can of tuna fish closely approximates the size and weight of something like a large alloy-framed .25 automatic. A large Milk Bone nicely approximates the size of a lockblade folding knife. In other words, you can improvise. Stash these items – the guns and knives and the comestibles, if you don't have enough guns and knives – on your body as artfully as you can, mindful of the fact that in the real world you would not only be hiding the object, but also going about your normal activities with these items in place, hidden under your clothes.

> ### Develop a regimen for having access to a firearm at all times without sacrificing safety.

After doing the best job you can of concealing these items, you effectively announce, "Okay, sweetheart, I'm wearing three guns and two knives (even if some of what you are concealing is quite a bit more mundane). Where are they hidden?" Stand, sit, move around, reach for things on the floor or above your head. Remember the places on your body that really worked, those places which proved more difficult or – hopefully – impossible to pinpoint. Try to get better and more creative with each attempt. Obviously, this is more of a thing where the guy dons the weapons and the girl looks for them; but, these days, women have a lot more freedom in what they wear and, hence, what guns or knives they might conceal.

Always remember safety concerns. As you practice your concealment related techniques, you'll want to work out your draw from various concealed carry positions and holsters. There's a great temptation, once you're armed and ready for the day, to try one more draw. Of course, your gun is loaded because you're about to walk out the door. Don't try that last draw. What if, in your enthusiasm, you accidentally trigger a shot? At the least, it's embarrassing; at the worst, it's manslaughter. If the middle ground is blowing holes in your walls and furniture, that's not so great an idea, either.

Depending on the kind of gun or guns you wear, you'll have to develop a regimen for having access to a firearm at all times without sacrificing safety in the least. If you hang out with armed friends, for example, and your plans to "party" include a little alcohol, not only have a designated driver, but have a designated armed person who doesn't drink on this occasion. When at home, if your drink but feel you might need ready access to your weapon, keep the gun unloaded and separate from the ammo. Maybe the ammo is in your pocket and the gun is on top of a bookcase in the next room. Whatever. Just try not to become a statistic.

The same applies – only moreso – if you live with children or adults who are not gun knowledgeable. You want your means of defense readily available, but only to you. That old line about not being able to put anything out of reach of a cat applies to children, too. If someone gets their hands on your weapon despite your best efforts to prevent someone doing so, make certain the gun is kept in a manner disallowing anyone to do any harm.

Being armed – especially if you are armed most or all of the time – demands pre-planning and healthy paranoia, in order for you and those around you to be safe. As I write this, our daughter and son-in-law and their daughter are literally on their way to our house. Sam and Danny are gun knowledgeable people. The impending arrival of their little girl – emphasis on little at just over three years old – necessitated re-arranging certain items in the house, ranging from where we put the pocket change – she likes to play with it – to where I habitually keep a few weapons. The alternative to taking sensible precautions is unthinkable.

No one single weapon will serve all purposes all the time.

We are armed for the protection of life. The greatest weapon any of us has is the human brain. Use it without reservation. Intelligence and common sense should never be kept concealed!

As someone who writes about firearms and weapons regularly and has done so since 1973, I have developed my own personal ideas concerning the essential elements needed in a concealed carry battery.

First, the concept of a weapons battery must be considered in the concealed carry context. Regardless of what one may hear from time to time, no one single weapon will serve all purposes all the time. If that were the case, the gun makers, holster makers and knife makers would go out of business, of course; but, the fact that no one weapon will do everything isn't the result of some vast conspiracy to keep up sales. Rather, it's just reality, and reality cannot be avoided. For example, as any reader already conversant with my writings likely knows, I find hot weather abhorrent. Why do I live in Georgia, you might ask? Summery temperatures aside, it's a wonderful place to live. As the thermometer goes up, the amount of clothing many will wear diminishes. If you are wearing shorts, you won't get much use out of that terrific handgun you like to carry in your ankle holster.

Reality. It cannot be ignored, try as some of us might.

Similarly, under normal circumstances, a particular gun may suit your needs perfectly. Perhaps there has been a string of particularly heinous muggings in your area, committed by multiple assailants. This might well dictate arming up.

Since life may well present a variety of concealed carry challenges, the wise person possessed of the financial wherewithal to carry out his or her intents, should consider possible concealed carry situations and acquire the equipment necessary in order to deal with them.

Each to his own, here are what I consider the essential elements of a concealed carry battery.

First, you need a small automatic in .32 ACP or .380 ACP or a mini-revolver in .22 Magnum. The automatics reload faster, which isn't usually a concern in personal defense shooting. Semi-autos are more easily fired accurately than the mini-revolvers because there is more to hold onto and automatics are generally easier to shoot accurately than revolvers. The revolver would be less likely to experience a critical malfunction. My old friend Ron Mahovsky, revolversmith par excellence and refinishing guru, says, "Six for sure!" In the case of a .22 Magnum mini, it's five.

Such a handgun – the automatics or the mini – should be carried in a front/side pocket holster, the best place for this type of gun, maximizing on its diminutive size and its concealability. Why take something that small and convenient and carry it any other way? Some people cannot abide any kind of handgun carrying not at the waist. For their needs, there are inside waistband holsters and similar devices.

I use either a Seecamp .32, a North American Arms .380 Guardian with Crimson Trace LaserGrips or the newer NAA .22 Magnum Pug for this application, always carried in a front/side pocket holster, regardless of which of the three guns I use.

Next up is something I feel is mandatory. Unless you just cannot afford one, you've got to have a snubby .38 Special revolver. There are lots of great ones on the used market. This can be carried at waist level with a Barami Hip-Grip or in an inside waistband holster or, if you cannot abide a handgun inside your waistband, get a nice, slender belt holster. This kind of gun swings both ways, as a belt level gun or a pocket gun. When carried in a pocket – not shot from within a pocket – always use a pocket holster.

My choice for this element of my personal battery is the Smith & Wesson Model 640 in .38 Special. For decades, I used a J-frame Smith & Wesson with the Barami Hip-Grip. Nowadays, I don't carry the gun as primary ordnance as I used to when I was in my twenties, but as a backup gun. In that capacity,

A mini-revolver such as any of these from North American Arms is an essential part of an effective personal defense system.

pocket or ankle carry is the order of the day. And, in the intervening nearly 42 years since I started using a J-frame, the Crimson Trace LaserGrips have appeared. These days, my 640 is often fitted with Crimson Trace LaserGrips and, when it is actually carried that way, I use one of our old Ahern Pocket Natural holsters or a Galco Ankle Glove. I have an old friend who keeps a gun set up just like mine – with the LaserGrips -- beside his bed at night and takes it into the shower with him inside a plastic bag. He's cautious, not paranoid, and we could all learn a lot from him; I have.

If a .38 Special snubby revolver is not available to you, but something of that size is not a problem when it comes to concealment, then a good, solid, medium frame .380 can be substituted. I always had great luck with Walther PPK and PPK/S pistols years back, in the Interarms days.

I rarely use a classic medium frame auto for anything but dropping in a pocket when I'm walking Honey the Wonderdog at night. That gun is a Walther PP .32, loaded with Silvertips. I have a Grandfather Oak inside waistband holster for the gun, should I need it, and a few other holsters that suit various writing/photography related tasks. One of my best friends carried a SIG .380 backup gun in an ankle rig on a daily basis. Lots of people carry classic medium frames as primary ordnance or backup. My PP .32 is something I do consider part of my battery, simply based on the fact that I use it. As this is written, .380 ACP ammunition is extremely scarce, .32 ACP less so. Persons who don't like revolvers or can't have certain calibers will likely use a classic medium frame in .32 ACP or .380 ACP to fill the snubby .38's slot in the battery and that's perfectly okay, if need be.

Next up is a handgun in a full-size pistol caliber, but in medium frame size. Years ago, an obvious choice would have been the 2-1/2-inch K-Frame .357 Magnum Smith & Wesson Models 19 and 66 or the 3-inch fixed sight Models 13 and 65. Those guns can still be found on the used market; but, for concealed carry, with the exception of snubby .38s, their overly recoiling .357 Magnum counterparts and NAA Minis, semi-autos have become the way to go.

My personal choice for a medium sized semi-auto in a larger caliber is the Detonics CombatMaster .45 ACP. Not always in production and not always easy to find, as this is written the guns should be, at last, returning to the market place on a regular basis. The CombatMaster I use regularly is one made in Pendergrass, Georgia. I've been a devotee of the CombatMaster .45 since it was made in Seattle, years ago. These days, it's being made by people in southern Illinois. There are other smallish .45s; I'll stick with the Walther PP-sized Detonics, as did the main character, John Rourke, in our long-running science fiction/adventure novel series, The Survivalist.

If you don't absolutely have to use a .45 and/or want something other than a single action autoloader, there are guns available from Kahr Arms, Glock, SIG-Sauer and others. The Elite versions of the Kahr MK-9 are superb shooters, but the ordinary versions aren't ordinary at all. Everyone knows that Glocks work extremely well. SIGs are world class firearms, as well, of course. Guns from these sources and others can be had in 9mm Parabellum, .40 S&W and .45 ACP.

I would not be unduly upset, were my Detonics pistols somehow not available to me, to utilize a Kahr or a Glock or a SIG of similar size.

The final level in the handgun battery is the full-size or compact full-size autoloader. The choices are wide and the field is rich in quality performers. I really like SIG-Sauer compact full-size pistols and use the .40 S&W SIG 229. I have a .357 SIG barrel and I have a modest amount of .357 SIG ammo, but normally use the SIG in .40. .40 S&W is a fine compromise caliber, approaching .45 in power, not much larger than 9mm Parabellum in size.

In .45, I use my Detonics Model 9-11-01, a full-size 5-inch barrel 1911-ish gun. One of these guns did 31,000 rounds without a parts-related jam or a cleaning in the space of five days using Black Hills 230-grain hardball reloads for the most part. Actually, there never was a jam, just a few slow feeds because of dirt and powder residue build-up.

As much as I like my Detonics 9-11-01, I would not be feeling at all put out with a Kimber .45, like the nearly full-size SIS, or a Glock, Taurus, Smith & Wesson or SIG Sauer.

I am not a huge fan of the 9mm in a full-size pistol. I'd just as soon have a larger caliber. If I had to carry a 9mm, some of my favorite choices would include the time-proven Walther P-38, oddly enough, and the SIGs.

Add a couple of good, lock blade folding knives to the mix and I've got my personal concealed carry battery, ready for whatever sort of situation I might encounter. Your choices will be different in some or all ways from mine. The important thing is to be at once familiar with and confident in those choices you've made. If anyone ever asks you why you take these choices seriously and why you are armed, tell them that keeping a fire extinguisher handy at home doesn't mean you're expecting or even hoping for a fire. In fact, you really hope you'll never have to use that fire extinguisher. But, it's very comforting to know that fire extinguisher is ready to hand just in case!

Appendix

HANDGUNS FOR PERSONAL DEFENSE

AUTOLOADERS

BERETTA MODEL 3032 TOMCAT PISTOL
Caliber: 32 ACP, 7-shot magazine. **Barrel:** 2.45". **Weight:** 14.5 oz. **Length:** 5" overall. **Grips:** Checkered black plastic. **Sights:** Blade front, drift-adjustable rear. **Features:** Double action with exposed hammer; tip-up barrel for direct loading/unloading; thumb safety; polished or matte blue finish. Made in U.S.A. Introduced 1996.
Price: Matte $435.00
Price: Inox $555.00

BERETTA MODEL PX4 STORM SUB-COMPACT
Caliber: 9mm, 40 S&W. Capacity: 13 (9mm); 10 (40 S&W). **Barrel:** 3". **Weight:** 26.1 oz. **Length:** 6.2" overall. **Grips:** NA. **Sights:** NA. **Features:** Ambidextrous manual safety lever, interchangeable backstraps included, lock breech and tilt barrel system, stainless steel barrel, Picatinny rail.
Price: $600.00

GLOCK 26 AUTO PISTOL
Caliber: 9mm Para. 10/12/15/17/19/33-shot magazines. **Barrel:** 3.46". **Weight:** 19.75 oz. **Length:** 6.29" overall. Subcompact version of Glock 17. Pricing the same as Model 17. Imported from Austria by Glock, Inc.
Price: Fixed sight $690.00

KAHR K SERIES
AUTO PISTOLS
Caliber: K9: 9mm Para., 7-shot; K40: 40 S&W, 6-shot magazine. **Barrel:** 3.5". **Weight:** 25 oz. **Length:** 6" overall. **Grips:** Wraparound textured soft polymer. **Sights:** Blade front, rear drift adjustable for windage; bar-dot combat style. **Features:** Trigger-cocking double-action mechanism with passive firing pin block. Made of 4140 ordnance steel with matte black finish. Contact maker for complete price list. Introduced 1994. Made in U.S.A. by Kahr Arms.
Price: K9093C K9, matte stainless steel $855.00
Price: K9093NC K9, matte stainless steel w/tritium
    night sights $985.00
Price: K9094C K9 matte blackened stainless steel $891.00
Price: K9098 K9 Elite 2003, stainless steel $932.00
Price: K4043 K40, matte stainless steel $855.00
Price: K4043N K40, matte stainless steel w/tritium
    night sights $985.00
Price: K4044 K40, matte blackened stainless steel $891.00
Price: K4048 K40 Elite 2003, stainless steel $932.00

KAHR MK SERIES
MICRO PISTOLS
Similar to the K9/K40 except is 5.35" overall, 4" high, with a 3.08" barrel. Weighs 23.1 oz. Has snag-free bar-dot sights, polished feed ramp, dual recoil spring system, DA-only trigger. Comes with 5-round flush baseplate and 6-shot grip extension magazine. Introduced 1998. Made in U.S.A. by Kahr Arms.
Price: M9093 MK9, matte stainless steel .. **$855.00**
Price: M9093N MK9, matte stainless steel, tritium
    night sights $958.00
Price: M9098 MK9 Elite 2003, stainless steel $932.00
Price: M4043 MK40, matte stainless steel $855.00
Price: M4043N MK40, matte stainless steel, tritium
    night sights $958.00
Price: M4048 MK40 Elite 2003, stainless steel $932.00

KAHR PM SERIES
PISTOLS
Caliber: 9x19, 40 S&W, 45 ACP. Similar to P-Series pistols except has smaller polymer frame (Polymer Micro). Barrel length 3.08"; overall length 5.35"; weighs 17 oz. Includes two 7-shot magazines, hard polymer case, trigger lock. Introduced 2000. Made in U.S.A. by Kahr Arms.
Price: PM9093 PM9 ....$786.00
Price: PM4043 PM40 ....$786.00
Price: PM4543 (2007) $855.00

KAHR P380

Very small double action only semiauto pistol chambered in .380 ACP. Features include 2.5-inch Lothar Walther barrel; black polymer frame with stainless steel slide; drift adjustable white bar/dot combat/sights; optional tritium sights; two 6+1 magazines. Overall length 4.9 inches, weight 10 oz. without magazine.
Price: Standard sights **$649.00**

KEL-TEC P-32 AUTO PISTOL

Caliber: 32 ACP, 7-shot magazine. **Barrel:** 2.68". **Weight:** 6.6 oz. **Length:** 5.07" overall. **Grips:** Checkered composite. **Sights:** Fixed. **Features:** Double-action-only mechanism with 6-lb. pull; internal slide stop. Textured composite grip/frame. Now available in 380 ACP. Made in U.S.A. by Kel-Tec CNC Industries, Inc.
Price: From **$318.00**

KEL-TEC P-3AT PISTOL

Caliber: 380 ACP; 7-rounds. **Weight:** 7.2 oz. **Length:** 5.2". **Features:** Lightest 380 ACP made; aluminum frame, steel barrel.
Price: From **$324.00**

KIMBER PRO CARRY II AUTO PISTOL

Similar to Custom II, has aluminum frame, 4" bull barrel fitted directly to the slide without bushing. Introduced 1998. Made in U.S.A. by Kimber Mfg., Inc.
Price: Pro Carry II, 45 ACP **$888.00**
Price: Pro Carry II, 9mm **$929.00**
Price: Pro Carry II w/night sights **$997.00**

KIMBER ULTRA CARRY II AUTO PISTOL

Lightweight aluminum frame, 3" match grade bull barrel fitted to slide without bushing. Grips .4" shorter. Low effort recoil. Weighs 25 oz. Introduced in 1999. Made in U.S.A. by Kimber Mfg., Inc.
Price: Stainless Ultra Carry II 45 ACP **$980.00**
Price: Stainless Ultra Carry II 9mm Para. (2008) **$1,021.00**
Price: Stainless Ultra Carry II 45 ACP with night sights (2008) **$1,089.00**

KIMBER COMPACT STAINLESS II AUTO PISTOL
Similar to Pro Carry II except has stainless steel frame, 4-inch bbl., grip is .400" shorter than standard, no front serrations. Weighs 34 oz. 45 ACP only. Introduced in 1998. Made in U.S.A. by Kimber Mfg., Inc.
Price: **$1,009.00**

KIMBER CDP II SERIES AUTO PISTOL
Similar to Custom II, but designed for concealed carry. Aluminum frame. Standard features include stainless steel slide, fixed Meprolight tritium 3-dot (green) dovetail-mounted night sights, match grade barrel and chamber, 30 LPI front strap checkering, two-tone finish, ambidextrous thumb safety, hand-checkered double diamond rosewood grips. Introduced in 2000. Made in U.S.A. by Kimber Mfg., Inc.
Price: Ultra CDP II 9mm Para. (2008) **$1,359.00**
Price: Ultra CDP II 45 ACP **$1,318.00**
Price: Compact CDP II 45 ACP **$1,318.00**
Price: Pro CDP II 45 ACP......................... **$1,318.00**
Price: Custom CDP II (5" barrel, full length grip) **$1,318.00**

KIMBER ECLIPSE II SERIES AUTO PISTOL
Similar to Custom II and other stainless Kimber pistols. Stainless slide and frame, black oxide, two-tone finish. Gray/black laminated grips. 30 lpi front strap checkering. All models have night sights; Target versions have Meprolight adjustable Bar/Dot version. Made in U.S.A. by Kimber Mfg., Inc.
Price: Eclipse Ultra II (3" barrel, short grip) .. **$1,236.00**
Price: Eclipse Pro II (4" barrel, full length grip) **$1,236.00**
Price: Eclipse Pro Target II (4" barrel, full length grip, adjustable sight) **$1,236.00**
Price: Eclipse Custom II 10mm **$1,291.00**
Price: Eclipse Target II (5" barrel, full length grip, adjustable sight) **$1,345.00**

KIMBER ULTRA CDP II
Compact 1911-syle semiauto pistol chambered in .45 ACP. Features include 7-round magazine; ambidextrous thumb safety; carry melt profiling; full length guide rod; aluminum frame with stainless slide; satin silver finish; checkered frontstrap; 3-inch barrel; rosewood double diamond Crimson Trace lasergrips grips; tritium 3-dot night sights.
Price: **$1,603.00**

NORTH AMERICAN ARMS GUARDIAN DAO PISTOL

Caliber: 25 NAA, 32 ACP, 380 ACP, 32 NAA, 6-shot magazine. **Barrel:** 2.49". **Weight:** 20.8 oz. **Length:** 4.75" overall. **Grips:** Black polymer. **Sights:** Low profile fixed. **Features:** Double-action only mechanism. All stainless steel construction. Introduced 1998. Made in U.S.A. by North American Arms.
Price: From **$402.00**

OLYMPIC ARMS MATCHMASTER 5 1911 PISTOL

Caliber: 45 ACP, 7-shot magazine. **Barrel:** 5" stainless steel. **Weight:** 40 oz. **Length:** 8.75" overall. **Grips:** Smooth walnut with laser-etched scorpion icon. **Sights:** Ramped blade, LPA adjustable rear. **Features:** Matched frame and slide, fitted and head-spaced barrel, complete ramp and throat jobs, lowered and widened ejection port, beveled mag well, hand-stoned-to-match hammer and sear, lightweight long-shoe over-travel adjusted trigger, shaped and tensioned extractor, extended thumb safety, wide beavertail grip safety and full-length guide rod. Made in U.S.A. by Olympic Arms, Inc.
Price: **$903.00**

OLYMPIC ARMS ENFORCER 1911 PISTOL

Caliber: 45 ACP, 6-shot magazine. **Barrel:** 4" bull stainless steel. **Weight:** 35 oz. **Length:** 7.75" overall. **Grips:** Smooth walnut with etched black widow spider icon. **Sights:** Ramped blade front, LPA adjustable rear. **Features:** Compact Enforcer frame. Bushingless bull barrel with triplex counter-wound self-contained recoil system. Matched frame and slide, fitted and head-spaced barrel, complete ramp and throat jobs, lowered and widened ejection port, beveled mag well, hand-stoned-to-match hammer and sear, lightweight longshoe over-travel adjusted trigger, shaped and tensioned extractor, extended thumb safety, wide beavertail grip safety and full length guide rod. Made in U.S.A. by Olympic Arms.
Price: **$1,033.50**

PARA USA LDA HI-CAPACITY AUTO PISTOLS

Similar to LDA-series with double-action trigger mechanism. Polymer grips. Available in 9mm Para., 40 S&W, 45 ACP. Introduced 1999. Made in U.S.A. by Para USA.
Price: High-Cap 45, 14+1 . . . .**$1,279.00**

PARA USA WARTHOG

Caliber: 9mm Para., 45 ACP, 6, 10, or 12-shot magazines. **Barrel:** 3". **Weight:** 24 to 31.5 oz. **Length:** 6.5". **Grips:** Varies by model. **Features:** Single action. Big Hawg (2008) is full-size .45 ACP on lightweight alloy frame, 14+1, match grade ramped barrel, Power extractor, three white-dot fixed sights. Made in U.S.A. by Para USA.
Price: Slim Hawg (2006) single stack .45 ACP, stainless, 6+1 . . . .**$1,099.00**

RUGER SR9C COMPACT PISTOL

Compact double action only semiauto pistol chambered in 9mm Parabellum. Features include 1911-style ambidextrous manual safety; internal trigger bar interlock and striker blocker; trigger safety; magazine disconnector; loaded chamber indicator; two magazines, one 10-round and the other 17-round; 3.5-inch barrel; 3-dot sights; accessory rail; brushed stainless or blackened allow finish. Weight 23.40 oz.

Price: **$525.00**

SIG SAUER P220 CARRY AUTO PISTOLS

Caliber: 45 ACP, 8-shot magazine. **Barrel:** 3.9". **Weight:** NA. **Length:** 7.1" overall. **Grips:** Checkered black plastic. **Sights:** Blade front, drift adjustable rear for windage. Optional Siglite night sights. **Features:** Similar to full-size P220, except is "Commander" size. Single stack, DA/SA operation, Nitron finish, Picatinny rail, and either post and dot contrast or 3-dot Siglite night sights. Introduced 2005. Many variations availble. From SIG SAUER, Inc.

Price: P220 Carry, from .... **$975.00**; w/night sights **$1,050.00**

Price: P220 Carry Elite Stainless (2008) **$1,350.00**

SMITH & WESSON M&P AUTO PISTOLS

Caliber: 9mm Para., 40 S&W, 357 Auto. **Barrel:** 4.25". **Weight:** 24.25 oz. **Length:** 7.5" overall. **Grips:** One-piece Xenoy, wraparound with straight backstrap. **Sights:** Ramp dovetail mount front; tritium sights optional; Novak Lo-mount Carry rear. **Features:** Zytel polymer frame, embedded stainless steel chassis; stainless steel slide and barrel, stainless steel structural components, black Melonite finish, reversible magazine catch, 3 interchangeable palmswell grip sizes, universal rail, sear deactivation lever, internal lock system, magazine disconnect. Ships with 2 magazines. Internal lock models available. Overall height: 5.5"; width: 1.2"; sight radius: 6.4". Introduced November 2005. 45 ACP version introduced 2007, 10+1 or 14+1 capacity. **Barrel:** 4.5". **Length:** 8.05". **Weight:** 29.6 ounces. **Features:** Picatinny-style equipment rail; black or bi-tone, dark-earth-brown frame. Bi-tone M&P45 includes ambidextrous, frame-mounted thumb safety, take down tool with lanyard attachment. Compact 9mm Para./357 SIG/40 S&W versions introduced 2007. Compacts have 3.5" barrel, OAL 6.7". 10+1 or 12+1 capacity. **Weight:** 21.7 ounces. **Features:** Picatinny-style equipment rail. Made in U.S.A. by Smith & Wesson.

Price: Full Size, from.................................**$719.00**
Price: Compacts, from **$719.00**
Price: Midsize, from **$758.00**
Price: Crimson Trace Lasergrip models, from **$988.00**
Price: Thumb-safety M&P models, from **$719.00**

SMITH & WESSON MODEL 908 AUTO PISTOL

Caliber: 9mm Para., 8-shot magazine. **Barrel:** 3.5". **Weight:** 24 oz. **Length:** 6-13/16". **Grips:** One-piece Xenoy, wraparound with straight backstrap. **Sights:** Post front, fixed rear, 3-dot system. **Features:** Aluminum alloy frame, matte blue carbon steel slide; bobbed hammer; smooth trigger. Introduced 1996. Made in U.S.A. by Smith & Wesson.
Price: Model 908, black matte finish **$679.00**
Price: Model 908S, stainless matte finish **$679.00**
Price: Model 908S Carry Combo, with holster **$703.00**

SMITH & WESSON MODEL 3913 TRADITIONAL DOUBLE ACTIONS

Caliber: 9mm Para., 8-shot magazine. **Barrel:** 3.5". **Weight:** 24.8 oz. **Length:** 6.75" overall. **Grips:** One-piece Delrin wraparound, textured surface. **Sights:** Post front with white dot, Novak LoMount Carry with two dots. **Features:** TSW has aluminum alloy frame, stainless slide. Bobbed hammer with no half-cock notch; smooth .304" trigger with rounded edges. Straight backstrap. Equipment rail. Extra magazine included. Introduced 1989. The 3913-LS Ladysmith has frame that is upswept at the front, rounded trigger guard. Comes in frosted stainless steel with matching gray grips. Grips are ergonomically correct for a woman's hand. Novak LoMount Carry rear sight adjustable for windage. Extra magazine included. Introduced 1990.
Price: 3913TSW **$924.00**
Price: 3913-LS **$909.00**

SMITH & WESSON MODEL 1911 SUB-COMPACT PRO SERIES

Caliber: 45 ACP, 7 + 1-shot magazine. **Barrel:** 3". **Weight:** 24 oz. **Length:** 6-7/8". **Grips:** Fully stippled synthetic. **Sights:** Dovetail white dot front, fixed white 2-dot rear. **Features:** Scandium frame with stainless steel slide, matte black finish throughout. Oversized external extractor, 3-hole curved trigger with overtravel stop, full-length guide rod, and cable lock. Introduced 2009.
Price: **$1,304.00**

SPRINGFIELD ARMORY XD POLYMER AUTO PISTOLS

Caliber: 9mm Para., 40 S&W, 45 ACP. **Barrel:** 3", 4", 5". **Weight:** 20.5-31 oz. **Length:** 6.26-8" overall. **Grips:** Textured polymer. **Sights:** Varies by model; Fixed sights are dovetail front and rear steel 3-dot units. **Features:** Three sizes in X-Treme Duty (XD) line: Sub-Compact (3" barrel), Service (4" barrel), Tactical (5" barrel). Three ported models available. Ergonomic polymer frame, hammer-forged barrel, no-tool disassembly, ambidextrous magazine release, visual/tactile loaded chamber indicator, visual/tactile striker status indicator, grip safety, XD gear system included. Introduced 2004. XD 45 introduced 2006. Compact line introduced 2007. Compacts ship with one extended magazine (13) and one compact magazine (10). From Springfield Armory.
Price: Sub-Compact OD Green 9mm Para./40 S&W,
  fixed sights **$543.00**
Price: Compact 45 ACP, 4" barrel, Bi-Tone finish (2008) **$589.00**
Price: Compact 45 ACP, 4" barrel, OD green frame,
  stainless slide (2008) **$653.00**

Price: Service Black 9mm Para./40 S&W, fixed sights **$543.00**
Price: Service Dark Earth 45 ACP, fixed sights **$571.00**
Price: Service Black 45 ACP, external thumb safety
(2008) **$571.00**
Price: V-10 Ported Black 9mm Para./40 S&W **$573.00**
Price: Tactical Black 45 ACP, fixed sights **$616.00**
Price: Service Bi-Tone 40 S&W, Trijicon night sights (2008) . .**$695.00**

SPRINGFIELD ARMORY XDM-3.8

Double action only semiauto pistol chambered in 9mm Parabellum (19+1) and .40 S&W (16+1). Features include 3.8-inch steel full-ramp barrel; dovetail front and rear 3-dot sights (tritium and fiber-optics sights available); polymer frame; stainless steel slide with slip-resistant slide serrations; loaded chamber indicator; grip safety. Black, bi-tone or stainless steel finish. Overall length 7 inches, weight 27.5 oz. (9mm). Also available with 4.5-inch barrel as Model XDM-4.5.
Price: . . . . **N/A**

STI ECLIPSE PISTOL

Compact 1911-style semiauto pistol chambered in 9x19, .40 S&W, and .45 ACP. Features include 3-inch slide with rear cocking serrations, oversized ejection port; 2-dot tritium night sights recessed into the slide; high-capacity polymer grip; single sided blued thumb safety; bobbed, high-rise, blued, knuckle relief beavertail grip safety; 3-inch barrel.
Price: . . . . **N/A**

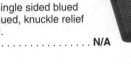

TAURUS MODEL PT-22/PT-25 AUTO PISTOLS

Caliber: 22 LR, 8-shot (PT-22); 25 ACP, 9-shot (PT-25). **Barrel:** 2.75". **Weight:** 12.3 oz. **Length:** 5.25" overall. **Grips:** Smooth rosewood or mother-of-pearl. **Sights:** Fixed. **Features:** Double action. Tip-up barrel for loading, cleaning. Blue, nickel, duo-tone or blue with gold accents. Introduced 1992. Made in U.S.A. by Taurus International.
Price: PT-22B or PT-25B, checkered wood grips. **$248.00**

TAURUS MODEL 22PLY SMALL POLYMER FRAME PISTOLS

Similar to Taurus Models PT-22 and PT-25 but with lightweight polymer frame. Features include 22 LR (9+1) or 25 ACP (8+1) chambering. 2.33" tip-up barrel, matte black finish, extended magazine with finger lip, manual safety. Overall length is 4.8". Weighs 10.8 oz.
Price: . . . . **TO BE ANNOUNCED**

TAURUS 138 MILLENNIUM PRO SERIES

Caliber: 380 ACP, 10- or 12-shot mags. **Barrel:** 3.25". **Weight:** 18.7 oz. **Grips:** Polymer. **Sights:** Fixed 3-dot fixed. **Features:** Double-action-only, polymer frame, matte stainless or blue steel slide, manual safety, integral key-lock.
Price: 138BP. **$419.00**

TAURUS SLIM 700 SERIES

Compact double/single action semiauto pistol chambered in 9mm Parabellum (7+1), .40 S&W (6+1), and .380 ACP (7+1). Features include polymer frame; blue or stainless slide; single action/double action trigger pull; low-profile fixed sights. Weight 19 oz., length 6.24 inches, width less than an inch.
Price: . . . . **N/A**

WALTHER PPK/S AMERICAN AUTO PISTOL

Caliber: 32 ACP, 380 ACP, 7-shot magazine. **Barrel:** 3.27". **Weight:** 23-1/2 oz. **Length:** 6.1" overall. Stocks: Checkered plastic. **Sights:** Fixed, white markings. **Features:** Double action; manual safety blocks firing pin and drops hammer; chamber loaded indicator on 32 and 380; extra finger rest magazine provided. Made in the United States. Introduced 1980. Made in U.S.A. by Smith & Wesson.
Price: **$605.00**

DOUBLE–ACTION REVOLVERS

CHARTER ARMS OFF DUTY REVOLVER

Caliber: .38 Spec. **Barrel:** 2".
Weight: 12.5 oz. **Sights:** Blade front,
notch rear. **Features:** 5-round cylinder,
aluminum casting, DAO. American made by
Charter Arms, distributed by MKS Supply.
Price: Aluminum **$438.00**

CHARTER ARMS UNDERCOVER REVOLVER

Caliber: .38 Special **Barrel:** 2".
Weight: 12 oz. **Sights:** Blade front,
notch rear. **Features:** 6-round cylinder.
American made by Charter Arms, distributed
by MKS Supply.
Price: Blued **$438.00**

ROSSI MODEL R351/R352/R851 REVOLVERS

Caliber: .38 Spec. **Barrel:** 2" (R35),
4" (R851). **Weight:** 24-32 oz. **Grips:**
Rubber. **Sights:** Fixed (R35), Fully
Adjustable (R851). **Features:** DA/SA, 3
models available, +P rated frame, blue carbon
or high polish stainless steel, patented Taurus
Security System, 5-shot (R35) 6-shot (R851).
Price: From **$352.00**

RUGER SP-101 REVOLVERS

Caliber: 327 Federal, 6-shot;
.38 Spec. +P, 357 Mag., 5-shot.
Barrel: 2.25", 3-1/16". **Weight:**
(38 & 357 mag models) 2.25"-25 oz.; 3-
1/16"-27 oz. **Sights:** Adjustable on 327, fixed
on others. **Grips:** Ruger Cushioned Grip with
inserts. **Features:** Compact, small frame, double-
action revolver. Full-length ejector shroud. Stainless steel only.
Introduced 1988.
Price: KSP-321X (2.25", 357 Mag.) **$589.00**
Price: KSP-331X (3-1/16", 357 Mag.) **$589.00**
Price: KSP-821X (2.25", 38 Spec.) **$589.00**
Price: KSP-32731X (3-1/16", 327 Federal, intr. 2008) **$589.00**
Price: KSP-321X-LG (Crimson Trace Laser Grips, intr. 2008) . **$839.00**

SMITH & WESSON M&P REVOLVERS

Caliber: .38 Spec., 357 Mag., 5 rounds (Centennial), 8 rounds (large
frame). **Barrel:** 1.87" (Centennial), 5" (large frame). **Weight:** 13.3
oz. (Centennial), 36.3 oz. (large frame). **Length:** 6.31" overall (small
frame), 10.5" (large frame). **Grips:** Synthetic. **Sights:** Integral U-
Notch rear, XS Sights 24/7 Tritium Night. **Features:** Scandium alloy
frame, stainless steel cylinder, matte black finish. Made in U.S.A. by
Smith & Wesson.
Price: M&P 340, double action **$869.00**
Price: M&P 340CT, Crimson Trace Lasergrips. **$1,122.00**
Price: M&P R8 large frame **$1,311.00**

SMITH & WESSON MODEL 442/637/638/642 AIRWEIGHT REVOLVERS

Caliber: .38 Spec. +P, 5-shot. **Barrel:** 1-7/8", 2-1/2". **Weight:** 15 oz. (37, 442); 20 oz. (3); 21.5 oz.; **Length:** 6-3/8" overall. **Grips:** Soft rubber. **Sights:** Fixed, serrated ramp front, square notch rear. **Features:** Aluminum-alloy frames. Models 37, 637; Chiefs Special-style frame with exposed hammer. Introduced 1996. Models 442, 642; Centennial-style frame, enclosed hammer. Model 638, Bodyguard style, shrouded hammer. Comes in a fitted carry/storage case. Introduced 1989. Made in U.S.A. by Smith & Wesson.
Price: From **$600.00**

SMITH & WESSON MODELS 637 CT/638 CT/642 CT
Similar to Models 637, 638 and 642 but with Crimson Trace Laser Grips.
Price: **$920.00**

SMITH & WESSON MODEL 60 CHIEF'S SPECIAL

Caliber: 357 Mag., .38 Spec. +P, 5-shot. **Barrel:** 2-1/8", 3" or 5". **Weight:** 22.5 oz. (2-1/8" barrel). **Length:** 6-5/8" overall (2-1/8" barrel). **Grips:** Rounded butt synthetic grips. **Sights:** Fixed, serrated ramp front, square notch rear. **Features:** Stainless steel construction, satin finish, internal lock. Introduced 1965. The 5"-barrel model has target semi-lug barrel, rosewood grip, red ramp front sight, adjustable rear sight. Made in U.S.A. by Smith & Wesson.
Price: 2-1/8" barrel, intr. 2005 .... **$798.00**
Price: 3" barrel, 7.5" OAL, 24 oz. **$830.00**

SMITH & WESSON MODEL 317 AIRLITE REVOLVERS

Caliber: 22 LR, 8-shot. **Barrel:** 1-7/8", 3". **Weight:** 10.5 oz. **Length:** 6.25" overall (1-7/8" barrel). **Grips:** Rubber. **Sights:** Serrated ramp front, fixed notch rear. **Features:** Aluminum alloy, carbon and stainless steels, Chiefs Special-style frame with exposed hammer. Smooth combat trigger. Clear Cote finish. Introduced 1997. Made in U.S.A. by Smith & Wesson.
Price: Model 317, 1-7/8" barrel **$766.00**
Price: Model 317 w/HiViz front sight, 3" barrel, 7.25 OAL **$830.00**

SMITH & WESSON MODEL 340/340PD AIRLITE SC CENTENNIAL
Caliber: 357 Mag., .38 Spec. +P, 5-shot. **Barrel:** 1-7/8". **Weight:** 12 oz. **Length:** 6-3/8" overall (1-7/8" barrel). **Grips:** Rounded butt rubber. **Sights:** Black blade front, rear notch **Features:** Centennial-style frame, enclosed hammer. Internal lock. Matte silver finish. Scandium alloy frame, titanium cylinder, stainless steel barrel liner. Made in U.S.A. by Smith & Wesson.
Price: Model 340 .... **$1,051.00**
Price: Model 340PD **$1,122.00**

SMITH & WESSON MODEL 438

Caliber: .38 Spec. +P, 5-shot. **Barrel:** 1-7/8". **Weight:** 15.1 oz. **Length:** 6.31" overall. **Grips:** Synthetic. **Sights:** Fixed front and rear. **Features:** Aluminum alloy frame, stainless steel cylinder. Matte black finish throughout. Made in U.S.A. by Smith & Wesson.
Price: $624.00

SMITH & WESSON MODEL 442/642/640/632 PRO SERIES REVOLVERS

Double action only J-frame with concealed hammers chambered in .38 Special +P (442 & 642), .357 Magnum (640) or .327 Federal (632). Features include 5-round cylinder, matte stainless steel frame, fixed sights or dovetail night sights (632, 640), synthetic grips, cylinder cut for moon clips (442, 642, 640).
Price: . . . . $640.00 (standard) to $916.00 (night sights)

SMITH & WESSON K-FRAME/L-FRAME REVOLVERS

These mid-size S&W wheelguns come in a variety of chamberings, barrel lengths, and materials, as noted in individual model listings.

TAURUS MODEL 94 REVOLVER

Caliber: 22 LR, 9-shot cylinder; 22 Mag, 8-shot cylinder **Barrel:** 2", 4", 5". **Weight:** 18.5-27.5 oz. **Grips:** Soft black rubber. **Sights:** Serrated ramp front, click-adjustable rear. **Features:** Double action, integral key-lock. Introduced 1989. Imported by Taurus International.
Price: From $369.00

TAURUS JUDGE PUBLIC DEFENDER POLYMER

Single/double action revolver chambered in .45 Colt/.410 (2-1/2). Features include 5-round cylinder; polymer frame; Ribber rubber-feel grips; fiber-optic front sight; adjustable rear sight; blued or stainless cylinder; shrouded hammer with cocking spur; blued finish; 2.5-inch barrel. Weight 27 oz.
Price: . . . . N/A

TAURUS MODEL 605 REVOLVER

Caliber: 357 Mag., 5-shot. **Barrel:** 2". **Weight:** 24 oz. **Grips:** Rubber. **Sights:** Fixed. **Features:** Double-action, blue or stainless or titanium, concealed hammer models DAO, porting optional, integral key-lock. Introduced 1995. Imported by Taurus International.
Price: From $403.00

TAURUS MODEL 651 PROTECTOR REVOLVER

Caliber: 357 Mag., 5-shot. **Barrel:** 2". **Weight:** 17-24.5 oz. **Grips:** Rubber. **Sights:** Fixed. **Features:** Concealed single-action/double-action design. Shrouded cockable hammer, blue, matte stainless, Shadow Gray, Total Titanium, integral key-lock. Made in Brazil. Imported by Taurus International Manufacturing, Inc.
Price: From $411.00

Arm Yourself with Knowlege

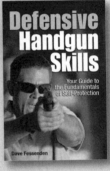
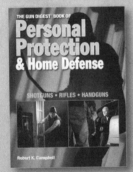